D0734844

BEFORE Brooklyn

THE UNSUNG HEROES WHO HELPED BREAK BASEBALL'S COLOR BARRIER

TED REINSTEIN

Guilford, Connecticut

An imprint of Globe Pequot, the trade division of
The Rowman & Littlefield Publishing Group, Inc.
4501 Forbes Blvd., Ste. 200
Lanham, MD 20706
LyonsPress.com

Distributed by NATIONAL BOOK NETWORK

British Library Cataloguing in Publication Information available

Library of Congress Cataloging-in-Publication Data

Names: Reinstein, Ted, author.
Title: Before Brooklyn : the unsung heroes who helped break baseball's color barrier /
    Ted Reinstein.
Description: Guilford, Connecticut : Lyons Press, 2021. | Includes bibliographical references
    and index. | Summary: "This book tells the story of the little-known heroes who fought
    segregation in baseball"— Provided by publisher.
Identifiers: LCCN 2021020537 (print) | LCCN 2021020538 (ebook) | ISBN
    9781493051212 (cloth) | ISBN 9781493051229 (epub)
Subjects: LCSH: Negro league—History. | African American baseball players—History. |
    Baseball—Social aspects—United States—History. | Discrimination in sports—United
    States—History.
Classification: LCC GV875.N35 R45 2021 (print) | LCC GV875.N35 (ebook) |
    DDC 796.357/640973—dc23
LC record available at https://lccn.loc.gov/2021020537
LC ebook record available at https://lccn.loc.gov/2021020538

For Anne-Marie, Kyra, and Daisy—my own unsung heroes. I remain so grateful for your support. With much love and deep appreciation.

Contents

Preface

On April 16, 1945, a startling scene unfolded on the field at Boston's Fenway Park. It had never happened before. It would be nearly 15 years before it happened again.

At midmorning on that sunny but brisk early spring day, three Black professional baseball players ran out to take positions on the field. There were no other teammates. It was not a game. The stands were empty, save for a few small groups of white men in suits and hats.

It was a tryout.

The three Black men were being given what seemed to be an unprecedented opportunity: to showcase their talents and skills, and hopefully impress the Red Sox enough to make the team's roster—and break Major League Baseball's longstanding color barrier.

The three players proceeded to field balls, run the bases, and take batting practice. Some of the men in suits took notes. Others simply looked on, as if they were observing something at once both familiar and strange. After about 90 minutes, a tall, lanky man in a suit walked to the edge of the stands, signaled that the proceedings were over, thanked the players for their time, and promised that the Red Sox would be in touch.

The players never heard from the team again.

Two years later (nearly to the day), in another city, on another field, one of those same three players ran out and took his position at first base. This time, it was a real game. The stands were full. Photographers ringed the infield, flashbulbs popped like fireworks as they recorded the moment. This time, the player hadn't merely made the team, he was making history. The royal blue "42" on the back of his Brooklyn Dodger uniform that day will never be worn by another major-league player. Such was the impact that Jackie Robinson had on both baseball and the long struggle for civil rights in America.

The question of why the Boston Red Sox passed on the opportunity to sign Jackie Robinson is one that has dogged the team, and to an extent its city, ever since that long-ago April morning. The short answer is that the team (and more specifically, its then-owner) was simply not willing, in April 1945, to hire a Black ballplayer. Nor, for that matter, at that time, was any other Major League Baseball team. (The Dodgers would, however, sign Robinson a scant six months later; the Red Sox would become the very last major-league team to integrate, in 1959.) Given the stark and simple fact that Jackie Robinson could have conjured the second coming of Babe Ruth that day and still be sent on his way, the more interesting question is why did the Red Sox hold an obviously sham tryout to begin with?

Because they had to.

In holding the tryout, Boston's hand was essentially forced by two remarkable men who today are mere historical footnotes. In 1945, Isadore "Izzy" Muchnick was a Jewish Boston city councilor at a time when Boston politics was still dominated by Irish Catholics. Wendell Smith was a well-respected Black reporter for the *Pittsburgh Courier*, then one of the nation's most successful African-American newspapers. No strangers to some of the same bigotry that bedeviled Robinson, the pair became unlikely allies, collaborating to cleverly exploit a legal loophole that left the Red Sox with little choice but to accede to their demands. The tryout they forced may have been a farce, but the larger, longer drama they were part of—and how it ultimately played out—was very real.

In fact, the long, lurching, unlikely path to Fenway Park that day was, in many ways, far more fascinating than the event itself. For while the result of the Robinson tryout was entirely predictable, the fact that it actually *took place* was something no one could have foreseen. Today, few know that it happened at all. Even fewer are aware of the long struggle that preceded it, or that it was one that transcended sports.

Muchnick and Smith were only among the last in a long line of similarly unsung heroes who, for decades, had taken on the same outsized foes in the same, seemingly lopsided struggle. Laced with politics, violence, cunning, and courage, the bitter, relentless battle to break baseball's color barrier spanned several decades, as well as much of America.

It was fought first on fields that, while green, saw only Black players between the white lines. The famed and fabled Negro Leagues were formed in direct response to Major League Baseball's color barrier. Negro League stars like Satchel Paige, Josh Gibson, and Cool Papa Bell knew their talents equaled—or exceeded—many of their major-league counterparts. Yet, neither the higher pay and broader fame they never received, nor the endless, exhausting road trips on rickety buses ever diminished these player's passionate calls for equality, or dimmed their more personal, poignant longing to play as truly free men on baseball's biggest stage.

Sometimes wielding pens instead of bats, the battle also enlisted the critical help of Black (and many white) journalists and Black newspapers nationwide to press for change. For decades before it finally fell, African-American papers like the *Courier* and the *Chicago Defender* tirelessly pressed the case for abolishing baseball's color barrier. The African-American press was not alone. In New York, the Communist *Daily Worker* hired its first-ever sports editor in the 1930s, and Lester Rodney—white and Jewish—became one of the most outspoken and effective journalists to battle baseball's color ban.

Some of the battle's foot soldiers were indeed uniformed, but not in khaki, or blue. Black Pullman porters who worked America's passenger trains became an ingenious if invisible distribution system for those same Black newspapers, newspapers that otherwise would never have had such national reach, and without which countless Black communities along their routes would not have been as fully informed and engaged on the issue of integration.

And some of those who fought the long fight against baseball's segregation did wear real military uniforms. They carried real guns, faced real bullets, and many died young in bloody deaths on real battlefields. Unable to enjoy at home the very freedoms for which they were prepared to sacrifice their lives overseas, they were nonetheless determined, by that very act of patriotism, to achieve the "double victory" of freedom over both Adolf Hitler and Jim Crow.

The sham tryout at Fenway Park took place less than a month before the end of the War in Europe. By itself, it didn't break the color barrier. But it did help set the final stage for that to happen shortly thereafter.

Branch Rickey and the Brooklyn Dodgers deserve great and lasting credit for signing Jackie Robinson, and for being first to fix an unforgiveable wrong. But that credit was never theirs alone. And the path that Robinson himself first trod out onto Ebbets Field had been prepared by earlier trailblazers, none of whom were famous or photographed or applauded on that landmark day. Some 75 years later, their names are largely lost to history. But the battle to break baseball's color barrier was won by them as much as Rickey or Robinson. And it began long before Brooklyn.

Prologue: A Most Unlikely Meeting

As he turned right off of Boston's busy Commonwealth Avenue, past the main buildings of Boston University, and proceeded to shuffle down Babcock Street, not a single passerby would have guessed where the short, slightly stooped pedestrian with an armload of papers was headed. After all, it was 1938, and what possible business would a Black man have with the white, well-known owner of a Major League Baseball team?

But the bespectacled young man was, in fact, headed to Braves Field, and the executive offices of the newly renamed Boston Bees.* There, he was to meet with the team's president and part-owner, Bob Quinn.

It's hard to imagine a meeting of more striking contrasts. The two participants themselves were as different as night and day, their backgrounds of entirely other worlds. One man's father had been an immigrant from Ireland. The other's had been born into slavery. Having never met, they shared little more than the air they breathed. But there was baseball. And barriers, and grievances. And on this day, a rare and extraordinary opportunity. And Mabray Kountze was determined to take advantage of it.

Physically, even at 28, he was the very opposite of imposing. Slight (just over 5'5"), with wiry hair, an upturned nose, and big, expressive eyes that stared from behind strong glasses, he looked soft-spoken and bookish. Which he was. Words were the way he would distinguish himself. He loved sports, but unlike his brothers, he was not athletic. He'd been frail, even sickly as a child. And shy. None of which was helped by the fact that he'd been saddled with a full name—Mabray Kountze—that defied easy pronunciation ("MAY-bree COUNTS") at either end. Later in life he acquired the nickname "Doc," which spoke to his local stature as a

---

* In advance of the 1936 season, the National League Boston Braves changed their name to the "Bees." (And their field to the "Bee Hive.") Although the "Bees" were back to being the "Braves" in 1940, they still stung the city when they skipped town and moved to Milwaukee in 1953. They remain the Braves today (in Atlanta).

Mabray "Doc" Kountze at home, West Medford, Massachusetts, c. 1970
KOUNTZE FAMILY COLLECTION/MEDFORD TRANSCRIPT

dependable authority on a little bit of just about everything, and it made "Mabray" (shortened by family to "Mabe") a bit less of a hindrance.

"He was very quiet and unassuming," says Shirley Kountze of the man she knew as "Uncle Mabe." But the diminutive gentleman seemed to command an outsized level of respect. "He was really something of a 'guru,' people would say. He was very wise, and he made you feel good, good to be around."

In terms of physical stature, James Aloysius Quinn wasn't a big man, either. But with broad shoulders, red hair, and a ruddy complexion, he looked every inch the rugged, solid Irishman that his father, a stonecutter, had been. His mom was an Ohio native, which is where Quinn grew up, and where as a young man he began calling himself "Bobby." By that time, he had discovered baseball. In 1884, at 14, he was playing on an Irish team in Columbus called the Shamrocks. Alas, no particular good luck seems to have rubbed off on his career as a ballplayer. A sturdy catcher, he was known for being better at handling the ball than hitting it. But the bond with baseball was permanent, and Quinn made a lifelong professional attachment with the game in a variety of front-office roles. He was general manager for several major-league teams, including the St. Louis Browns, the Brooklyn Dodgers, and the Boston Braves. In 1923, he headed a group that bought the Boston Red Sox, succeeding previous owner Harry Frazee's infamous reign of ruin.*

Making the meeting at Braves Field that day all the more unlikely was the fact that Mabray Kountze was decidedly a homebody, and not much of a traveler. Even the 45 minute or so bus ride from his home just outside of Boston proper, to Kenmore Square in the city's Back Bay section, was not a common jaunt for Kountze. In the early 1900s, his father, Hillard Kountze, had moved his large family from Boston to working-class West Medford, seven miles north of the city. There, in addition to his other jobs, the "Chief," as the elder Kountze was known, opened up a small real estate business in a small building behind his house, becoming the only Black real estate broker in the wider Medford community. By drawing new Black residents to a safe, thriving community of color, the elder Kountze helped make West Medford the uniquely integrated neighborhood it continues to be today.

For his son, Mabray, this would be home, and essentially the larger world for his entire life. Never married, he worked at the West Medford post office. At the same time, he was a tireless researcher, with an unquenchable thirst for acquiring knowledge. Through sheer diligence and a lifelong passion for writing and history, he retired early and carved out a role as a contributing journalist for a variety of African-American press outlets. When he was older, he lived first at a nephew's home, then at his sister, Vivien's, all in West Medford. And yet, for a homebody, he seemed very much a man of the world. In a sense, as a voracious reader and a ham radio operator, he actually was. It was a defining irony—at once a familiar, beloved if peculiar fixture of his small, insular neighborhood, but perceived as someone who somehow transcended it, possessed of a wisdom that ranged far beyond it.

---

* Frazee, a Broadway producer, is most remembered for selling off his team's best players, including a budding star named Babe Ruth, sent to the Yankees in 1919.

Aerial view of Braves Field, Boston, 1933
COURTESY LESLIE JONES COLLECTION/BOSTON PUBLIC LIBRARY

"Doc was eccentric, but we all knew he knew everything," says Terry Carter matter-of-factly. Carter, a writer and poet who's head of elder services today at the West Medford Community Center, was a kid in the 1960s, and remembers Kountze riding his bike around the neighborhood. "It had a basket on it and the basket was always full of papers," laughs Carter.

"Doc would have been a great teacher—he wanted people to grow themselves," says Adele Travisano, an artist and longtime West Medford friend. "He was constantly interested in learning new things, constantly."

Little seemed to escape Kountze's keen and boundless curiosity. He was especially drawn to history and sports, mostly in the context of the long, painful struggle that was the Black experience in America. And he wrote about it ceaselessly. He wrote books, he wrote essays and articles, and he wrote letters—endlessly, to everyone: family, friends, foes, editorial pages, and anyone or any entity that Kountze felt would benefit from what he might share.

"Oh, the letters," exhales Travisano with a breath of bemused wonderment. "He really was just an incredible letter writer."

"He wrote to everyone," says Ione Vargus, former dean of Temple University's School of Social Administration, and a niece of Kountze. "He wrote to the Pope, he wrote to world leaders."

And he wrote to the team offices of the Boston Braves.

"The visit was to talk over the previous contact with club secretary Edward Cunningham," Kountze recounted later in his book, *50 Sports Years Along Memory Lane*. "It was relative to bringing Colored baseball clubs to Braves Field."

The letter to Cunningham led to the meeting with Quinn. Clearly, Kountze was able to persuade. And persist.

"He was keenly aware that he was a Black man in America," says Carter. "He knew that because of his intelligence he would have access to certain things. But because of his skin, there is certain access he wouldn't have."

On this special day, he had access. And he used it.

There is no verbatim transcript of the meeting between Kountze and Quinn on that day at Braves Field in 1938. But, from Kountze's own writing years later, we get a good sense of what was discussed, and what his impressions were. The meeting's specific agenda item centered on a request that the Braves allow their ballpark to be used by more Black baseball teams. By the 1930s, it had become commonplace for many Negro League and other Black teams to occasionally play games in major-league ballparks when that city's team was on the road. There was nothing magnanimous (much less free) in the arrangement; the otherwise empty ballparks represented an easy source of extra revenue for the major-league clubs. (And for the booking agents.) So Bob Quinn would not have been entirely disinterested in the discussion, if only from a purely financial perspective.

Kountze had been asked (also by letter) to seek the meeting to begin with by Burlin White, a Black baseball player and catcher of some renown at that time. Kountze had interviewed White previously for a newspaper piece, and had struck up a correspondence.

"The letter requested me to visit President Bob Quinn, Sr., of the National League Boston Braves . . . relative to bringing Colored baseball clubs to Braves Field and which business-like Burlin White had agreed to promote."

For his part, in meeting Quinn, Mabray Kountze relished the opportunity to reach for his papers, and pull out pages and pages of notes and clippings, referencing both local and national teams that could be booked immediately to play at Braves Field. He pointedly underscored some of the star Black ballplayers on those teams—players like Burlin White—who were already well known even to white baseball fans, and who by themselves would be legitimate and significant draws at the ticket gate. He emphasized that some of these Black ballplayers had special appeal as local sports celebrities in Boston and across the New England region. Their legions of fans proved it: fans that paid good money and filled up seats. And as Quinn well knew, huge major-league ballparks like Municipal Stadium in Cleveland and Yankee Stadium in New York were already hosting (and making money from) Black baseball games when the major-league Indians and Yankees were on the road. So it wasn't a foreign, first-time subject for Quinn. And it's not hard to imagine Quinn listening with genuine attention and interest, gazing down at the stadium below him, imagining just how many of those empty seats might be filled with essentially "found" money. Kountze also knew that the Braves might be doubly intrigued; the National League team was not doing well financially in what its own executives referred to as "an American League city."

But Kountze had other things on his mind as he sat in that executive suite above the field. Unlike Quinn, he didn't stand to make a dime on anything they were discussing. Besides, his real interest lay with a much wider question than the momentary, narrow one of how many Black ballgames could fit on the schedule of the Boston Braves or any other all-white team. The long game was much bigger. It wasn't about Blacks merely playing at Braves Field when the team was away. It was about playing at Braves Field when the team was *home*. It was about Blacks playing *on the Braves*, and every other major-league team. It was about undoing what had been done more than 50 years earlier and which kept them from doing just that.

"I was only one of a legion of black sportswriters throughout the nation voluntarily united to attack the color ban," wrote Kountze. "These thoughts were in my mind," he recalled, after having been "cordially received" by Quinn.

It's easy to imagine that, at some point in the discussion, Mabray Kountze paused and sat back for a moment. He may have smiled wanly as he rearranged the papers on his lap, clearing his throat and glancing out the window for a moment before bringing his gaze back to Quinn. Kountze knew that Quinn, even for 1938, was no kneejerk segregationist. He'd had professional contact with Negro League owners. And now he'd invited a Black man to meet in his office to discuss some serious issues of substance and sensitivity. (Something his American League counterparts down the street at Fenway Park had declined to do.) In 1938, that was not nothing. But the two men had entirely different experiences and perspectives. And agendas. No amount of cordiality could overcome that.

Kountze, with his expansive sense of historical context, wanted to make sure that Quinn understood that simply having Blacks play baseball at his Braves Field when the team was not home was, in and of itself, not such a big deal. It was already happening elsewhere. What Kountze wanted to underscore was something less well known: that even the bigger, more momentous goal of playing integrated Major League Baseball had *also* already happened. Some 50 years earlier. For Kountze, and his compatriots, the goal ahead was to *re*-integrate baseball.

"As a learned, lifelong man of baseball," Kountze gently prodded Quinn, "surely you are familiar with Moses Fleetwood Walker. . . ."

ONE

The American Pastime Takes Root (and Even Looks Like America for a While)

Baseball was the earliest, most organized black sport in America. It was black baseball . . . that finally toppled the color barrier.
—Mabray "Doc" Kountze

When it comes to the past and the origins of America's national pastime, the public has always faced a bit of a curveball. (Perhaps "doctored pitch" is more apt.)

What's most remarkable about baseball's birth story is how remarkably made-up it is.

Almost nothing is factual about the game's creation story—including its supposed creator and its alleged place of birth—other than the fact that Abner Doubleday was a real person, and Cooperstown is a real place. That's pretty much it. Call it baseball's own "birther" issue. (Although this was a lie to cover for an invented truth, rather than a lie intended to impugn something that was actually true.) It's worth looking at because it makes clear that, from the beginning, those in positions of power in professional baseball have often lacked the courage to face inconvenient truths, from where and when the game was invented, to who gets to play it and, more to the point, who doesn't.

Maj. Gen. Abner Doubleday
LIBRARY OF CONGRESS/WIKIMEDIA COMMONS

Baseball's Hall of Fame opened in Cooperstown, New York, on June 12, 1939. The date was chosen in order to mark what was said to be the sport's centennial: the date that the game's "founder," Abner Doubleday (who did not grow up in Cooperstown), laid out the very first baseball diamond, right there in a Cooperstown cow pasture. (It's a wonder there's no record of the cows' reaction; why limit the fiction to humans?)

The first problem with the Hall's hagiography is that in 1839, Abner Doubleday was 145 miles from Cooperstown. He was enrolled at West Point, having been appointed to the military academy a year earlier. (He had been a student of the Cooperstown Classical and Military Academy.) He did go on, no question, to have a military career of genuine distinction. He saw combat in both the Mexican War and the American Civil War, by which time he had become a general. Ironically, there was never any need to pad Doubleday's resume, or claim achievements that weren't his. He had plenty. But then, it wasn't Doubleday that did the padding. Nor did he live to know about it.

In 1861, under Doubleday's orders, the first shot of the Civil War was fired in defense of Fort Sumter in Charleston, South Carolina. Two years later, he led an infantry division during the first hours of the Battle of Gettysburg. Assigned to duties in the defense of Washington, Doubleday became friendly with President Abraham Lincoln, and later accompanied him on his trip to give the Gettysburg Address. He remained in the military after the war and was posted to San Francisco. An engineer by training, he received a patent for what became the city's famous cable cars. He dropped his involvement with the project when he was reassigned to Fort McKavett, Texas, in 1871. There, he took command of the 24th US Infantry—an all African-American regiment. After leaving the military, Doubleday moved back to New York where he wrote, and practiced law. He died of heart disease in 1893. His obituary made no mention of baseball, which shouldn't surprise, since Doubleday had essentially nothing to do with the sport (and never claimed to), much less invented it.

The connection was forged posthumously. The Doubleday story stems from the work of a commission formed in 1905 by sporting goods magnate Albert Spalding, in order to definitively determine baseball's origins. Spalding's preferred narrative was evident from the outset, and his ultimate "conclusion" (made clear before any actual investigating began) was that the sport's roots were American, not foreign. To that end, the Doubleday story, though sheer myth, was settled on, and the rest, as they say, is heresy. (Especially in Cooperstown.) The actual history? Baseball unquestionably has roots in England, in the games of both cricket and "rounders." Baseball's fundamental rules, however, were first laid out in America—and for-real in New York—by Alexander Cartwright, in the 1840s.

Regardless of how the sport of baseball in America began, what's both remarkable *and* true is how far back it goes (considerably further than 1839),* and how fast it caught on. Documents refer to "Base Ball" being played in 1823 on Saturdays in the area of what is today New York City's Greenwich Village. (At the time, Abner Doubleday would have been four years old.) The first organized baseball club to play under the original rules set out by Alexander Cartwright was the amateur New York Knickerbockers, formed in 1845 as a social club. (New Yorker Cartwright was a founding member.) The first competitive game between two baseball clubs took place in 1846 in New Jersey at Hoboken's Elysian Fields. (Although the Knickerbockers lost 23–1 to another New York club, they did ultimately make some tweaks to the rules of play, one of which has made baserunners grateful ever since.†) In 1857, 16 New York area baseball clubs formed the National Association of Base Ball Players (NABBP). Although the NABBP was formed as an amateur organization, compensation for players was allowed in 1869, at which point over 400 teams were competing nationally, from the Northeast and Atlantic seaboard, to the Deep South, and west to California. By 1871, the NABBP had spun off the breakaway National Association of Professional Base Ball Players and, in fits and starts, a major league of two rival "associations" (the forerunners of today's National and American Leagues) had begun to emerge. Thus, its murkier origin stories aside, only six years after the end of the American Civil War, baseball had established itself as a thriving professional sport in America, and was well on its way to truly becoming the "national pastime."

---

* In 2004, researchers in Pittsfield, Massachusetts, released a document showing that a 1791 bylaw there prohibited the playing of baseball within 80 yards of the town's new meeting house.

† Prior to the updated "Knickerbocker Rules," a fielder could record an out by throwing the baseball at a runner. Thankfully, the ball was a bit softer in this era.

And, for a time, early on, America's national pastime actually looked somewhat like America. For a brief period, professional baseball was not all white.

"To a black player just starting out, these pioneer leagues of organized baseball were the minor and major leagues of that time," writes "Doc" Kountze. "It was played by both armies during the Civil War, and may have been played then by both freemen and slaves."

BORN IN FORT PLAINS, NEW YORK, IN 1858, JOHN W. JACKSON'S FAMILY moved to Cooperstown when he was a child. The son of a freeman who became a barber, Jackson was playing baseball by the time he was 10. By the time he was 20 his professional name had become "Bud" Fowler. "Bud," apparently, was an all-purpose name he bestowed on others. There's no clear explanation for the change of last name. Some researchers, like Brian McKenna of the Society of American Baseball Research (SABR) have speculated that he did it to avoid trouble with his parents, who likely looked with disfavor on their son's chosen profession. After all, he could have followed his father into barbering, a thoroughly respected middle-class job at the time, particularly in the African-American community. Instead, Fowler chose to be a community of one. On a field of nine.

He was a versatile baseball player, to be sure. Known primarily as a second baseman, he played every position at one time or another. In 1878, he was pitching for an amateur team in Chelsea, Massachusetts, an industrial city less than five miles from Boston. On the state's North Shore, the Lynn Live Oaks, which played in the then-International Association, were in need of a replacement pitcher. Fowler answered the call. On May 17, he suited up, took the mound, and made history—becoming the first African American to play in a professional baseball game. Only 15 years after slavery had been abolished—and nearly 70 years before Jackie Robinson—professional baseball in America was integrated.

While Fowler generally stood alone on the professional teams he would play for, he was not alone as a Black man playing pro baseball, as the game's various organized leagues expanded and multiplied, spreading all across America. By the late 19th century, the game was taking root everywhere, with baseball diamonds sprouting like kudzu in every corner of the country, from fresh-mown prairie fields in the shadow of purple mountains, to rubble-cleared city lots in the shadow of gray tenements. No part of the nation was untouched by baseball, each region proving fertile ground for the new game, including areas like New England, where the actual ground seemed inhospitable even for farming, never mind sport.

Tucked in the very northeast corner of America, the six states of New England would seem to be more suited to football and hockey than baseball. For farmers, the growing season is short and as unforgiving as the soil itself. Many of the farm fields that exist today are still ringed by low, stone walls. The stones for those walls came from the fields they surround, having been dug up hundreds of years earlier so that the region's earliest farmers could till the stubborn ground to begin with. By Thanksgiving, New England's north country can be covered with snow. Even as late as April, ball fields as far south as Rhode Island and Connecticut can still be hard, brown, and brittle, the promise of green grass and warm sun still more than a month away. (A wry Vermonter once summed up his state's calendar year thusly: "Eight months of winter, and four months of pretty poor sledding.") In short, it is far more challenging to play and excel at baseball in New England than it is in Florida or Southern California, where ball fields are accessible, green, and snow-free year-round. Given the dramatically shorter "growing season" for good players, it's a wonder that any native New Englanders make it to the major leagues at all. But they do. Always have.* Beginning with Frank Grant.

"Frank Grant appears to have been the first great black ball player to come out of New England, and perhaps the entire Eastern Seaboard," wrote Kountze. "Grant was known as the 'Black Dunlap,' thus comparing him to Fred Dunlap, one of the greatest second basemen in Major League history."

He was born in 1865, just four months after the Civil War ended. Growing up in western Massachusetts in the Berkshire Hills town of Pittsfield, Grant seems to have impressed as a ballplayer from the time he first picked up a bat and ball. By 17, he was playing for the Greylocks,

---

* Carlton Fisk, Tony Conigliaro, "Happy" Jack Chesbro, and the legendary Connie Mack come quickest to mind. Though, for memorable names alone, mention should be made of Snooks Dowd, Shanty Hogan, Adonis Terry and, sweetest 'n' dicey of all, Candy LaChance.

a semipro team in neighboring Williamstown. (Mount Greylock, rising 3,489 feet above the nearby town of Adams, is the highest point in Massachusetts.) He certainly left a lasting impression on one contemporary Black player, Sol White, who was himself a notable figure in the African-American experience with early baseball.*

"In those days, Frank Grant was the baseball marvel," wrote White. "His playing was a revelation to his fellow teammates, as well as the spectators. In hitting, he ranked with the best, and his fielding bordered on the impossible. Grant was a born ballplayer."

By the age of 20, Grant was playing on his first professional team, the Eastern League's club in Meriden, Connecticut. Although the Meriden club eventually folded for financial reasons, Grant had established himself as a genuinely talented second baseman. A year later, in 1887, playing for Buffalo, he was among the best hitters in the league. In an exhibition game against Pittsburgh, the *New York Times* described Grant's play as "brilliant." While the March 14, 1888, edition of *Sporting Life* described Grant as "the colored lad," it also raved about his stellar play at second base. At bat, Grant hit .340, the third highest average in the league. And he wasn't alone.

In the East, during this time period, several Black ballplayers were establishing themselves as legitimate standouts on otherwise all-white professional clubs. In addition to Frank Grant, Bud Fowler was playing for Binghamton in New York. A pitcher, George Stovey ("a fabulous southpaw," according to Kountze) reached the highest level of the then-minor leagues in 1886 at age 20. Pitching in New Jersey, he won 50 games over the course of two seasons, and struck out more than 300 batters. Famed writer and historian Robert Peterson† later called Stovey "the first great Negro pitcher."

---

* King Solomon ("Sol") White (1868–1955) was a professional African-American baseball player and manager from the 1880s through the turn of the century. After playing, he became a baseball executive for a variety of teams, and a sportswriter. He is the author of *History of Colored Baseball*, published in 1907, and was an influence in the creation of the Negro Leagues. In 2006, he was elected to the National Baseball Hall of Fame.

† Peterson led a pioneering study of baseball history that was central to raising awareness and recognition of the vanished Negro Leagues. His 1970 groundbreaking book, *Only the Ball Was White*, was named by *Sports Illustrated* as one of the 20th century's best sports books.

Needless to say, that kind of pitching dominance would attract attention. And it did. Several major-league teams scouted the tall, thin, light-skinned Stovey. None signed him. But in the late 19th century, and the period of baseball's national boom, one Black ballplayer did, however briefly, crack the pearly white major-league gates.

"Moses Fleetwood Walker was no ordinary man, and in the 1880s he was no ordinary baseball player." Thus wrote David W. Zang, biographer and author of *Fleet Walker's Divided Heart: The Life of Baseball's First Black Major Leaguer.* It's intriguing to speculate on the influence Walker's birthplace may have had on the path of his early life. Located in the eastern part of the state, Mount Pleasant, Ohio, was a well-known stop on the Underground Railroad, the secret network of routes, transports, and safe houses that, prior to the Emancipation Proclamation, spirited escaped slaves to free states and Canada in the early to mid-1800s. But Mount Pleasant's reputation for tolerance goes back even further. The *Philanthropist,* a Quaker-connected publication, and the first American newspaper to call for the abolition of slavery, began publishing in Mount Pleasant in 1817. Walker's parents were both of mixed-race. His father, who was also an Episcopal minister, was one of the first Black physicians in Ohio. Nicknamed "Fleet" from early youth, Walker was the third son of a large family of six or seven children. (Accounts vary.) He began playing baseball as a boy in Steubenville, Ohio. At 20, he was enrolled in a preparatory program at Oberlin College, and was playing catcher and batting leadoff for its baseball team. In 1881, Oberlin fielded its first intercollegiate baseball team, and it featured two Walkers: Fleet, and his younger brother Weldy. It was an auspicious debut in many ways. The Walker brothers impressed onlookers repeatedly over the season, and ultimately both would go on to play pioneering roles in professional baseball.

The University of Michigan was impressed enough with Fleet Walker to invite him to transfer there for the upcoming academic year and the 1882 baseball season. But first, there was the summer of 1881. Call it a summer job. Walker was hired as a catcher for a semipro baseball team representing the White Sewing Machine Company out of Cleveland, Ohio. On August 21 that summer, the club was in Louisville, Kentucky, set to play a strong local team, the Eclipse. (The following year,

Moses Fleetwood Walker with the Toledo Blue Stockings, 1884

The Oberlin College baseball team in 1881: Moses Fleetwood Walker is in the second row, far left (#6); his younger brother, Weldy, is standing, third from left (#10). COURTESY OBERLIN COLLEGE ARCHIVES

the Louisville team would enter the brand-new major-league American Association as a charter member.) Before the game began, several Louisville players objected to the fact that their opponent was set to field a "negro" player. There was nothing against the rules in having an integrated team, and a forfeit, if it came to that, would have been Louisville's. Just the same, in what likely felt to Walker like a weak and humiliating gesture, his team agreed not to play him. An injury, however, to Cleveland's replacement catcher forced them to reconsider. Walker came out to warm up, and prepared to finally enter the game. Apparently even extenuating circumstances wouldn't mollify Louisville. After several players walked off the field in protest of Walker sharing it with them, Cleveland had Walker leave the field, too, and tapped its third baseman to take over as catcher. Lacking in both offense and backbone, they lost the game. Also lost, presumably, was whatever innocence Walker had held onto from home; he wasn't in Mount Pleasant anymore.

At Michigan in 1882, Walker flourished athletically, academically, and personally. The Ann Arbor baseball team went 10-3, he began studying law, and he married his sweetheart, Bella Taylor. The sting of the previous summer's experience in Louisville aside, the pull of professional baseball continued to be strong and incessant. By the spring of 1883, Walker had been signed by Toledo of the professional Northwestern League. Before he'd played an inning, however, or absorbed his first violent slide into home plate, he collided instead with more bigotry. This time, in his home state.

A motion was made by a representative from Peoria that no colored player be allowed in the league.
—FROM THE NOTES OF THE NORTHWESTERN LEAGUE'S EXEC-UTIVE COMMITTEE, MEETING AT THE BOODY HOUSE HOTEL IN TOLEDO, OHIO, MARCH 14, 1883

The notes from that preseason meeting also indicate that the Peoria motion "was fought bitterly and finally laid on the table."

At any rate, Walker opened the 1883 season on Toledo's official roster. Good thing.

The Toledo Blue Stockings, with Walker catching, won its first game, then went on to win the Northwestern League pennant. Walker was also winning over cynics and skeptics with his play. The *Toledo Daily Blade* wrote on August 11, 1883, "Walker has played in more games and has been of greater value behind the bat than any other catcher in the league." (The *Sporting Life*, ever a stickler for detail, referred to Walker in 1883 as "Toledo's colored catcher," though it did add that he was "Looming up as a great man behind the bat.")

Spring-boarded by its rousing success, Toledo moved up, shifted leagues, and entered the 1884 season as part of the vaunted 10-team American Association. Fleet Walker was still a Blue Stocking, and proudly took the field for Toledo on May 1, 1884.

In an irony as striking as the day itself, it was an away game—in Louisville, against the the Eclipse. Walker, understandably, may have been feeling more than a few nerves. He was making a reappearance in the same city in which he had been shunned and forced to leave the field just three summers earlier. He had a lousy game, and Toledo lost 5–1. The box score would show that Walker went hitless in all three at-bats, in addition to committing four errors. The box score made no mention, however, of the history that was recorded that day: Moses Fleetwood Walker had just become the first Black baseball player in the major leagues. His name, as it turns out, was eerily prophetic. For him, and others, the breakthrough would indeed be fleeting.

TWO

The White Lines Become a Wall

Stovey was by no means the first black player to show up on a white team, although there were never many at one time, and the Negro player usually stood out in splendid isolation as the only African-American on the field.
—LAWRENCE D. HOGAN, *SHADES OF GLORY*

IT WAS A STARKLY SMALL FRATERNITY. YET TWO OF THE BEST BLACK players during baseball's professional rise in the late 1800s found themselves on the same team. Pitcher George Stovey and catcher Moses Fleetwood Walker both began the 1887 season with Newark, of the International League. It was an auspicious start. Stovey won his first 10 decisions of the season; Walker had cemented his reputation as one of the best catchers in the league. When Walker caught Stovey, there was the rare sighting of not one, but two Black players on the same field—battery mates, no less—in an otherwise almost entirely white ballgame, white ballpark, and white league. And as Walker and Stovey were about to find out, playing on a mostly white team even in a northern city in the late 1800s could be illusory. Despite their official presence on the roster, there was no guarantee of real acceptance, and no real refuge from the lack of it. But then, by 1887, Walker should have been used to it: the slights, the scars, both inside and out. It was there from the beginning. On September 5, 1884, in advance of a road trip to Richmond, Virginia, the below letter was received by Walker's manager, Toledo's Charlie Morton:

Manager Toledo Base Ball Club:
Dear Sir: We the undersigned, do hereby warn you not to put up
Walker, the Negro catcher, the evenings that you play in Richmond, as
we could mention the names of 75 determined men who have sworn to
mob Walker if he comes to the ground in a suit. We hope you will listen
to our words of warning, so that there will be no trouble: but if you do
not, there certainly will be. We only write this to prevent much blood
shed, as you alone can prevent.

As it happened, Walker was injured and was ultimately released by Toledo prior to the Richmond trip. Beset by injuries for much of the historic season, he played in only six games over most of the summer. Just four months earlier, on May 1, 1884, Walker had been the first African American to play in a major-league game. Officially released on September 22, he would never play in another one.

Not that there weren't pockets of tolerance, and places where professional Black ballplayers on white teams felt more accepted and welcomed for simply doing what they, like their teammates, were there to do—play baseball. New Castle, Pennsylvania, was one such place. Located about 50 miles north of Pittsburgh, the town was home to a semipro team, the Neshannocks. In the summer of 1882, Fleet Walker was hired to catch for the "Nocks," as they were known locally. On his arrival, local press reports described him as "one of the best catchers in the country," and "a gentleman in every sense of the word, both on the field and off." Walker's biographer, David Zang, described the New Castle–area newspapers as being unique in that, "unlike those in every other city where Walker played professionally, they never made reference to Fleet Walker's color." (Nor, presumably, to any of the other players' colors.)

For professional Black ballplayers in most other places not named New Castle, references to their color were made routinely, and often obscenely. But name-calling was the least of it. Physical injury stung a bit more.

As a second baseman, Bud Fowler was often in a dangerous position anyway, as runners bore down to the bag and slid, spikes high, in an attempt to beat a throw or break up a double play. But as any infielder

Bud Fowler (second row, far right) in 1894 with the Findlay, Ohio, unaffiliated minor league team (Grant "Home Run" Johnson, is second row, far left)
NATIONAL BASEBALL HALL OF FAME AND MUSEUM

knows, there are "clean" slides and "dirty" slides—slides that are intended to merely avoid a tag, or slides that are intended to "take out" the tagger. For Fowler, it was invariably the latter. Both he and fellow infielder Frank Grant adapted to baserunners bent on malice by fashioning wooden slats, which they wore under their socks to protect themselves. For catchers, it can be even rougher. A baserunner barreling full-speed around third base and attempting to score at home plate represents a potentially dangerous threat, especially if the catcher is trying to prevent a run by blocking the plate. Even in modern-day baseball, violent collisions at home plate aren't uncommon. Nor did 19th-century catchers wear the extensive protective gear of today. Fleet Walker often faced runners less intent on scoring a run, and more intent on driving him out of the game. Over time, they nearly succeeded.

"When the 1884 season ended," wrote Doc Kountze, "Walker was so cracked up, including broken ribs, that Toledo had to release him for his own good."

Looking back, what's more striking is not that a small number of Black players made their way into early professional and major-league baseball, but that those who made it often chose to stay with it over multiple seasons, and for some, for as long as they could. Even while, as Lawrence Hogan writes in *Shades of Glory*, "Events were making life for black players in white baseball more tenuous."

The "integration" of early professional baseball, such as it was, was a fact. But only barely. From the outset, even in small numbers, it was a brittle and uneasy stasis, frequently jolted by bursts of the raw bigotry that ran just underneath it all, like the shallow roots of the grass that covered the ball fields. Sometimes it seeped, sometimes it spat. But it was always there.

Why would it have been otherwise? Baseball, after all, was not something separate from the larger society and culture in which it was played. It was a part of it. It reflected it. It represented it. And it cannot be overstated that the rapid, national growth of professional and major-league baseball took place only a decade or so removed from the end of the Civil War, and slavery. States and cities that had been Confederate strongholds (and had fought to hold onto their slaves) had only recently had their first exposure to baseball.* There is a frequent narrative regarding baseball's early history, that the growth of the sport at this particular time made it something of a balm for a recently fractured nation, that baseball itself became a building block of new unity during the period of Reconstruction.

In his book, *Baseball and American Culture: A History*, author John P. Rossi observes, "A leading sports publication, *Wilke's Spirit of the Times* argued that baseball 'was destined to close national wounds opened by the late war. It is no idle pastime which draws young men, separated by two thousand miles, together to contest in friendship, upon fields but lately crimsoned with their brothers' blood in mortal combat.'"

---

* Captured Union army soldiers were often allowed to play baseball in southern prisoner of war camps, thus introducing the game to a region of the country that had not been part of its earlier, more northerly development. By the end of the 19th century, more and more players from below the Mason-Dixon Line were represented in professional baseball.

Baseball game between Union prisoners at Salisbury, North Carolina, 1863
LIBRARY OF CONGRESS

Wilke's Spirit gets points for prose, but not for accuracy. There's little doubt that the rise of a truly national sport was a healthy development in a nation that had just nearly torn itself in two. Or that nonviolent athletic contests on a ball field were preferable to violent engagement on a battle-field. But "wounds opened by the late war" is a bit of Hallmark hooey before there was Hallmark. The wounds were willfully opened by Americans who insisted on enslaving humans, and were intent on destroying one country and creating a new one of their own in order to keep doing it. The "young men" drawn together to "contest in friendship" were almost exclusively young *white* men. And "friendship" most certainly would not describe what was commonly experienced by the relatively few Black players who *did* venture onto these new ball fields. Nor, for that matter, were the contests always nonviolent.

Other than that, *Wilke's* nailed it.

What *can* be agreed on is that the Union held, slavery was ended, and if former foes (and sons of former slaves) could find common cause around a new national pastime, well, that's all a net plus. In 1868, three years after the Civil War's end, the 14th Amendment was passed, officially conferring citizenship on all Black Americans. (More far-reaching equality and civil rights would take more than another century—and counting.) Professional baseball by the 1880s was, on balance, only marginally more integrated than medical schools, metropolitan suburbs, or the US Congress.* Which is to say, sparingly.

Just the same, professional baseball in America was not yet all white. The Jim Crow† era was taking shape, but had not completely taken root. There was some racial fluidity with respect to color barriers. That said, for Blacks at this time, it required courage, skill, talent, and, above all, an intense will and passion to play professional baseball. It required these qualities in degrees far greater than their white counterparts. Once arrived at the professional level, it required additional determination and will to withstand the ongoing, unrelenting, and often hostile pressure to leave.

But it also required something of whites.

"For African Americans to play in white organized baseball," writes Lawrence Hogan, "three groups had to agree: team management, the fans, and the rest of the players." Fans, Hogan writes, "were for the most part color blind—they applauded a good performance and booed a bad one." In its own way, management largely took the same approach—filling rosters with the best players available. But as a growing pool of good Black ballplayers competed with white players, racism was a ready wrench to throw into the advance of further integration.

"Baseball had created a situation nearly unknown in the American society of the time: Black men were taking white men's jobs," writes Hogan. "When enough white players on a team complained to management, the officials almost always wound up siding with the white ballplayers."

In reality, even before (or even without) competing for jobs with whites, Black ballplayers entered the game with two strikes against them:

---

* During the period of American Reconstruction (1865–1877), 16 African Americans were elected to and served in the US Congress. As of 2018, a total of only 10 have served in the US Senate.

† "Jump Jim Crow" was a racist African-American character stereotype, often performed onstage, starting in the 1830s. By the late 1870s, the phrase "Jim Crow" came to describe the entire period and practices of American racial segregation.

They were Black. And they were Black. Despite the temptation to see the game's early days as more integrated or more tolerant, that's the way it was from the start.

Even before the start.

The first organized ban of Black baseball players occurred in 1867— four years *prior* to the creation of the first professional league. The Civil War had ended only two years earlier. Reconstruction was in full swing. It was just 10 years after Bud Fowler was born. In the Berkshire Hills of western Massachusetts, future second-base standout Frank Grant had not yet wielded a bat; he was two. In Ohio, Fleetwood Walker was 11 years old, beginning to play baseball, but still 17 years away from his historic first major-league game.

In Philadelphia, by 1867, the Pythians were already a well-established, unique, and talented all-Black baseball club. They were led by a remarkable man whose very name suggests the classical pursuit of something lofty and civic-minded—which is what the Pythians represented to founder, Octavius Catto. He was a native of South Carolina whose family ("free people of color") had moved to Philadelphia when he was a child. A graduate of the Institute for Colored Youth, he later taught there and became an assistant principal. He was a Civil War veteran, passionate about education, abolitionism, civil rights, and baseball. The Pythians club (so named as many were also members of the Black Knights of Pythias Lodge) was conceived as a men's social organization as well as a baseball team, much like the groundbreaking New York Knickerbockers had been some 20 years earlier. The club had rigid rules forbidding drinking, gambling, cursing, and "unbecoming conduct." Club members, Catto insisted, were to be seen as upstanding gentlemen first, ballplayers second.

Led by Catto's skills as both player and manager, the Pythians did, in fact, become a very good baseball team. In so doing, they succeeded in persuading several equally good white ballclubs from various cities, such as Washington and Chicago, to play them. In Harrisburg, however, on October 16, 1867, neither their baseball skills nor their powers of persuasion could spare them a defeat that no amount of runs would have changed.

Having established themselves as a well-respected ballclub both on and off the field, the Pythians had applied to join the Pennsylvania Base Ball Association. Seemed like a reasonable thing to do, and all in line with the steady progress that had been the club's path in the Keystone State so far. The nominating committee of the Pennsylvania Base Ball Association saw things differently. The Pythians' application was denied. In addition, the committee ensured that no future Pythians would trouble themselves (or the Pennsylvania Base Ball Association) by seeking membership. By a unanimous vote, the Association barred "the admission of any club which may be composed of one or more colored persons." (Zero seems to be the figure they were aiming for.) And, lest the rejection seem tinged with bigotry, rather than the sensitivity that they apparently wanted to suggest, the committee hastened to share its peculiar (if not quite Solomonic) reasoning: "If colored clubs were admitted, there would in all probability be some division of feeling, whereas, by excluding them, no injury could result to anyone."

'Cause, you know, who minds being excluded?

Not to be outdone by a lowly state organization, the National Association of Base Ball Players also subsequently barred the Pythians from membership. For their part, the Pythians forged ahead with the same determined organization and strong team ethic that had been their hallmark thus far. Barred from membership in white leagues, their own membership swelled, eventually expanding to four separate teams, all based in Philadelphia, where the city's Black population was expanding, also. On September 16, 1869, they achieved a historic first: In defeating the City Items, a Philly team representing a local newspaper, they became the first all-Black baseball team to defeat an all-white one. It was the same year that saw the formation of the nation's first professional baseball team, the Cincinnati Red Stockings. Thus, two years before the official beginning of professional baseball, color barriers had already been placed before Black ballplayers. These early bans did not yet fully affect professional leagues. But, even at the beginning, even with some degree of integration, there were ominous signs of what was to follow.

"The Pythians . . . were barred from membership in two amateur organizations," writes Neil Lanctot, author of *Negro League Baseball: The*

Rise and Ruin of a Black Institution, "foreshadowing the eventual de facto exclusion of African Americans from white professional baseball later in the century."

The Pythians, alas, did not make it to the end of the century, and neither did their beloved founder and leader, Octavius Catto. October 10, 1871, marked the first Election Day in Philadelphia in which Blacks were legally able to vote. The days leading up to the election itself in the city were marked with heightening racial tension and violence. Catto, who was teaching at the Institute for Colored Youth, allowed his students to leave early in order to get home safely. An officer of a Black unit of the Pennsylvania National Guard, Catto himself headed home in order to both vote, and potentially be called to help keep order in the city. Before reaching home, he was shot and killed in the street by a white assailant. His killer was later acquitted by an all-white jury. The Pythians disbanded as a team shortly after Catto's death.

The irony of the 19th century's last couple of decades is that even as integration, as measly as it was, reached its highest point, the walls were closing in on Black players. Or, more likely, the walls were always there to an extent; but for a time, however briefly, there seemed to be paths through them.

And yet, 20 years after Octavius Catto's murder and the disbanding of the pioneering Pythians, early professional baseball's standout Black ballplayers were now firmly established in the game. Players like Frank Grant, Bud Fowler, George Stovey, and Fleet Walker—on almost entirely white teams—were enjoying the greatest success that Black baseball players had ever had. Yet, at the same time, like some sort of insidious inversion, they also encountered relentless, steadily mounting racism and bigotry meant to drive them out.

Bud Fowler, generally regarded as the first Black to play in organized baseball, had a career that was bracketed by bigotry. In 1881, at just 23, he was signed to pitch for the semipro Guelph Maple Leafs in Guelph, Ontario. A number of his white teammates were so adamantly opposed to playing with him that Fowler was forced to leave. Six years later, now as a skilled second baseman and standout hitter playing for Binghamton, New York, in the International League, the same situation repeated itself.

As Lawrence Hogan (*Shades of Glory*) writes, Fowler's team, "although struggling in the bottom of the standings, mysteriously found it could get along without its .350-hitting colored second baseman."

The "mystery" in Binghamton was one that cropped up repeatedly across professional baseball in the late 1800s: The most talented and productive Black ballplayers were regularly released or sold to other takers by teams that otherwise would never relinquish such productive, valuable assets to their rosters. Of these players, few seem as confounding to consider as George Stovey.

Often called the greatest Black pitcher of the 19th century, Stovey grew up and began playing baseball in rural Pennsylvania. A tall, lanky, light-skinned left-hander, he was already playing for a semipro team in the Williamsport area by the time he was 18.

His talent and passion for pitching was clear from the start.* He is known to have repeatedly recorded 10 or more strikeouts in a game. Blessed with both natural athleticism and speed, he was considered one of the best-fielding pitchers of his time.

His reputation grew quickly, as did aggressive competition for his services. He started the 1886 season with a Canadian team, but before June was over, his contract had been bought out by the fabled Cuban Giants, whose manager had traveled to Canada to personally accompany his new star back to the Giants' new home in Trenton, New Jersey.† Although Stovey's first game for the Giants was a one-run (4–3) four-hit loss to Bridgeport, he impressed nonetheless. The *Trenton Evening Times* wrote of Stovey, "If he may be judged from yesterday's game, he is all that has been said of him." And that was, in fact, all that the *Trenton Times* would be able to say about the new pitcher's time in Trenton. Stovey had also deeply impressed others. Like a scene out of a movie, the manager of the Eastern League's Jersey City team arrived in Trenton at midnight, cash in hand, in an attempt to lure Stovey, and spirit him out of town. Stovey

---

* In an article for SABR (Society for American Baseball Research), Brian McKenna writes that, "One of his friends decades later declared that Stovey was so excited to join the club that he offered to tend the ball grounds for free."

† The Cuban Giants were the first all-Black professional baseball team. Created in 1885 by the merger of three existing teams, they played initially for guests at the Argyle Hotel in Babylon, New York.

turned the offer ($200 a month) down, but Jersey City persisted, using tactics both above and below board, and ultimately a cash offer to Trenton secured Stovey's release. His first game for Jersey City was a tough 1–0 loss to Newark. More significantly, he had essentially gone overnight from an all-Black team to an all-white team, clearly a detail not lost on the *New York Times* in its coverage of Stovey's Eastern League debut: "The home nine, for the first time, played Stovey, formerly pitcher for the Cuban Giants of Trenton. He is a colored player."

Although the *Times* seemed to have missed it, he also pitched a scoreless game into the ninth inning, all while batting cleanup, striking out eight, and allowing only four hits.

For Stovey, though, racial tensions seemed to mount as steadily as the innings he was racking up. Although he pitched in 31 games for Jersey City, winning 16 and striking out over 200 batters, some had no trouble looking past his glittering stats. What they couldn't look past was Stovey's skin.

"'Tis said the other Eastern League clubs don't fancy Jersey City's employment of a colored pitcher," reported *Sporting Life* in 1866. In truth, his own *teammates* didn't much fancy it, either. When Stovey pitched, some of his white teammates, infielders in particular, simply didn't play as hard behind him as they normally might. Clearly, it was noticeable. "If the team would support him, they would make a far better showing," observed the *Sporting News*. Nor was Stovey alone in facing this phenomenon; it dogged other Black players on white teams, sometimes with more serious implications than an extra hit or run in a box score.

When Moses Fleetwood Walker was catching for Toledo (after becoming the first Black major leaguer), one of his battery mates was a white pitcher, Tony Mullane. Years later, in a January 11, 1919, interview with the *New York Age*, Mullane admitted, "I had it in for him." Ironically (or not), Mullane also admitted that Walker "was the best catcher I ever worked with." Nonetheless, Mullane would routinely throw whatever he wanted to Walker, regardless of the catcher's signs. It's a potentially dangerous thing for a pitcher to cross up and surprise a catcher with a blazing fastball when, for example, a slower, breaking pitch (like a curveball) has been called for, and expected. And it was even more dangerous in the

1880s when catchers wore minimal protective gear. Mullane recounted that, after one harrowing cross-up, Walker came to the mound and said, "Mr. Mullane, I'll catch you without signals, but I won't catch you if you are going to cross me when I give you a signal."

The deliberate crossing apparently stopped. But the chilly détente only marginally reduced the danger. "All the rest of that season he caught me," Mullane reminisced. "And caught anything I pitched, without knowing what was coming."

It wasn't only some teammates and fellow players that had it in for Black players. Sometimes those entrusted with calling the balls and strikes and enforcing the rules of the game made a bigoted mockery of both. "Eastern League umpire Billy Hoover," writes Brian McKenna (SABR), "admitted to calling close plays against clubs that fielded black players. Imagine the tight strike zone Stovey was working with when Hoover was behind the plate."

Robert Higgins could easily imagine that. And worse. Like George Stovey, Higgins was a living asterisk, a walking aberration: He was an accomplished Black pitcher making his way in a white profession. Growing up playing strictly segregated baseball in Memphis, Higgins was among those who'd integrated the International League, and by 1887 was playing for Syracuse. (He was one of seven Black ballplayers in the IL that year, including Stovey, Fleet Walker, Frank Grant, and Bud Fowler.) In the previous offseason, Syracuse had made some roster moves that made life harder on Higgins even before the season's first inning was played. After the Southern League folded, Syracuse management signed a number of the defunct league's white players. They became notoriously difficult to handle, and their open resentment and distaste for Higgins roiled the team as the season wore on. As with Stovey's experience, many of these players made little effort in the field behind Higgins when he pitched. Sometimes, there was no effort at all. In a game against Toronto, Syracuse lost 28–8 with Higgins on the mound. How glaringly obvious was the lack of effort by some of the Syracuse fielders? Only *seven* runs were earned, meaning that an incredible *21* opposing baserunners who scored were not on base because of any fault or failing of the pitcher. Indeed, the open hostility to Higgins by some of his white teammates, particularly the southerners, moved the *Sporting News* to describe them as the "Ku-Klux-Coterie" on May 25–26, 1887. The racial animosity festered off the field too. At one point early in the season, the team was to meet at a studio and sit for an official team photograph. Two of the southerners boycotted the session, citing their refusal to be photographed with a Black man. "I am a Southerner by birth," said one. "And I tell you, I would have my heart cut out before I would consent to have my picture in the group."

To his credit, Syracuse manager Joe Simmons suspended the player. But truthfully, it wasn't a team photograph that many of these white players didn't want to share with a Black man. It was a team itself. And it wasn't about undermining them on the field; it was about keeping them off the field to begin with. All 19th-century Black professional baseball players competing in white leagues had experienced lack of support, some degree of ugly racial jeers, physical intimidation, and violence and, for some, outright death threats. But this was small-bore, penny-ante stuff for the racists with power to influence league policy. Besides, these types of tactics were failing to deter the George Stoveys and Bob Higgins, the Frank Grants, Bud Fowlers, and Moses Fleetwood Walkers. Far from it—by 1887, the International League had its highest number of Black players.* Fowler was hitting .350, Grant was the league's home-run leader, Higgins had won 20 games, and there was genuine interest by some white owners in promoting George Stovey to the majors. For some, who recoiled at the notion of both Black success and increased integration in professional baseball, more deterrence was clearly necessary: not on the fields, but in the front offices. By the late 1880s, the crossing-up, the grumbling, the jeering, and the threats were inexorably moving toward a more sweeping, conclusive, and effective action: barring Black players from white leagues. Period.

Enter, Cap Anson.

Or rather, re-enter. By 1887, Anson's storied career had already intersected with some early Black professional ballplayers, most notably with Moses Fleetwood Walker. To say that theirs was a fateful meeting would be a ballpark-sized understatement. David Fleitz, writing for the Society

---

* Between 1878 and 1899, it's estimated there was a total of 33 Black players competing on clubs in organized white baseball.

Cap Anson, baseball card, 1888

of American Baseball Research, summed up the significance: "The beginning of the end of African-American participation in Organized Baseball may have begun when Cap Anson brought his Chicago White Stockings to Toledo for an in-season exhibition game on August 10, 1883."

The Cap Anson that stepped off the train with his team in Toledo after traveling the 250 or so miles from Chicago was the nearest thing to baseball's then-biggest star and most well-known personality. His was a quintessentially American, up-from-nothing, small-town-boy-makes-good story. In fact, his town was so small, it wasn't officially created until a year after he was.

Born in a log cabin in rural Iowa in 1852, Adrian Constantine Anson's family were genuine pioneers. His father, Henry, brought his wife, Jeanette, and their first child west from New York State in a covered wagon, and founded the very town (Marshalltown) his children grew up in. (And which still exists today.) Surrounded by a family of brothers following his mother's death, neither school nor much else seemed to take for the youngest Anson, until baseball reached Marshalltown in the late 1860s. At 15, he was playing second base for a team that won the Iowa State Championship. At 19 and a stocky 6 feet, he was playing semipro ball (batting .325), and by 20 he was a major leaguer, batting .415 for the Philadelphia Athletics of the brand-new National Association. Filling-out at 6-feet-2 and nearly 200 pounds, he was one of the most physically imposing players of the time. Like the powerful line drives he seemed to spray to all sides of the field, Adrian Anson was launched. By 1876, having formed a friendship with Chicago White Stockings manager Albert Spalding, he moved to Chicago where their team won the first National League pennant. By 1879, with Spalding taking over the role of club president, Anson became player-manager, as well as team captain. "Cap" became his enduring nickname. Many of his baseball achievements have endured as well. To this day, Anson, who died in 1922, still holds Cubs career records for hits, doubles, and RBIs. Like Spalding, Cap Anson was inducted into the Baseball Hall of Fame by a special committee in 1939. But while his plaque in Cooperstown justly memorializes him as the "Greatest hitter and greatest National League player-manager of 19th century," it makes no mention of what else Anson is famous for. He was also a vicious, unrepentant racist with a big, foul mouth to match. And in that infamous regard, quite likely also the "greatest" in 19th-century baseball.

FOR HIS PART, "DOC" KOUNTZE CERTAINLY KNEW ALL ABOUT CAP ANSON. The hitting exploits, and the racist ones, too. Back in that executive suite meeting above Braves Field in Boston, having broached the beginnings of professional baseball, and having found his unerring way to Moses Fleetwood Walker, Kountze may have reminded Bob Quinn of who was lurking malevolently in history.

"Cap Anson may have been a baseball hero to some white fans," wrote Kountze. "But he does not hold a high place in Colored Baseball history."

Why would he?

"The records seem to indicate that following the 1887 'high point' of Negro achievement in the minor leagues," continued Kountze, "a white revolt was instigated against blacks led by not only southern players, but also a certain 'Cap' Anson of Chicago. . . ."

What could Bob Quinn say? A decent man and a keen student of baseball history himself, he knew all about Anson, Walker, and Toledo. He knew all about what came later, too. After all, it had everything to do with why the young Black man was sitting across from him now. It might have been Quinn who now turned to gaze out the window in silence. Really, what could he say?

"Facts," as John Adams sagely observed, are indeed "stubborn things." They're still there, still facts, even if it's a half-century later. Even if they've been left off a plaque in Cooperstown that people otherwise still read in reverence today.

MOSES FLEETWOOD WALKER, AS INTENSELY PASSIONATE ABOUT BASE-ball as Anson, must have felt doubly lucky to have simply been on Toledo's roster on August 10, 1883. After all, he almost wasn't. And not for any lack of hustle or production in the field. Less than five months earlier, Walker had survived an attempt by the Peoria club, meeting with the executive committee of the Northwestern League, to consider a motion to bar "colored players" from the league. "This action was made specifically to expel Walker," writes John R. Hussman (SABR). "After a bitter fight, the motion was defeated, allowing Walker to play."

The game in Toledo was considered an in-season exhibition game. (An unusual practice by today's standards, such games in baseball's early days were almost entirely about generating extra income for the competing teams.) Anson's Chicago White Stockings were the defending National League champions. Toledo was still a new entrant to the major leagues' American Association. New or not, Chicago—and Anson— knew that Walker was on the Toledo team and, they assumed, would be behind the plate. And they apparently were not happy about it. The only surviving original source of the game's events is in the August 10, 1883, edition of a local paper, the *Toledo Daily Blade*:

> *Walker, the colored catcher of the Toledo club . . . was a source of contention between the home club and . . . the Chicago club. Shortly after their arrival in the city . . . the Toledo club was . . . informed that there was an objection in the Chicago club to Toledo's playing Walker.* *

Toledo, in turn, informed the Chicago club that their objection was moot, as Walker was nursing a sore hand, and would not be in the lineup that day. According to the *Daily Blade*, this did not mollify Anson and his team: "Not content with this, the visitors . . . declared with the swagger for which they are noted, that they would play ball "with no d----d nigger."

It didn't happen often. It hardly ever happened. But on this day, at this game, a white team, in a white league, led by its white manager (Charlie Morton), stood up for its sole Black player.

> *The order was given, then and there, to play Walker, and the beefy bluffer was informed that he could play or go, just as he blank pleased. Anson hauled in his horns somewhat and "consented" to play, remarking, "We'll play this here game, but won't play never no more with the nigger in."* (Daily Blade, *Toledo, Ohio, August 10, 1883*)

---

* Courtesy of Society of American Baseball Research

In agreeing to play the game, Anson wasn't second-guessing his incendiary behavior. Rather, a racist lout with a business sense, he knew that pulling his team off the field meant a costly double forfeit: of both the game, and of Chicago's share of the day's ticket receipts. It hardly matters today that upstart Toledo nearly beat the champion White Stockings, losing by one run (7–6) in 10 innings. What matters still today is what happened before the first pitch was thrown—for Cap Anson would hold true to his ugly pregame promise.

"NEWARK'S COLORED BATTERY IS DOING FINELY." ACTUALLY, IN EARLY June 1887, that seemed a bit of understatement from the sports page of the *Brooklyn Eagle*. The pitching half of that battery, George Stovey, didn't lose his first game until June 4. (He'd eventually win over 30 games for the season.) The catching half, Fleet Walker, was also on his way to a career year. So when the vaunted Chicago White Stockings of the National Association came to play the International Association's Newark for an exhibition game on July 14, one would have expected arguably the league's best battery to be in place. They weren't. This wasn't Toledo. On this day, at this game, a white team, in a white league, led by its white manager (Charles Hackett), did *not* stand up for its two Black—and two of its best—players.

It's unclear whether or not Stovey wasn't feeling well that day. What is known, is that a day before the game (Chicago had an off day between series in Washington and New York), Hackett had received a telegram from Chicago's fiery captain/manager, Cap Anson, informing Newark that his team would not play if Stovey and Walker took the field. This was becoming Anson's crude calling card around the game, as surely as his trademark line drives. Black players of the period came to focus not on Anson's considerable baseball skills, but on someone who, as former Black player and baseball historian Sol White recollected, was a man with "repugnant feeling, shown at every opportunity, toward colored ball players."

Newark manager Hackett claimed Stovey was ill, and inserted a substitute pitcher. Without explanation or comment, Walker was simply held out of the lineup. Although Newark went on to win the game 9–4, the headline should have read, "Newark Folds." But the day wasn't over. There was more folding to do. By an entire sport.

While the timing was coincidental, on the same day as the Chicago-Newark game, International League officials were meeting in Buffalo. The assemblage at the city's Genesee House that day didn't need a live update from Newark to be apprised of Cap Anson's threats before the game. Especially given his standing in the game, Anson's bitter and hateful haranguing about Black players in professional baseball had been having an effect. But they'd heard the same from others. The refusal of many white players to play with Blacks was becoming endemic. In late June, nine white players of the Binghamton, New York, team signed a petition demanding that the club's two Black players—Bud Grant and William Renfro—be released.

Needless to say, at the July 14 meeting in Buffalo, the "Colored element" was front and center on the agenda. A contemporaneous report describes what transpired when it came up: "Several representatives declared that many of the best players in the league are anxious to leave on account of the colored element." With dissent only from two clubs (Buffalo and Syracuse), the board then voted to direct (the aptly named) "Secretary C.D. White" to approve "no more contracts with colored men."

It was done.

With that single vote, what had been sporadic, if increasing, hostility by some white players and club officials became official policy. A July 15, 1887, story in the *Newark Evening Journal* about the decision was headlined, "Color Line Drawn in Baseball." The door which had allowed Black players to enter professional baseball, and which had been at least partly, if grudgingly ajar, was now closing. Fast. And while the International League's decision on July 14, 1887, did not immediately or completely end Black participation in the league or in professional baseball, it did put in place the beginning of the end. It would be more than half a century before what happened in Buffalo—and in Newark—would begin to be reversed.

"Cap Anson was not entirely responsible for baseball's more than half-century of segregation," writes John R. Husman, "but he had a lot to do with it."

Following that momentous day, the few Black players already playing, including the established standouts—Walker, Hovey, Higgins, Fowler, Grant—were allowed to honor their existing contracts and continue to play in the league.

Professional baseball's racial divide, which was always present but implicit, was now out in the open and official. Or rather, it only *felt* that way to Black players. In truth, there was nothing open or official about what had taken place in Buffalo. To be sure, the ban on signing Black ballplayers was very real, and the color barrier that formed in its wake was as stark and impassable as if it loomed up in actual concrete and concertina wire. But nothing was written down. No public positions had been laid-out, no baseball-wide vote had been taken, no edict-for-the-ages had been announced, its contents published, to be viewed, vilified, or defended. And never would be. Not in 1887, not in 1947, not to the present day. It was an unspoken, tacit, secret pact wordlessly adhered to throughout major- and minor-league baseball: Blacks would not be signed, and not allowed to play. "The Gentleman's Agreement" in baseball held for nearly six decades. It remains the national pastime's original sin.

A year after the color barrier was drawn, Weldy Wilberforce Walker, Fleet Walker's younger brother, became the first ex-Black major-league ballplayer to make an official statement, of sorts, about the segregation that had now overtaken professional baseball. Weldy had continued to try and make a go in professional baseball. In the footsteps of his older brother, he had also played with Toledo in 1884, becoming the second Black major-league baseball player.* A good player, but lacking his brother's standout skills, Weldy Walker's last brief, recorded stints in organized ball were in 1887, with Akron of the Ohio State League, and with the Pittsburgh Keystones (an all-Black team). Out of baseball, Weldy Walker partnered on several business ventures, including a restaurant, and a hotel. He also became active politically on racial and civil rights issues. In Steubenville, Ohio, he was part of an effort to integrate a roller rink.

---

* Weldy Walker remained history's second Black major-league baseball player until April 15, 1947, when just the third Black major-league player in 63 years took the field in Brooklyn, New York: Jack Roosevelt Robinson.

(Denied admittance, they won damages in court.) He and his brother Fleet became co-editors of the *Equator*, a Black newspaper. Increasingly outspoken on issues of race, Weldy Walker frequently wrote open letters to various publications. On March 5, 1888, he wrote one such letter to the *Sporting Life*, in the form of an appeal to the president of the Ohio Tri-State League, which, a month earlier, had repealed a league provision allowing for the signing of Black players.

> *I am convinced beyond doubt that you all, as a body of men, have not been impartial and unprejudiced in your consideration of the great and important question—the success of the "National game . . ."*
>
> *The law is a disgrace to the present age, and reflects very much upon the intelligence of your last meeting, and casts derision at the laws of Ohio—the voice of the people—that say all men are equal. I would suggest that your honorable body, in case that black law is not repealed, pass one making it criminal for a colored man or woman to be found in a ball ground.*
>
> *There is now the same accommodation made for the colored patron of the game as the white, and the same provision and dispensation is made of the money of them both that finds its way into the coffers of the various clubs.*
>
> *There should be some broader cause—such as want of ability, behavior, and intelligence—for barring a player other than his color. It is for these reasons and because I think that ability and intelligence should be recognized first and last—at all times and by everyone—I ask the question again, why was the "law permitting colored men to sign repealed, etc.?"*
>
> *Yours truly,*
> *Weldy W. Walker*

For Weldy Walker's older brother, walking away from baseball was tougher. Staying in it was tougher still. Now 31, Walker signed on with the International League's Syracuse Stars for 1888. But the strain and struggle of the past five years, both physically and emotionally, was evident. Although he played well enough to help the team win the pennant, his hitting was weak. The following season it dropped off even further, and his catching skills diminished, too. Worse, in a sad sign of things to come, Walker had developed a gambling habit, frequently owing large sums of money. (During an 1888 Syracuse trip to Toledo, the Stars signed over their share of the game's receipts in order to pay off Walker's debts in the city.) He was released by Syracuse on August 23, 1889. He'd be the International League's last Black player for 57 years.*

In 1888, Frank Grant had the unenviable experience of staying on with Buffalo, in the very city where the color ban had been enacted a year earlier. To further protect his bruised and battered legs from the flashing spikes of malevolent baserunners, Grant began playing in the outfield. In July, he injured his arm running into an outfield wall. Metaphorically, that also described his continuing effort to play in the white minor leagues. That same year, the *Louisville Post* summed up Grant's challenge just within his own team: "The players of the club are said to feel keenly having to play with a colored man."

(Or pose with one. No official team photo was taken for the season, "on account of the nigger," offered a teammate.) In a blatant acknowledgement of not playing their best with Grant on the field, the *Sporting Life* reported in 1888 that some players vowed that the team's fortunes wouldn't improve "until the colored man is fired."

As it turns out, the team's fortunes apparently involved more than just jettisoning "the colored man." In 1889, unsuccessful in seeking his former salary ($250 per month), Grant left Buffalo. A year later, without their best hitter, and following what the *Sporting Life* called a "dreary and disastrous season," the Buffalo Bisons left Buffalo too.

Following his 20-win season for Syracuse in 1887, Robert Higgins had another good season in 1888, helping Syracuse win the International League title. A year later, tired of the taunts and the pay disparity, Higgins was running a barbershop in Memphis. No more baseball. But also no more having to pose for a picture with people who didn't want him in it.

---

* After signing with the Brooklyn Dodgers in the fall of 1945, Jackie Robinson was assigned to Brooklyn's Triple-A minor-league team, the Montreal Royals, which played in the International League.

George Stovey's 1888 summer sojourn in New England was no day at the beach. "Stovey, Worcester's colored pitcher," wrote the *Boston Globe* in 1888, "has fine curves, but no head for working a batsman." What the *Globe* didn't add was that, as Stovey knew from painful experience, it was tough to work an opposing batsman when your own infielders might or might not try to field the ball a batsman hit. Over 11 games, he went 6-5 for Worcester of the New England League, before being released in July.

But of all the early Black baseball pioneers, even after the color barrier descended, none had a longer, more extraordinary go of it than Bud Fowler. Which seems either ironic, unlikely, or both. At age 20, in 1878, Fowler was the first in. That May, he was picked up as a pitcher by the Lynn (Massachusetts) Live Oaks of the newly formed International Association. When he took the mound, he became the first African American to integrate a white team, and the first to play professional baseball. Incredibly, his career would wind through another 30 years, from east to west, north into Canada, and south to Texas. Fowler seemed to never stop playing baseball, sometimes playing on half a dozen different clubs, in different climates, all in the same calendar year. Later in his career, he claimed to have played baseball in every state. Even a quick look at his biography suggests that's entirely plausible, not to mention exhausting. He lived, it seems, for baseball. Crisscrossing America, he played in many top minor leagues but, unlike the Walker brothers, never had the chance to play for a major-league team. It certainly wasn't for lack of trying. Or lack of talent. By the time he was 25, his speed, hitting, and defensive wizardry all over the diamond had become the buzz around baseball. Alas, his one overriding hurdle was the one he could do nothing to overcome.

"He is one of the best general players in the country," commented the *Sporting Life*. "And if he had a white face would be playing with the best of them."

Playing second base with Montpelier (Vermont) of the Northeastern League, he became the first Black captain of an integrated baseball team. From the Green Mountains to the Rockies, Fowler left an impression as a particularly amiable man and a strikingly talented ballplayer whose glowing reputation, even long before electronic media, often preceded him. In 1885, having been hired based only on such second-hand newspaper accounts, Denver, of the Colorado League, sure seemed surprised to find out more details about Fowler.

"Fowler," reported the *Rocky Mountain News* on August 16, 1885, "turns out to be an African American gentleman, Black as the ace of spades, but a crack baseball player." Over time, Denver's "surprise" was clearly looked back on as a pleasant one. "Fowler will always be a favorite in Denver," observed the *News* a year later.

At other times, the same surprise played out much less pleasantly, especially after 1887 and the ban on Black players. With his relentless travels around the country and extensive experience in professional baseball, Fowler was keenly attuned like no other Black player to the rapidly tightening vise of segregation. Indeed, that may have been part of his thinking in putting together the New York Gorhams in 1887. It would be the first of his many all-Black barnstorming teams, and originated a tradition that would later become common in Negro League Baseball. He planned to make New York his base and continue with the Gorhams the following season. But as a fierce and talented competitor, Fowler found it hard to give up the larger and more prominent stage that was white professional baseball.

In 1888, similar to what happened in Denver three years earlier, Fowler signed on to play with the Lafayette, Indiana, team—whose scouting report *also* apparently did not include the fact that their new signee was Black. "It was thought that Fowler was a white man," reported the *Logansport Pharos Tribune* in 1888, "and quite a surprise was in store for the Lafayette players when they discovered that he was a genuine darkey."

For Lafayette, unlike Denver, the surprise was clearly too much. The team cancelled Fowler's contract. In turn, Fowler publicly called out the Lafayette management. "As a body of businessmen, who contract with players and pay them advance money," said Fowler, "they ought to know enough to find out who and what they are getting for their money."

As documented by Brian McKenna for the Society for American Baseball Research, Fowler then signed with the nearby Crawford Hoosiers of the Central Interstate League.

Crawford clearly did know who and what they were getting for the money, and Fowler shined as a Hoosier, even as erstwhile compliments on his play were jarring in their casual ugliness.

"Fowler is playing a great game at second, and it is a very unusual thing for a ball to get by him," commented a writer for the *Sporting Life*. "I shall be very much surprised if the 'coon,' as he is called, does not have a record equal to any in our National League in his position."

Considering that Mr. *Fowler* (as he was actually called) hit nearly .300 in just over 53 games, that would have been a very safe assumption. Not that Fowler then, in 1890, was getting anywhere near the major leagues. For that matter, his continued efforts to find a new landing spot in the minors were also becoming a miserable experience. As McKenna writes, "A quote in the *Dubuque Daily News* in July [1890] cited Fowler's plight in the predominantly white minor leagues: 'As [IL] president Atherton said yesterday, if only he had been painted white, he would be playing with the best of them.'"

That was an opinion widely shared, not just about Bud Fowler, but about many of the early Black ballplayers, by both their contemporaries and those that researched the period later.

"Frank Grant, Bud Fowler and George Stovey," declared baseball researcher and author Robert Peterson, "were unquestionably of major-league star caliber."

"In no other profession has the color line been drawn more rigidly than in baseball," wrote Sol White, a former teammate of Fowler's, an accomplished early Black ballplayer in his own right, and later author of *Sol White's Official Baseball Guide*. "Were it not for color, many would be playing in the big league."

Decades later, Mabray "Doc" Kountze was even more emphatic. "By the 1880s," he wrote, "Negro baseball players knew they could equal, and even surpass, many white ball players, including those in the Major Leagues."

Bud Fowler undoubtedly felt that way. And over the decade of the 1890s, he kept looking, tirelessly, ceaselessly, for just a shot at showing it. Amply fulfilling Brian McKenna's description of him as a "baseball nomad," Fowler, between about 1891 to 1902, either played for teams and/or appeared in games in Michigan, Nevada, New Mexico, Texas, California, Missouri, Illinois, Indiana, Ohio, Wisconsin, Nebraska, and Michigan. He had also developed a talent for marketing himself. And, as

McKenna writes, what was now the stuff of legend around baseball certainly gave him plenty to promote himself with: "He regaled writers with stories of playing match games for trappers' furs and playing in farming communities, pioneer settlements, mining camps and Old West towns. In a few years, he would add to the mystique by tweaking his age and billing himself as the oldest active ballplayer in the game."

In 1894, in Adrian, Michigan, he partnered with two white businessmen, and the white owner of the Page Woven Wire Fence Company, to form the Page Fence Giants. Traveling around the country in a custom-built train car, playing mostly white semipro teams, the Giants truly became the first genuinely successful Black barnstorming baseball team, and offered both a template and a glimpse of what dozens of Negro League teams would begin replicating in earnest by the 1920s. Fowler was player and manager for the new team that may have won over 100 games in its first season. But he left before the debut season was over. Once more, ignoring all the present racial reality, Fowler felt the familiar and seemingly incessant tug to try to hook on with a white minor-league team. And one more time, he did.

He caught on with the Michigan State League. (This was his second go-round with the MSL; the first had been with Greenville in 1889.) He played first with Adrian, and then, finally, with Lansing. It would be his last official roster spot as a Black player on an otherwise all-white team.

By 1900, Fowler was focusing his still immense energy on creating Black barnstorming teams. In Findlay, Ohio, he and a partner formed the All-American Black Tourists, which, like the Page Fence Giants, traveled and played other semipro teams for several years. By 1904, Fowler began efforts to establish a Black professional baseball league, but investors balked, and the project stalled and ultimately fell apart. "One of these days," Fowler lamented to the *Cincinnati Enquirer* in 1904, "a few people with enough nerve to take the chance will form a colored league of about eight cities and pull off a barrel of money." Fowler was seeing the future. Accurately. But he wouldn't quite live to see the birth of the Negro Leagues. He died of a blood disorder in Frankfort, New York, in 1913.

He was only 55.

Bud Fowler's gravestone, Frankfort, New York
COURTESY SOCIETY FOR AMERICAN BASEBALL RESEARCH

His unmarked grave told not a word of a truly extraordinary life.* For years since the color ban began to spread in 1887, Fowler had relentlessly fought for a place in organized baseball. Along with the other early Black professional players, he had continued to try and play in the shadow of

---

* In 1987, the American Society of Baseball Research purchased and placed a headstone on Fowler's grave. The inscription reads, "John W. Jackson: 'Bud Fowler,' Black Baseball Pioneer."

the descending barrier, as teams shed Black players and refused to sign more. Fowler had uncommon talent, no question. But often it seemed his greatest skill was in seeming to somehow doggedly outrun the inescapable end. As if he simply willed himself to persevere, to compete and play and even excel in an increasingly hostile landscape that, move about as he might, expelled him at shorter and shorter intervals. In Michigan, Fowler was finally was out of options. They all were. But he had outlasted the others.

"My skin is against me," Fowler had written in 1895. "If I had not been quite so black, I might have caught on as a Spaniard or something of that kind. The race prejudice is so strong that my black skin barred me."

Now, as the 20th century unfolded, it barred them all. The color barrier was complete. It would take another 50 years of fierce Fowler-like will and determination to break through again.

THREE

Separate, Not Equal

You would have to have seen them brown boys play,
to believe the legends from back in the day . . .
Made to play the national pastime,
on the "no coloreds" side of the Jim Crow line.
—Terry E. Carter,
"Of Black Diamonds and Brown Legends"

The first week of May 1887 was not a good one for the Boston Resolutes. It had been an unusually rainy late spring up and down the Eastern Seaboard. From Boston down to Baltimore, baseball games were postponed and rescheduled. But getting a game in wasn't the Resolutes' biggest concern. Getting home was. While visiting in Louisville, Kentucky, for two scheduled games, the new league in which the Resolutes played suddenly folded and went out of business. Which must have come as something of a surprise to the team, since the league was only a week old. Nearly a thousand miles from home, the Resolutes had no league, no money, and no means of getting back to Boston. They were marooned in Louisville.

The Resolutes deserved better. But then, so did all Blacks in baseball. Established in 1870 by Marshall Thompson, they were Boston's first semi-professional Black baseball team. Well run and well managed, they played consistently good baseball, and were considered by many to be the best all-Black baseball team in New England. By 1887, as integrated baseball clubs grew scarce, and the pressure to segregate grew stronger, Blacks at all levels of baseball felt a pressure of their own: to find a viable outlet for the wide pool of talented players increasingly without an organized league to compete in. Late in 1886, Walter Brown, an African-American journalist,* organized a meeting between some of the leading Black baseball clubs. The result was a first: the brand-new, six-team National Colored Baseball League (NCBL). (Just before the season's launch in May, two more teams were added.) The kickoff was auspicious and encouraging, with a parade and a brass band concert preceding the game between New York and Pittsburgh (at Pittsburgh's Recreation Park), won 11–8 by the visitors, and watched by approximately 1,200 people. From there, alas, things went downhill in a hurry for the league, as it was hit by a perfect storm of events, only one of which actually involved the weather.

From Louisville, the Resolutes were scheduled to travel on to play in Baltimore. But the bad weather had caused so many cancellations that their week-long trip had already turned into two, and had already burned through their limited travel budget. In addition, their Louisville stay coincided with the Kentucky Derby, so railroads had hiked their rates to take full advantage. To make matters even worse, railroads were also fighting back against the recent passage of the Interstate Commerce Act,† causing general widespread confusion and uncertainty regarding train schedules and ticket prices. The Resolutes watched as their games, their season, their league, and their ability to get back home dissolved with each drenching downpour. Weeks later, on their own, team members were still steadfastly making their way home, affording each leg of the trip by working in barbershops and at hotels all along the route back to Boston. So much for auspicious beginnings.

As ironic it sounds, however, the 1887 fiasco that was the failed National Colored Baseball League nonetheless helped lead to an ultimately positive and pivotal event—the eventual creation of the fabled Negro Leagues three decades later. To be sure, the Negro Leagues would suffer their own fits and starts over their 30 years or so of existence. But collectively, the leagues also represent perhaps the single, greatest unsung

---

* Brown was a correspondent in Pittsburgh for the *Cleveland Gazette*, then one of the nation's most successful African-American newspapers.

† President Grover Cleveland signed the 1887 bill in order to rein in the monopolistic power the railroads had wielded, and to impose fairer rates and some degree of federal regulation.

hero on the road to returning Black ballplayers to their rightful place in the national pastime. Ray Dodson, vice president and curator of the Negro League Baseball Museum in Kansas City, Missouri, has a very short answer to the question: "Would baseball's color barrier have fallen without the Negro Leagues?"

"No."

Indeed, exactly 60 years after those dampened and disillusioned Resolutes made their soggy way back to Boston, Jackie Robinson himself would be the first former Negro Leaguer to again take the field with a major-league team.

But the Resolutes were hardly the first all-Black baseball club. (The Pythians in Philadelphia were a thriving ballclub by the late 1860s.) Neither, needless to say, were the Negro Leagues the first attempt at organizing multiple Black teams. As with other long and winding social struggles in history, change evolves gradually, in those same fits and starts. (Resistance to social change, however, is generally more immediate and continual, without the fits and starts.) But if there hadn't been a critical mass of talented Black baseball teams by 1887, the NCBL could not have been organized. And if there hadn't been the Cuban Giants, the path to that critical mass would have been less clear too.

The Cuban Giants were not based in Cuba, nor were they Cuban. They were, however, among the first Black baseball teams to call themselves "Giants," which represented a bit of trailblazing of its own. From Boston and New York, south to Philadelphia and Baltimore, and west to St. Louis and Chicago, the name "Giants" would become a conspicuously popular name for Black baseball teams. The Negro League Baseball Museum's Roy Dodson offers two thoughts.

"For one, and from early on, the major-league New York Giants baseball team proved to be very popular." But the more likely and persuasive explanation is that the name "Giants" also carried a hidden meaning. "Traveling black teams," says Dodson, "didn't always want to say on a poster or a placard that it was a black team; 'Giants' became a kind of code."

The Cuban Giants became history's first Black professional baseball team. Not bad for a roster that was originally filled out in part by hardworking hotel waiters.

Frank P. Thompson was a headwaiter at the Argyle Hotel in Babylon, New York, a summer resort on Long Island. He also loved playing baseball on off hours with his workmates. By 1885-1886, their pickup games had become a draw for the hotel's white visitors, who gathered eagerly to watch. Soon, Thompson and his mates started playing—and winning—against white amateur teams in the area. A local white promoter joined with a Black manager to help fill out the team with additional, experienced ballplayers. A busy schedule against white teams was arranged (along with salaries), and the Cuban Giants were launched. With nary a Cuban in the bunch.

"They were neither Cubans, nor Giants," underscored Sol White, who played with the team (among at least a dozen other Black teams), and later wrote about them in his book, *History of Colored Base Ball*. "When that first team began playing away from home, they passed as foreigners—Cubans, as they finally decided—hoping to conceal the fact that they were just American Negro hotel waiters."

The players, according to White, also embellished the ruse by talking "in a gibberish to each other on the field which, they hoped, sounded like Spanish."

Whatever it sounded like, it looked a lot like really good baseball. Their fame, and success grew, as did their travel. Their Black manager, Stanislaus Kostka "Cos" Govern, was a native of the Virgin Islands, and the team began making frequent playing trips to the South and warmer climes, where they could extend their playing schedule. They'd play their way down to Florida, waiting tables again if they needed to (often in St. Augustine at the Hotel Ponce de Leon). The Cuban-less Giants also played several winters in Havana, Cuba. (Presumably the "gibberish" sounded less like Spanish there.) In the spring, repeating the cycle, the team would play its way north again.

Over the first few years, the team went through several different owners and home bases, from New York, to New Jersey, to Pennsylvania. Players also came and went, lured by better offers, diluting further what had been the original team. In 1891, yet another new owner, E. B. Lamarr Jr. of Brooklyn, reconstituted the team and rebranded them as the "Cuban X Giants." (A rival edition—the "Original Cuban Giants"—continued to compete.) The Cuban X Giants played successfully in the East for 10 years and, like the first Cuban Giants, competed with fanfare in Cuba, also.* But their most important achievement was that they had formed at all, and then succeeded, with a roster of all Black, all salaried players. The Cuban Giants were never part of an established league, but were considered skilled and talented, and a consistently good draw, so were able to regularly fill their schedule with a wide range of opponents, from college teams, to amateur and semipro teams, to well-established professional minor-league teams. Their reputation attracted even some major-league teams to find open dates on their schedule for exhibition games.

Some regretted it.

During the summer of 1886, the American Association's Cincinnati Red Stockings had an opportunity to take advantage of an open date between series in Philadelphia and Baltimore. On July 21, in Trenton, New Jersey, before a standing-room-only crowd, the major-league (white) Reds squared off against the independent, all-Black Cuban Giants.

Nine innings later, the Reds were anxious to leave town. A day later, having not received it, the *Cincinnati Commercial Tribune* was still anxious for a detailed box score of the game. History records it as a 9–4 Giants win, their first victory over a major-league team. How talented were the Cuban Giants? "With the exception of Frank Grant, Moses Fleetwood 'Fleet' Walker, and John 'Bud' Fowler," Sol White wrote, "they had the best colored base ball the world could produce."

Ironically, when the Giants beat the Reds in 1886, those three Black baseball stars—Grant, Walker, Fowler—were still playing, or trying to remain playing, in white professional baseball. A year later, in the aftermath of Cap Anson, Buffalo, and the color ban, the three were still involved in white professional baseball only because their individual, active contracts were still being honored. There would be no more Black players joining them. Their final seasons in white baseball were more about fending off hate than playing a game they loved. In later years, rather than being able

---

* In Havana, in the spring of 1900, the Cuban X Giants played a series against a variety of native Cuban ballclubs on the island. The Giants won 13 of 15 games, but the two games won by Cuba's Criollo team—beating America's best "colored baseball team"—established that baseball had truly come of age on the island. The series, and Criollo's impressive play, led to both the rapid growth of baseball in Cuba, and to more talented Cuban players coming north to play.

to relish major-league memories, as their white former teammates did, the three found themselves apart, embittered, and mostly impoverished.

What matters most about the Cuban Giants, then, was that, despite the despair and disillusionment in the wake of the color ban, they pointed a way forward for talented Black ballplayers. The Giants, and the multitude of professional Black teams that would follow them, showed it was possible to still play baseball at a high level—indeed, even to beat white major-league teams—on their own clubs, in their own leagues. Yes, they had been shut out of the major leagues, but they would not be shut out from baseball. For the time being, however unfair and immoral, they would work with the landscape as it was, on their own, with what they had. It could be said, with some important distinctions, that Black ballplayers were "casting down their bucket" where they were. In fact, it was exactly what the most important Black leader of the time did say.

By any measure, Booker Taliaferro Washington was a truly transformational figure and, by the late 19th century, one of the most significant African Americans to have lived. Born in 1856 into slavery in Virginia, his life, career, and achievements unfolded and echoed as inspirations for more than a generation. His contributions to education are still felt today. Over the course of his life (he died at 59 in 1915), he became friends with powerful philanthropists and business leaders, and consulted with presidents.

Having taught himself to read as a child, Washington attended Hampton Normal and Agricultural Institute (Hampton University today) and Wayland Seminary (now Virginia Union University). In 1881, he became the first leader of Alabama's pioneering Tuskegee Institute, a role and relationship that both occupied and defined the rest of his life and career. Booker T. Washington's guiding philosophy was that education and learning a useful trade was key for Blacks, and he preached it tirelessly as the most prominent African-American spokesperson of the period.

In Atlanta, on September 18, 1895, Washington gave a historic speech on race relations. In it, before a mostly white audience (at the Cotton States and International Exposition), he called on Blacks to do everything they could to prepare for, and look for work. And he called on whites to hire Blacks, to allow them to aggressively compete for jobs with the waves of immigrants then arriving in America. Washington used the phrase, "Cast down your bucket where you are," which had great, if differing symbolism for both whites and Blacks, but was understood to be a call to make the most of one's situation, whatever and wherever it is. On relations between Blacks and whites, Washington also said, "In all things purely social, we can be as separate as the fingers, yet one as the hand in all things essential to mutual progress." Among some African Americans, Washington's tone was considered too accommodating to achieve meaningful progress on civil rights and racial equality. (NAACP cofounder W. E. B. Du Bois called the speech the "Atlanta Compromise.") A year later, that progress seemed further away than ever, no matter the approach. In a momentous and landmark decision, the US Supreme Court would ensure that, for Blacks, the "fingers"—and virtually everything else in American life, including baseball—would indeed be kept separate.

As train rides go, it was a short one. Heading out of New Orleans, Louisiana, it barely went a few city blocks before stopping. And yet, in its way, that train and what it symbolized really steamed on for four more years, over a thousand miles, and into history.

Homer Adolph Plessy boarded that train on June 7, 1892. A French-speaking Creole (the son of Haitian refugees), Plessy was a US citizen born in 1862 in New Orleans, where he was raised and spent his entire adult life, first as a shoemaker, then as an insurance collector. An early civil rights activist, he belonged to the New Orleans Citizens' Committee, which sought to address the loss of racial advances made in the wake of emancipation and the withdrawal of federal troops following the Civil War. During this period, the state of Louisiana (and others) began instituting its own state-mandated segregation laws and regulations. Among the more onerous of these involved transportation. While federal interstate commerce laws still prevented full-on segregation as it pertained to railroads, the East Louisiana Railroad ran only within the boundaries of that state, making it possible to enforce the state's new law requiring Blacks to sit in a "colored only" section of the train. Homer Plessy agreed to work with the Committee in creating a test case of the state's new law. He boarded the train in New Orleans and was quickly asked to take a seat in the "colored only" section. He refused, was removed from the train, arrested, and convicted of breaking state law. (Louisiana judge John Howard Ferguson presided.) His conviction was sustained through the state courts and ultimately made it to the US Supreme Court, where Plessy argued that both his 13th (abolishing slavery) and 14th Amendment (equal protection) rights had been violated. The Supreme Court saw things differently. With only one dissent (Justice John Marshall Harlan of Kentucky), the high court ruled in favor of Louisiana. Just two sentences from the majority opinion convey why the decision is still viewed as a particularly shameful moment in American democracy:

> *We consider the underlying fallacy of the plaintiff's argument to consist in the assumption that the enforced separation of the two races stamps the colored race with a badge of inferiority. If this be so, it is not by reason of anything found in the act, but solely because the colored race chooses to put that construction upon it.*

Today, thanks to this decision's legal contortions, moral abdication, and all that it presaged, *Plessy v. Ferguson* occupies a special place in infamy.* It re-created a legalized class system only 30 years after the end of slavery and the beginning of Reconstruction. Worse, it was no temporary setback; it would be over half a century before it was overturned.† Any incipient racial progress, including in baseball, now ground to a halt. In the ruling's wake, local segregation ordinances, which had already proliferated (as in baseball) but had lacked real legal muscle, now had it. Across America (including the North), in small towns and big cities, Jim Crow/"Whites Only" laws now moved into the open, and moved in to stay. For two entire generations of African Americans to come, virtually

---

* In 2009, a survey conducted for the American Bar Association found that Plessy was one of the two "worst cases" ever decided by the US Supreme Court. (The other was *Dred Scott v. Sandford*, the 1857 decision that upheld slavery.)

† In its landmark *Brown v. Board of Education* ruling in 1954, the Supreme Court found that "separate but equal" was not valid, and that no legal basis existed for racial segregation.

every facet of daily life—health care, housing, education, work, transportation, recreation—would now be defined by legalized, state-sponsored racism, segregation, and the doubly insidious doctrine of "separate but equal": insidious for both the raw bigotry that underpinned it, and for the ugly, blatant lie it always represented.

It didn't take long for Jim Crow to settle in and get comfortable with the American landscape. Only a few years after *Plessy*, a young catcher for the Ohio Wesleyan baseball team had his own bitter taste of the new normal in America. In South Bend, Indiana, with his team to play Notre Dame—and as the team's only Black player—he was refused a room at the team's hotel. The team's white manager asked for, and received, special permission to allow the catcher to sleep on a cot in his room. ("So long as this relationship of master and servant was obvious," the team manager recounted years later, "then it was perfectly all right with whites who otherwise would object to a Negro's staying in the hotel.")

The incident turned out to be a formative one for both men. Years later, the manager would movingly describe how he had returned to the

The 1904 Ohio Wesleyan University baseball team: Branch Rickey, manager, is rear row, far right. Charles Thomas is standing center, rear row.
COURTESY OHIO WESLEYAN UNIVERSITY

room after dinner, and found the young Black man in tears, clawing at his own hands.

"Black skin, black skin. If only I could make them white," he sobbed.

Four decades later, the young manager, Branch Rickey, had become president of the Brooklyn Dodgers. He would say that the scene in that South Bend hotel room that night haunted him his whole life. Seeing young catcher Charles Thomas's despair that night, Rickey later claimed, was a significant influence in his decision to sign Black Negro Leaguer Jackie Robinson, and break baseball's color barrier. By 1947, the (frequently repeated) Thomas anecdote certainly added some poignant and personal context to Rickey's role in a watershed moment in American history. And yet, however "haunted" he may have been by what he saw that night in South Bend, Rickey apparently was able to carry on, haunted and all. For nearly 50 years. Meanwhile, as the start of the 20th century unfolded, every Black baseball player in America was now Charles Thomas. No hotel had a room, no restaurant a table, no cab a ride. That was haunting, too. And Jackie Robinson was a long, long way off.

IN HIS PRIME, THERE IS NO RECORD OF RUBE FOSTER EVER ADMITTING to being haunted by much of anything. But then, looming up at 6'4" and 200 pounds, glaring from the pitcher's mound just prior to unleashing a screaming fastball, it was mostly Foster who did the scaring, and opposing batters who felt haunted.

But Foster's imposing physical stature is mirrored by the equally out-sized position he holds in baseball history. He is often referred to as the "Father of Negro Baseball."

"Jackie Robinson is considered by many to be the African-American who had the greatest impact on the integration of baseball," wrote Tim Odzer for the Society for American Baseball Research. "But perhaps the person with the greatest impact upon African-American baseball is the less renowned Andrew 'Rube' Foster. Despite facing immense racial prejudice, Foster persisted to carry out three distinctive baseball positions in his lifetime."

Indeed, Foster followed a playing career that established him as one of the best pitchers of the early 20th century by becoming an equally impressive and successful manager. Then, as an entrepreneur, Foster forged new and expanded opportunities for Black ballplayers. During the years of segregation, Foster's efforts provided them, if not a field of dreams, then at least the fields and the framework to keep the dream *alive* on. It was the Negro Leagues.

"The reason why Rube Foster was called "The Father of Colored League Baseball," Mabray "Doc" Kountze wrote, "obviously is because, after and even during his playing days, Rube had the typical Texas mind of big ideas, among them a plan to organize colored leagues throughout the country to train and ready them for the major leagues; a day he knew was inevitable."

As with so many Black ballplayers of the late 19th and early 20th century, Foster's pathway in baseball was full of twists and turns, but marked throughout by a determination to play the game however and wherever it was possible. He was born in 1879 in Calvert, Texas, a member of the first generation of African Americans born free of slavery. His mother was from Mississippi, his father was a preacher, and Foster, their fourth of six children, left school after the eighth grade to pursue a life in baseball. (He'd actually started earlier; in grade school Foster had formed and operated his own baseball team.) He pitched first for the Waco Yellow Jackets, an independent Black team. He moved next to Chicago to play for another Black team, the Chicago Union Giants. Still waiting to find his footing and true talent as a pitcher, Foster was released and caught on with an integrated semipro team in Otsego, Michigan. Here, he came fully into his own. Sought out by the Cuban X Giants in 1902, Foster won an astounding 44 games *in a row*, and pitched the team to a championship. A year later, Foster flipped over to the Philadelphia Giants, pitching them to a championship over the same team he'd played for the previous season. How far and how dazzling had Foster's reputation as a pitcher grown? The legendary manager of the New York Giants, John McGraw, is said to have sought Foster's help in working with his pitchers, including the future Hall of Famer, Christy Mathewson.* Among Foster's cagey

---

* Foster is said to have gained his nickname in 1902 by winning a game over another white future Hall of Fame pitcher, the Philadelphia Athletics' Rube Waddell.

and unorthodox tips for pitchers: mess with the batter's head—not with the ball, but with cunning. Especially when you're in trouble.

"Do not worry. Try to appear jolly and unconcerned," Foster suggested. "I have smiled often with the bases full with two strikes and three balls on the batter. This seems to unnerve."

Seems to have worked for Foster.

In demand, and hopscotching teams, Foster made his way back to Chicago, this time as player-manager for the Leland Giants, winners of 110 games and a Chicago City League championship in 1907.* Already the leading Black pitcher of the period, and having gained genuine respect as a strict but smart and strategic manager, Foster now set his sights on a new position: executive. He had in mind to own and run his own team. Having attempted and failed to gain ownership of the Leland Giants, he split with the team's owner, Black baseball executive Frank Leland, and in 1910, began putting together his own team, the Chicago American Giants. Foster was able to attract some of the greatest Black players of the period, such as shortstop John Henry "Pop" Lloyd,† and second baseman Grant U. "Home Run" Johnson. Overseeing a team brimming with talent, Foster pitched and managed the Chicago American Giants in 1910 to a staggering record of 128-6. With the 1911 season, Foster began a partnership with the son-in-law of Chicago White Sox owner Charles Comiskey. Foster's team was allowed to play at the Sox's former field, South Side Park, an arrangement that allowed Foster to significantly increase bookings for his team, and that boosted his status as a significant and respected mover and shaker in Black professional baseball. As owner, manager, and pitcher, his Chicago American Giants were a fearsome and dominant team for over a decade. By 1915, though, Foster himself was

---

* At the end of the Giants' 1907 season, Frank Leland, the team's Black owner and baseball executive, attempted to organize another Black professional league, the National Colored League of Professional Ball Clubs. The plan, for a midwestern league of 13 teams, never got off the ground. Other Black owners balked at both the financial investment, and the prospect of losing existing revenue from their many games with other Black and white midwestern semipro teams.

† Lloyd is considered one of the greatest shortstops ever. No less a baseball immortal than Hall of Fame shortstop Honus Wagner once said, "I am honored to have John Lloyd called the 'black Wagner.' It is a privilege to be compared to him." In 1977, Lloyd himself was posthumously inducted into the National Baseball Hall of Fame.

slowing down. Devoting more time to managing, to promotion, bookings, and the business of his team, he played less and less. He made his last official pitching appearance in 1917.

His playing days over, Foster now had the time, the position, and the experience to turn his attention to two things whose absence he had long lamented: the lack of any organizational structure for all the disparate, regional Black teams, and the lack of a national Black baseball championship. In addition, one element of Black baseball that *did* exist all too well—the frequent raiding of other team's rosters—was something that Foster (and other Black owners) was determined to address.* Not that these ideas were new, nor was Foster the first to push for them. The last years of the 19th century and the first decade of the 20th was a period of explosive growth for Black ballclubs. Many crisscrossed constantly much of the East and the Midwest, and (as we've seen) dipped down south as far as Florida, Mexico, and Cuba. Others, like the legendary Hilldale club in Philadelphia, created a winning tradition and loyal fan following by largely staying in place. Sporadically, attempts were made to loosely organize some of these powerhouse Black ballclubs. There were sound economic reasons for it. And there was survival. By this point, stability and cooperation had allowed white Major League Baseball to divide itself into two, well-organized, eight-team leagues.† All of which had turned the 16 major-league teams (and their individual owners) into enormously lucrative businesses.

Foster had no illusions that he and his fellow Black baseball owners could easily replicate this. The restrictive racial divide that ran across baseball ran clear across America and encompassed all of daily life. But Foster was determined to work with what he had. His goal, he said, was "to create a profession that would equal the earning capacity of other

---

* During the early days of Black professional baseball (and truthfully, through much of the later Negro Leagues as well), players were continually lured to rival teams with offers of higher salary, and/or a fuller schedule of games, which also translated into additional pay. For Black ballplayers, it was about maximizing both. Such was the tenuous nature of their game, and there was little owners could do to keep talented players from thus being "poached" by competitors. It was not uncommon for sought-after players to wear several different uniforms in a single season.

† The National League was created in 1876. Founded 25 years later (1901), the American League is still often referred to as the "Junior Circuit."

professions, and keep colored baseball from the control of whites."* For the future of Black professional baseball, Foster argued, "Organization is its only hope. With the proper organization, patterned after the men who have made baseball a success, we will, in three years, be rated as other leagues are rated . . . we could then let the best clubs in our organization play for the world's championship with other clubs, champions of their leagues."

Foster was certainly familiar with the futility of past efforts to organize Black baseball, including the unsuccessful attempt by his own former employer, Frank Leland.

Leland's successor as owner of the Leland Giants, Beauregard Moseley, also pushed hard for an organized Black baseball league in 1910. He made some progress, but despite putting together an association of eight cities, it failed to launch. By 1919, with the same steely sense of purpose and determination he'd shown on the mound, Foster set about conferring with other Black owners, promoting his grand vision: a viable, truly organized, and truly national Black baseball league.

"We will always be the underdog," Foster warned, "until we can successfully employ the methods that have brought success to the great powers that be in baseball of the present era: organization."

In the early innings of the effort, pitching the league idea proved considerably tougher for Foster than pitching a baseball had been. Progress was frustratingly slow, and initially, Foster could neither cobble together wide national agreement, nor easily attract investment from African-American financial sources.

"Few black entrepreneurs possessed the necessary capital, and even those with adequate resources were unenthusiastic about investing in something as uncertain as a professional baseball team," says Neil Lanctot in *Negro League Baseball: The Rise and Ruin of a Black Institution*.

---

* As segregation took hold, and Black baseball clubs grew in number and renown, several sports promoters and executives who had previously booked white semipro teams turned their attention and interest to include Black teams. Few were as prominent as Nathaniel Colvin "Nat" Strong. A white, New York sporting goods salesman, Strong had been involved in early Negro League baseball. By 1906, with ties to city political figures, Strong became the most indispensable (and unavoidable) booking agent for all Black and white semiprofessional clubs in the New York area. For nearly 30 years, if a team needed to arrange for a field to play on, Strong was the man to deal with. And pay.

"Moreover, because of rampant prejudice, Blacks at least initially needed whites to lease playing fields and arrange games with white opponents."

But a tide was turning for Foster. And while it didn't involve baseball directly, it would affect it—and Foster's fortunes—greatly. A social upheaval was underway, and Foster began to have the advantage of a growing "wind" at his back: the mounting, massive movement north of millions of his fellow African Americans.

It would become known as the Great Migration. Between 1915 and 1960, more than five million American Blacks uprooted from the South and moved northward. (By World War II, they were also moving westward.) It was fed by several factors: the rampant racism of a South unbound following reconstruction, and the deepening hopelessness of both entrenched segregation and the lack of any real economic opportunity for the future. At the same time, with America's entry into World War I in 1917, and with thousands of white workers having enlisted or been drafted, northern cities and factories faced sudden, crippling labor shortages.* Waves of African Americans responded. The growth of Black communities in Chicago, Detroit, Cleveland, Philadelphia, and New York was dramatic and significant. (Between 1910 and 1920, the Black population in Philadelphia rose from 84,000 to 134,000.) Seemingly overnight, the makeup of these major cities was changing, as was every facet of African-American life within them—including baseball.

The Great Migration spurred "unparalleled growth and development of Black enterprises," according to Neil Lanctot. "The burgeoning black 'metropolises' of the northeast and Midwest facilitated the establishment of separate hospitals, banks, self-help organizations, publications, and businesses, most notably the continued expansion and development of black baseball."

For his part, Rube Foster realized how significant these rapidly growing, urban Black communities were to his goal of advancing an organized, national Black baseball league. In these communities, African-American

---

* African Americans also had an active presence in the Allied war effort. With America's entry into the war in 1917, thousands of Black men volunteered for combat. By the time of Germany's surrender in 1918, nearly half a million African Americans had served—in segregated units—with America's Expeditionary Force in Europe.

World War I soldier with American flag

businesses were also growing, and prospering. At the same time, despite new empowerment within these growing Black communities, it was a source of continuing frustration for Foster (and other Black entrepreneurs) that links to white partners and white financial interests were still essential and unavoidable. It was a question of access. As in, access denied. And more proof that "separate but equal" guaranteed only the "separate" part. Without access to their own fields and stadiums, Black teams needed to rent or create partnerships with white teams who owned their own ballparks. (As Foster did in Chicago.) Without access to scheduling top white teams to play against, Black teams needed to engage white booking agents (like Nat Strong), who then took their own (often hefty) share of the team's profits. But Foster saw subtle changes that gave him hope. Whereas a decade earlier, it was mostly whites who turned out to see Black teams play, that was changing. By the second decade of the 20th century, with more and more African Americans migrating north, Black baseball teams looked out at crowds that were no longer all white. This was the wind that Foster was hoping to harness.

"I have fought against delivering Colored baseball into the control of whites," Foster said in 1919. "Thinking that with a show of patronage from the fans we would get together."

Events during that same year added to Foster's feelings of urgency in establishing a viable Black baseball league once and for all. In the summer of 1919, a race riot broke out in Chicago. Its causes were many: the influx of African-American arrivals, along with other European immigrants, all competing for sparse housing and jobs amid a war's end, an economic downturn, and wary, more-established immigrant communities determined to protect their turf. It lasted a bloody week, and resulted in 38 deaths and hundreds of injuries. Arson and looting were widespread and largely unchecked. In some Black neighborhoods, marauding white gangs torched entire blocks. Foster had seen enough. It had never seemed more vital to "get together."

On February 13, 1920, at a YMCA in Kansas City, Missouri, Foster convened a meeting of fellow Black team owners. It had not been the first. But Foster was determined it would be the last, and that this time, after years and years of trying, there would finally be an agreement.

A man with a keen sense of stagecraft and promotion—not to mention no lack of confidence—Foster had brought with him a legally executed charter document for the proposed new league. All it lacked was signatures. In entering into an official organization, several of the assembled owners continued to express worries about losing some of their individual autonomy. For their part, players, too, had concerns about their own freedom, and fears that an organization would affect their ability to individually seek out the best deals and highest pay. There were even concerns directed at Foster himself. Some owners worried that, in his new position, and as the owner of Chicago's American Giants, Foster might arrange schedules and games in ways that might benefit his team, and himself. Foster reminded his colleagues that, ultimately, their individual interests aside, they only had each other, and they needed each other. The wider world of white baseball was neither their salvation nor their refuge. It had rejected them. It certainly would not carry them to success. Only they could do that for each other, with each other. To further drive his argument, Foster unveiled the new league's motto: "We are the ship, all else the sea."

He carried the day. The ship was launched. Eight teams (the same as the major leagues' National and American Leagues), all in the Midwest, would begin the 1920 season. The Negro National League—forerunner of the fabled Negro Leagues—was born.

THERE WAS GREAT FANFARE WITH THE RISE OF THE NEWLY ORGANIZED Black baseball league. But the excitement about the new Negro League was part of a larger sense of energy and optimism that the Great Migration had spawned. Across the now swelling and bustling Black communities full of new arrivals, from Chicago to New York, there was a surge of Black creativity and achievement: in business, in politics, in the arts, and in sports. It was perhaps best exemplified in what became known as the Harlem Renaissance, where New York City's mushrooming Black community saw an explosion of new voices, new paintings, new music, new literature, and, above all, a new spirit. For many African Americans, it all spoke to a new way of thinking. About themselves. The "New Negro" was both a book by Alain LeRoy Locke, and a new term for the 1920s.

It was a statement of dignity and empowerment, a repudiation of meekness and of Jim Crow acceptance. But more broadly and importantly, it was as if a deep and stunning seam of skill and talent had been chipped away and revealed for both Black and white America to marvel at: writers like Locke, Langston Hughes*, and Dorothy West; painters and sculptors like Jacob Lawrence and Augusta Savage; musicians like Louis Armstrong, Ethel Waters, and Duke Ellington. And electrifying baseball stars like Smokey Joe Williams, Judy Johnson, Oscar Charleston, and James Thomas "Cool Papa" Bell.

By the 1920s, in their own way, Black baseball players had already been spearheading a drive for equality for decades. Theirs had been, and continued to be, a fight for the freedom to pursue a job for which many of them were as eminently qualified as their white counterparts, sometimes more so. When, despite their talent, segregation and Jim Crow forced them off the field and out of the game, they formed their own teams. And now, they had formed their own well-organized league. As it launched, the Negro National League carried with it high hopes, and high expectations.

"The workings of this league will be watched with more than passing interest by everyone," observed Ira Lewis, an African-American journalist for the Black newspaper, the *Pittsburgh Courier*. "If it is successful, as we all hope, look for a further merging of colored business interests on a national scale."

It was certainly an auspicious start. In the NNL's first year of operation, it's estimated that more than a million people turned out to see league games and support the various eight teams. By the second season in 1921, there were some growing pains. Two original teams dropped out of the league, but were replaced by two new ones. The fundamental elements that had drawn the owners together, however—more stable and dependable schedules, improved promotion, greater financial security— were holding. And eastern baseball owners noticed. On December 16, 1922, in Philadelphia (at another YMCA), a number of leading Black

---

* Writing about the period's emerging Black artists, Hughes wrote, "We will express our individual, dark-skinned selves without fear or shame. If white people are pleased, we are glad. If they are not, it doesn't matter. We know we are beautiful. And ugly too . . . if colored people are pleased we are glad. If they are not, their displeasure doesn't matter either . . . we build our temples for tomorrow . . . and we will stand on top of the mountain, free within ourselves."

James Thomas "Cool Papa" Bell, with the St. Louis Stars, c. 1930
National Baseball Hall of Fame and Museum

baseball team leaders met to discuss the possibility of doing what their counterparts in the Midwest had done: realigning from a loosely knit group of independent teams into an officially organized league.

The eastern owners, however, had even less incentive to organize. As Lawrence D. Hogan points out in *Shades of Glory*, "Strong, independent, prosperous teams had existed for several years in major eastern cities. These clubs had regular access to their own parks. Patronage had been built up. Good transportation by train over relatively short distances made travel an affordable operation."

In the end, in the East, where a large number of good teams shared regional rivalries, the lure of, and strong fan appeal for well-organized and regular, dependable scheduling settled the debate. Reliability was reassuring. The Eastern Colored League (ECL) would form a companion league for the National Negro League. For the first time, Black baseball had succeeded in creating an organized, national, two-league structure similar to the white major leagues from which they had been banished.

By 1923, with the leagues fully, if not perfectly, operational, half of Rube Foster's goal had been realized. A genuine "Negro Baseball World Championship" still seemed elusive. That was partly because there was still plenty to bicker about between respective owners. In fact, some of the most intense interleague competition was happening off the field. It was known as player "poaching," and it remained a charged and divisive issue. *Raids* was the term Foster used. His own Chicago team had already lost contracted players to Eastern League ballclubs, putting him in no mood to sit down and organize a World Series.* But by the 1924 season, a collective clamor for a championship series finally wore down, or at least pushed aside, owner enmities. On September 10, representatives of the NNL and ECL met in New York City at the 135th Street YMCA (naturally) to hammer out the details. Foster was happy that his dream was coming true. He was less enthused that, after a tight, season-long race, his own Chicago American Giants had lost out to the Kansas City

---

* Foster had also riled the feathers of even some of the biggest boosters for a Negro World Series, like Ed Bolden, Black owner of the successful Eastern Colored League Hilldale club. Renowned for aggressively attracting and signing talent (including those already signed elsewhere), Bolden accused Foster of financial improprieties. Foster denied it and called Bolden a liar. None of which helped their mutual dream of a World Series happen any faster.

Monarchs for the Western title. Worse, the Eastern League winners were none other than the Hilldales, from Darby, Pennsylvania. On the bright side for Foster, the meeting had also resulted in the formation of a commission to deal with inter-team contract disputes. So there was a bit of a salve for the tempestuous league creator who may otherwise have been tempted to take his bats and balls and go home.

The first Negro World Series began on October 3, 1924, in Philadelphia. For African Americans, it was regarded as a dramatic and truly meaningful milestone both for Black baseball in America, and for the American Black community. And it didn't disappoint. It took 10 games to produce a winner. The series star was Kansas City's player/manager, black Cuban pitcher José Méndez, who appeared in four games and won two, including a shutout in the final and deciding game.* While rockier days lay ahead for the Negro Leagues, it's ironic that, in victory, the Kansas City Monarchs pointed the way to further history, greatness, and ultimately the biggest victory of all: re-integrating Major League Baseball. The Monarchs would not only become one of the Negro League's most storied and successful teams, but the most famous Negro Leaguer of all time—Satchel Paige—would one day wear its uniform. And the last team Jackie Robinson played for before signing with Brooklyn was the same Kansas City Monarchs.

For a few more years, the leagues soldiered on, but financial stresses and dissension between owners and clubs were all growing. By the third Black World Series, following the 1926 season, trouble was gathering on the horizon, both for the Negro Leagues, and the nation. It seems bitterly ironic that Rube Foster's American Giants won the West that year, yet the team's leader—and the league's founder—was not in the dugout for the very event he had so long sought for, and had finally reached. Years of struggle and stress had taken a toll; Foster suffered a nervous

---

* By the time Méndez played for and managed the Monarchs, he was already a baseball legend in his native Cuba, where he was known as *El Diamante Negro* ("The Black Diamond"). A dominating pitcher for the island's Almendares club in the early 1900s, he awed—and beat—a succession of visiting American major-league teams. In 1912, famed New York Giants manager John McGraw, who compared Méndez with pitching greats Walter Johnson and Grover Alexander, candidly gushed, "If Méndez was a white man, I would pay $50,000 for his release from Almendares." And if McGraw had been a courageous white man, he might have done just that for even half the money.

First Colored World Series: October 11, 1924, Kansas City, Missouri: Rube Foster is standing center, light suit and white hat; J. L. Wilkinson is fourth to the left of Foster. LIBRARY OF CONGRESS

breakdown, and was placed in the Illinois State Hospital in Kankakee. He never recovered from mental illness, and died of a heart attack on December 9, 1930. At his funeral in Chicago, which was attended by thousands of people (3,000 of whom stood outside the church in the snow), he was properly eulogized as the "father of Negro baseball," the man without whom the Negro Leagues would not have existed.

With Foster gone, his American Giants faltered as a club, never seeming to recover their footing. Neither did the Negro Leagues more generally. Of broader concern, the entire American economy's footing suddenly seemed less steady, too. As the 1920s neared an end, what had been a roaring and record-setting decade had slowed to something decidedly more dark, anxious, and uncertain. By September 1929, the roof began to fall in.

FOUR

A Broke Nation, a Busted League,
a New Beginning

If stupidity got us into this mess, then why can't it get us out?
—WILL ROGERS

IN 1930, AS THE TIGHTENING TEETH OF THE GREAT DEPRESSION TRULY sunk into the bone of the American workforce, every day approximately 12,000 Americans lost their job and about 23,000 people committed suicide. One of them was a young man in Milwaukee who was found in a rooming house with four cents in his pocket, along with a note. It asked that his body not be removed until the rent was due.

In 1930, the US population was just over 123 million. Of that, more than 15 million were now unemployed. Over 10,000 banks failed during the Depression, wiping out the savings of millions and millions of Americans. In 1930, more than 20,000 businesses went bankrupt. A year earlier, the unemployment rate had been under 4 percent. Within a few years, it was 25 percent; fully one in four Americans were out of work. It's hard now to imagine what that landscape looked and felt like: the fear, the anxiety, the want, and the humiliation. For many families, the floor was gone. And pretty much everything else. It was not uncommon for kids as young as 12 or 13 to be encouraged to strike off on their own: one less mouth to feed, one less body to clothe.

"Depression," photograph by Mark Benedict Barry, 1934
LIBRARY OF CONGRESS

As bleak and brutal as the national landscape loomed in the Depression's wake, it was even worse for African Americans, who were worse off to begin with.

Prior to 1929, owing to institutionalized racism and segregation, the overwhelming majority of African Americans worked in low-skilled and low-paying jobs. They were also generally subjected to a rule of "Last Hired, First Fired." With the Depression, that call became louder and more aggressive, as unemployment soared and masses of white workers were now competing with Blacks for the same few jobs. In 1932, while the white unemployment rate hovered at an alarming 25 percent, Black unemployment in Chicago, Pittsburgh, and most urban areas reached 50 percent. In Philadelphia and Detroit, it was higher. In 1934, the jobless rate for Black workers in Atlanta reached an astounding *70 percent*.

Along with waves of others, Black-owned businesses were also decimated by the Depression. Often operating on much tighter margins and with far less capital, many of these businesses were extremely vulnerable even before the collapse. The growing Black banking industry was particularly hard hit. By 1938, only about a dozen of the 135 Black banks founded between 1888 and 1934 were still in operation. Theater owners, barbers, Realtors, grocers, even the (then) relatively few independent Black farmers were devastated by the Depression.*

The business of baseball was not exempt from the economic ravages of the Great Depression. It was, however, exempt from widespread sympathy. After all, it was a *game*, and most people in the nation's struggling cities were a bit more focused on food, family, or rent payments. For most, tickets for a ballgame became an extravagance that was quickly and easily dropped. During the Depression years, the white major leagues saw a dramatic drop in attendance. While the 1920s had been the most exciting decade in the game's existence, the Depression years saw major-league stadiums that sat 45,000 dotted at many games with only a 10th of that.

But the major leagues soldiered on. Many teams were owned by extremely wealthy men whose deep, established business holdings and broad investment portfolios made them less vulnerable to the economic crisis of the moment. In 1933—one of the toughest Depression years— young Tom Yawkey bought the Boston Red Sox for $1.25 million. It barely dented his fortune. He'd recently turned 30, and inherited $40 million.

The Negro Leagues were hardly in the same position. As businesses, the teams that Rube Foster had cobbled together 10 years earlier had lived hand-to-mouth existences, entirely dependent on playing enough games over the course of a year to generate enough money to meet salaries. (Which were continually reduced.) Indeed, the Eastern Colored League had folded in 1928, a year before the crash. In 1929, an effort was made to create a new league, the American Negro League (ANL), composed of five of the six original ECL clubs that were still viable. Sixty

---

* Dearfield, on the plains of eastern Colorado, was founded in the early 1900s by Black entrepreneur Oliver T. Jackson, who wanted to create a community where Blacks could buy property and farm their own land. By the 1920s it was a thriving town of over 700 residents. But by the 1930s, the combination of the Great Depression and the Dust Bowl that followed forced most people to leave the town and seek work in Denver. Dearfield's last official resident, a niece of its founder, died there in 1973.

of the planned 80 games were played before the fledgling league also collapsed. Although most of the cities involved—Baltimore, Brooklyn, Philadelphia, and New York—had strong fan bases, alas, compromise and cooperation had never been the calling card of many of these teams' owners. And needless to say, 1929 was hardly a good year to open so much as a lemonade stand, never mind a multi-city, professional baseball league.

For Foster's creation, the Negro National League, the crushing economic climate was proving equally merciless. Once the most profitable organization in the NNL, Foster's own former team, Chicago's American Giants, withdrew from the league in 1931. A year after Rube Foster died, his dream of a national Negro baseball league was expiring as well, one struggling and overextended team at a time. A year later, the pride of Darby, Pennsylvania, the once dominant and trendsetting Hilldale club, was forced to disband for lack of fan support. In fairness, fans never actually *withdrew* their support; they had nothing to support their beloved team with. In 1932, the unemployment rate in neighboring Philadelphia hit 60 percent.

"By late 1932," wrote Neil Lanctot (*Negro League Baseball: The Rise and Ruin of a Black Institution*), "black professional baseball in the east and Midwest had virtually returned to its pre-1920 status of a handful of unaffiliated professional teams scheduling exhibition games on little more than an ad hoc basis."

And yet, as grim as the landscape was in the early 1930s, it would ironically be in Pennsylvania that the beaten-down business of Black baseball would make a comeback.

Even in the depths of the Depression, one could draw a straight line from the events that began to unfold in Allegheny County in 1932 through the golden age of the Negro Leagues, and straight to Jackie Robinson and the fall of the color barrier. The greatest Black baseball talent ever seen was about to be concentrated between two teams, in one single, greater metropolitan area. The two teams would rival each other for some of the greatest success in baseball, perhaps all of sports history. The two owners responsible for these two teams—and for the rebirth of a lame and limping game—could not have been more different. In fact, they detested each other. But Black professional baseball survived the

Depression largely because of them. The legends that came to define the Negro Leagues and who truly set the stage for Robinson—Satchel Paige, Josh Gibson, Cool Papa Bell—all played for these two men. In the same city. Before Brooklyn, there had to be Pittsburgh.

It's a city that seems to have always been a bridge between places: from the Northeast to the Midwest, from the South to the North, from two large rivers (Allegheny, Monongahela) to a larger one (Ohio). Before Emancipation, runaway slaves from southern states called the Ohio the "River Jordan." Such was its near biblical significance in coming out of more modern bondage. For many, traveling northward along the Underground Railroad and crossing the Ohio River in Pennsylvania was the watery passage between slave states and free states, and the symbolic bridge between flight and freedom.*

It seems altogether fitting that Cumberland Willis Posey Jr. and William Augustus Greenlee would both establish their careers in Pittsburgh. In the most unlikely of ways, they ended up as the Allegheny to the other's Monongahela: two entirely separate streams, two dramatically different and distinct currents of life, ultimately contributing to one larger river of richer, shared history.

Homestead, Pennsylvania, is a borough of Pittsburgh, less than 10 miles southeast of the city's downtown. A relatively integrated and booming steel town by the late 1800s, it was here that Cumberland Willis Posey Sr. and his wife, Angelina, a teacher, settled and began a family. The elder Posey's rise was remarkable in itself. The son of former slaves, he first found work as a deck sweeper on a river ferry in Virginia. Fascinated with boat engines, he studied and worked his way up to assistant engineer. In 1887, continually overcoming racism, he became the nation's first officially licensed African-American ship engineer and river pilot, earning the title, "Captain." "Cap" Posey, as he became known, eventually broadened his career to include boat building, general manager of one coal company, and owner of another, and a partner of industrialist Henry

---

* Known today as the "City of Bridges," Pittsburgh has three more bridges (446) than Venice, Italy, and ranks fourth in the world for cities with the most bridges.

Clay Frick.* Posey became a leader of Pittsburgh's Black community, as well as the first president of the *Pittsburgh Courier*, a Black newspaper that began publishing in 1910. The Poseys were among the wealthiest of western Pennsylvania's elite Black families.

In 1890, Cumberland Willis Jr. was born in a huge home on a Homestead hillside street. The youngest of three (two boys and a girl), "Cum" Posey Jr. grew up in Homestead and seemed to be a natural athlete, playing football, basketball, and baseball as a teenager on local teams. Despite being only 5-foot-9 and a compact 140 pounds, Posey was tough and quick, and a particular standout in basketball, leading his high school team to a city championship in 1908. A year later, he entered Penn State, where he became the school's first Black student athlete. He also seemed more focused on hoops than books, and withdrew after two years. Back in Homestead, Posey put together the Monticello Athletic Association basketball club and began playing whatever games he—as the club's manager, promoter, and booker—could put together. They were good. In 1911, the club beat Howard University's basketball team and began to attract a local following. They had few resources, or places to practice. Urban neighborhoods weren't dotted with courts; basketball as a sport was then only about 15 years old. (Pittsburgh's first public playground wasn't created until 1908.) As in most places, the city's few indoor gyms were whites-only. But Posey was wily and resourceful. He found ways, and, by all accounts, it was during this period that he first developed the traits and the toughness that he would draw on later in putting together the professional teams he drove to excellence. In 1912 his team won the Colored Basketball World's Championship. In the wake of its growing success, the team found sponsorship and became professional. Which became an issue in 1915, when Posey enrolled at Pittsburgh's Holy Ghost College (today Duquesne University). In order to play for the school's basketball team and maintain his amateur status, he played there under the name of "Charles W. Cumbert." He needn't have worried; ultimately the pull

---

* A fabulously wealthy industrialist, financier, and a founder of U.S. Steel (as well as a patron of the arts), Frick also played a questionable role in both the calamitous Johnstown Flood in 1889 (Frick was an owner of the failed South Fork Dam), and the Homestead Steel Strike in 1892, which resulted in nearly a dozen deaths of strikers and strikebreakers.

of professional competition was too great. In addition to a brief foray at the University of Pittsburgh in 1915, Posey had attended three different colleges, but never graduated. At any rate, the most relevant education for the career he was launching had been gathered on the vacant lots, city streets, and the gyms he and his teammates had secretly slipped into at odd hours to practice. And no class could have taught him how to build and promote a team, and finesse a schedule that would attract both well-known and established opponents, as well as fans and spectators willing to pay good money. Young Cum Posey seemed as tireless as he was fearless, and ready to turn his athletic talents and business skills to baseball.

There had been an organized ballclub in Homestead, Pennsylvania, since 1900, when a group of Black men in Pittsburgh came together to create the Blue Ribbon Industrial League Team. For 10 years, the Blue Ribbons played other sandlot teams in the Pittsburgh area, mostly on weekends. In 1910, turning semipro, the team changed its name to the Murdock Grays. A year later, Cum Posey joined the team, his above-average speed and natural athleticism finding a perfect place in center field. In 1912 the team officially became the Homestead Grays.

Cum Posey had clearly found a home. What's striking is how quickly he made it his own. He became team captain in 1916, and was the on-field manager only a year later.

The experience he'd gained booking and promoting basketball games allowed him to begin scheduling wider and more varied competition for the Grays. By 1920, Posey had partnered with a local businessman, Charlie Walker, to purchase the team. The 1920s saw the team transition from semipro to a salaried club, and in 1922, Posey was able to contract with the major-league Pittsburgh Pirates for use of their Forbes Field. The Eastern Colored League had just been formed, the East Coast's equivalent of Rube Foster's midwestern Negro National League. Although Pittsburgh fell between both regions, both leagues wanted the Grays. But Posey and Walker made the determined decision to remain unaffiliated. The team made its money by keeping up a near-constant barnstorming schedule of its own making, and Posey wasn't about to give up that independence, or revenue. So he didn't. He did seek out the best talent he could get though, and it showed. The Grays became a regional powerhouse. In 1926, they played 153 games; they lost only 13. During the season they went on a 43-game winning streak. (By comparison, the longest regular-season win streak ever by the New York Yankees is 19 games in 1947.) At one point during the following season, they won 31 straight games.

In 1929, the Grays did join the short-lived American Negro League (which had replaced the Eastern Colored League), and it marked the last season in which Cum Posey appeared as a player. When the ANL folded, Posey went on something of a spending spree, signing the core of players who would, within a season or so, make up arguably the greatest baseball team of all time. Center fielder Oscar Charleston was already a famed Black ballplayer, as was slick-fielding third baseman William Julius "Judy" Johnson. Six-foot-four Smokey Joe Williams threw a fearsome fastball.* In 1930, Cum Posey was able to poach a coveted young catcher from a crosstown rival, the Pittsburgh Crawfords. A year later, in a neat bit of symmetry, 20-year-old Josh Gibson caught a pitching staff that counted *four* 20-game winners. He also hit nearly .400 with 40 home runs. If those were virtually the only stats one knew about the 1931 Homestead Grays, one would think they must have had a pretty good season. They most certainly did.

"You could safely say this," observed Negro Leagues authority Brian Carroll, a professor at Berry College in Georgia. "Rarely, if ever, have more of the very best that the Negro Leagues have ever had [worn] the same uniform at the same time."

The Grays' final season record in 1931 was an extraordinary 143-29-2.

Although Posey had lured star slugger Gibson to the Grays this time, the rivalry with the Crawfords was only in the first inning. As dominant as the Grays seemed in 1931, the lead would change hands. Power would shift. So would players. The owners were digging in.

His nickname was "Big Red"—just one of many quirks of a Black kid born in rural North Carolina in the shadow of the Blue Ridge Mountains. His mother's dad was a white businessman; her mom was Black.

---

* A Texan who was half African American and half Native American, Williams once struck out 27 hitters in a 12-inning, one-hit win. Awed by his sheer speed and pitching power, Hall of Famer Ty Cobb said if Williams had pitched in the major leagues, he'd have won 30 games a season.

Aerial view of The Point, Pittsburgh, Pennsylvania, 1930
ARCHIVES & SPECIAL COLLECTIONS, UNIVERSITY OF PITTSBURGH

William Augustus Greenlee was born light-skinned with reddish hair to Samuel and Julia Greenlee in Marion, North Carolina.* The couple had seven children (three girls, four boys); Sam made a decent living as a masonry contractor. A big and broad-shouldered young man, Gus Greenlee no doubt disappointed his parents when he dropped out of college after two years. His three younger brothers, however, salved that somewhat by each going on to careers in law and medicine. Ironically, without ever earning a degree, Gus Greenlee may have made as much money as any of them. Or more. Although, his line of work was definitely not what you hang out a shingle for.

In 1916, at 20 years old, Greenlee rode a freight train north to Pittsburgh, where he found odd jobs, and a place to live in the city's Hill District. He shined shoes, worked in a steel mill, and labored for a

---

* Greenlee's birth year is variously listed as 1893, 1895, 1896, or 1897. Curiously, there seems to be a general agreement it was definitely not 1894.

73

construction company. With some money saved up, he bought his own taxi cab. He also married a local young woman named Helen. (They had no children.) A year later, with the United States at war, Greenlee enlisted and served with the Black 367th infantry regiment as a machine gunner. He saw combat at Verdun, was injured (he sustained shrapnel in his leg), and was discharged in 1919. Returning to Pittsburgh, Greenlee seemed determined to find something more lucrative than taxi tips.

With the beginning of Prohibition in 1920, he found it.

A private taxi, it turns out, was the perfect delivery vehicle for running illegal liquor to illegal speakeasies. With a white partner (Joe Tito, co-owner of the famed Latrobe Brewery), Greenlee added, "Bootlegger" to his ever-diversifying professional resume. Soon, it became more diverse still. The partners opened up their own club on Pittsburgh's Wylie Avenue. It was raided and closed in 1922. They reopened two years later, bigger and better, with live music. Greenlee seemed to have found a niche owning entertainment properties, so he expanded. He opened a pool hall, a small cafe, and then, back in his neighborhood Hill District, at the corner of Crawford Street and Wylie Avenue, the Crawford Grill. Few (if any) properties figure quite so prominently in the history of Black baseball and the road to integration. A former hotel, it was a three-floor building that itself comprised most of a block. Well-known singers and musicians began to visit and perform there. The bar was a lively convivial place, and the busy restaurant clattered and hummed, filled with locals and visitors passing through. From the time it opened, the Grill developed a reputation for being a welcoming place of unusual (for its time) racial diversity. "The grill was a melting pot," said Nelson Harrison, a musician who played there. "It had a peaceful, loving atmosphere."

The Grill also became the perfect pot in which to mix and launder money from Greenlee's newest illegal venture: the numbers racket.

Greenlee and his partners (Tito, plus William "Woogie" Harris) quickly proved as adept at the numbers game as they'd been with bootlegging. Their operation covered all of Pittsburgh and most of Allegheny County. In control of nearly a hundred separate betting locations, it's estimated the partners were bringing in close to $25,000 a day. A lot of money in any era, it represented an avalanche of daily cash during the Depression.

Flush, but ever mindful of how best to use his money, Greenlee actively engaged himself in the city. He'd amassed a bit of a local, little empire, a mix of illegal financial activities, and a range of legit properties, including the Grill and two hotels. He became involved politically, in his own (Third) Ward, with several leading Republican politicians, and wielded enormous influence with Black voters.* By 1930, Greenlee became drawn to sports promotion. He managed several Black boxers, including John Henry Lewis, who would become light heavyweight champion in 1935.

At the same time, Greenlee developed a deserved reputation as a very real benefactor in Pittsburgh's African-American community. With Blacks often shut out of white banks, Greenlee provided vital financing for many local minority businesses, as well as loans and lines of credit for countless individuals in his Hill District. During the Depression, Greenlee opened up a local soup kitchen. Accounts are many of Greenlee helping families in need with rent, food, heating, and medical expenses.

"A big man who puffed big cigars, Gus Greenlee was something of a Robin Hood figure in Pittsburgh's Hill District," writes Tom Dunkel in *Color Blind: The Forgotten Team That Broke Baseball's Color Line.* "A shady character to be sure, but one who employed hundreds of people, ran soup lines, and gave generously to hospitals and the NAACP. Black athletes and fans flocked to his Grill after games."

It was some of those local Black athletes who first persuaded Greenlee to step in and help the local semipro baseball team. The Crawford Colored Giants had formed in 1925, taking their name from the Crawford Bath House, a municipal recreation center that had sponsored the team in a 1926 baseball tournament. Gus Greenlee bought the team in 1930, a low point for the Crawfords, after emerging star slugger Josh Gibson had bolted the team for Cum Posey's Homestead Grays, then the predominant Black baseball team in Pittsburgh. (Some would say the predominant baseball team in Pittsburgh, period.) Greenlee went all in. He put the team's players on a professional salary. He hired a new manager, Bobby Williams (former shortstop for the Atlantic City Bacharach Giants), and tasked him with

---

* Into the 1930s, African Americans were still largely aligned with the GOP, which was still seen as the "party of Lincoln" and of Emancipation. That would change dramatically with the more racially progressive administration of Franklin D. Roosevelt.

Homestead Grays, 1931: Cumberland Posey Jr. standing far left; Oscar Charleston standing second from right; Josh Gibson standing fourth from right; Smokey Joe Williams standing center WIKIMEDIA COMMONS

scouting and recruiting top-notch players to fill out a winning roster. And Williams did. He acquired talented veterans like Lefty Streeter, Jimmie Crutchfield, and a gangly but gas-throwing young pitcher named Satchel Paige. But Greenlee was just warming up. In the grip of the Depression, while most surviving businesses were struggling, Gus Greenlee was flourishing, able to tap his deep and diverse revenue streams for ready cash. In 1932, he bought a brand-new Mack bus to transport his team. The new bus didn't actually drive over to nearby Homestead to pick up Greenlee's newest prize players. But it might as well have.

Waving wads of money with which to lure them back, Greenlee was able to re-acquire Judy Johnson, Cool Papa Bell, and, yes, even Josh Gibson. The tables had turned. Now it was Homestead Grays owner Cumberland Posey who was left to decry having been raided, his championship lineup ransacked by his most bitter rival.

Nonetheless, the two teams were both brimming with talent. The Grays, however diminished, were still a fearsome team with a winning ethos. The Crawfords were dramatically reloading, and poised to make a new impact. Like enemy warriors on opposite sides of a river, the two teams' owners regarded each other's moves warily. Which, in fact, aptly describes the physical nature of their feud. (Right down to the river and the raiding parties.) Two potent teams, competing for the same fans, separated by a mere six miles, and too close for comfort.

In this real-life chess game of bats, balls, and bucks, Cum Posey made a move. With the final collapse a year earlier of the last remnant of Rube Foster's Negro National

Gus Greenlee, c. 1938 COURTESY NEGRO LEAGUES BASEBALL MUSEUM

League, Posey cobbled together a new East-West League, anchored by the Homestead Grays. The Pittsburgh Crawfords were to be included in the new league only if they met two absurd and laughable demands: The Crawfords' local schedule would be controlled by the Grays, and they would be managed by Posey's older brother, Seward. Needless to say, Greenlee had his laugh, and Posey had his Crawford-less new league. But Gus Greenlee also had something of a *last* laugh, too.

For one thing, the spending spree he'd sprung for new players was just getting started. Frustrated and angry that Black teams were perpetually forced to pay sizeable chunks of their uncertain revenue to major-league teams for use of their ballparks, he decided he wouldn't. He'd build his own ballpark.

On land owned by a local brick company, Greenlee paid an estimated $100,000 to build a concrete and steel structure with 7,500 seats, and the added impressive extra luxury of lights. (It's also estimated that half the cost was paid in cash by the owner.*) It would be the first ballpark built

---

* The new ballpark also afforded Greenlee yet another convenient outlet with which to launder profits from his illegal numbers business.

expressly for a Black team, and financed largely by Black capital. Needless to say, the odds against a Black ballclub, in the midst of the Depression, building its own park, were less than slim. They didn't exist. Teams often now didn't have money to make a road trip or meet payroll, never mind pay contractors.

"Black teams were not owned by titans of industry," reminds Dr. Ray Doswell, vice president and curator of the Negro Leagues Baseball Museum. "Among the struggling black teams, there were no Wrigleys, no Buschs, no Rupperts."

On April 29, 1932, Greenlee Field officially opened. The Crawfords faced the New York Black Yankees, who won 1–0, despite Pittsburgh's Satchel Paige giving up only six hits and striking out 10. In time, Paige would get his wins.

Observing his rival's new ballpark and newly resurgent team—which starred several of his own former players—Cumberland Posey was not happy. He was even less happy when his new East-West League fell apart and disbanded before it had played a first, full season. Greenlee's team—in the midst of the Depression, no less—now had a brand-new park of their own to play in, while Posey was paying out dwindling revenue to white major-league teams in both Pittsburgh and Washington in order to rent their ballparks for his own team's home games. A year later, Greenlee was more than happy to make Posey less happy still.

In 1933, Gus Greenlee spearheaded the formation of yet another new Black professional baseball league. This one would be an attempt to essentially resurrect Rube Foster's Negro National League. At the same time, he also was the driving force to create an East-West Black baseball All-Star Game. (In time, the East-West Game would evolve into the most celebrated annual event of the Negro Leagues.) It all sounded good—and wearily familiar. It also sounded like too tough a sell and too hard a lift to get off the ground during the crushing early years of the Depression. But, ever the gambler, Greenlee sized up the odds and made his bet. The dice rolled, the fledgling league lurched and swayed, but came fitfully to life. Looking at being left league-less and unaffiliated, Posey had little choice but to throw in his lot as well with the new NNL. The tables had turned yet again. But for both the Pittsburgh rivals and Black baseball generally, there was a sense that this time, however unlikely, it simply had to work. How many more times could it be attempted? At the same time, there couldn't possibly have been a worse time to try.

In many ways, 1933 was, according to many economic indexes, the worst year of the Great Depression. It was the year when it seemed things could go no lower, the year that the American economy bottomed out, like a great, sinking ship coming to rest on the ocean floor. Rock bottom.

There's no record in 1933 of Gus Greenlee ever cheerfully exclaiming, "Well, no time like the present!" Just as well. No one could have believed that, anyway. But people did believe, or want to believe, in this "big man, a great big man," as a former player described Greenlee. It was just harder than ever to have new faith in this new, audacious effort, at this hellacious time.

"As 1933 loomed, the position of Black professional baseball appeared tenuous, despite the heightened involvement of Greenlee, a relative newcomer to the industry," wrote Neil Lanctot. But newcomer or not, he was the man of the moment, however fraught the moment was. "Greenlee had emerged as a larger-than-life figure possessing a considerable bankroll and an abundance of street smarts, toughness, and bluntness."

To some, Greenlee seemed even larger than life. Russ Cowans, a *Detroit Tribune* sportswriter, described Greenlee as "the Moses for Negro Baseball . . . attempting to lead the owners out of the wilderness of depression."

Whether it was emotional or national/economic depression, or likely both, the point was made. Gambler or savior, or both, there was a lot of wilderness to get through. And even a skilled gambler couldn't like the odds.

"Negro Baseball is at a low ebb," observed *Pittsburgh Courier* sportswriter Rollo Wilson. "Both owners and players must make sacrifices and more sacrifices to maintain it until such a time as the fans are again in funds and able to storm the ball yard ramparts as they were wont to do in the yesteryears."

In the past, for Black baseball owners, regional independence had been the driving financial necessity. For struggling ballclubs, the freedom to schedule as many games and against whatever teams was the sole priority. Not that individual teams themselves didn't know all about sacrifice. Black ballplayers might be paid as professionals, but they never confused their paychecks with those of major leaguers. They never mistook their rickety buses running on scraped-up gas money with the comfortable overnight sleeper cars of the major-league teams. Still, it had always proved nearly impossible to cobble together real and lasting league-wide cooperation and organization. But the now dire economic landscape seemed to change that; owners seemed to sense that this time required something different, some degree of collective sacrifice that had not been forthcoming previously. Gus Greenlee, trusted for his can-do confidence and business acumen (even though parts of his business were illegal), was unanimously elected league president. Even more encouraging, his crosstown rival, Cum Posey, enthusiastically supported the new chairman.

Major challenges remained. Aside from the overarching and most punishing problem of the ruinous economy, the next biggest issue for the league's teams was an ongoing lack of home fields at which to play. Greenlee's own Crawfords were uniquely fortunate that they owned their own new park. No other league team was remotely in the same situation. Some clubs—like Nashville, Indianapolis, and Columbus—were confident in existing relationships with white-owned parks. Others, like Rube Foster's former team, the Chicago American Giants, had virtually no place to play in the city, and were looking at the disheartening prospect of playing no "home" games at all. In Pittsburgh, an interesting twist to the park problem: Cum Posey, under pressure to rent from a Black owner instead of a white one, temporarily rescheduled his home games from the Pittsburgh Pirates' Forbes Field to Greenlee Field. Those payments could not have been easy for Posey to make. It was one thing to support his rival's position as new league chairman, quite another to support his business too.

In the bigger picture, though, the Negro League's rebirth, however difficult, was happening. It was happening in the very depths of the Depression. It was happening when people least expected it to succeed, but also when people most desperately wanted and needed it to. And it was happening in a city that was among the hardest hit by the Depression. The waves of now-unemployed African-American steelworkers who'd been the victim of "Last hired, first fired," were the very fans who could no longer even think of buying a ballgame ticket. But Pittsburgh, it turned out, was as tough as the steel it forged. And two of its best-known Black success stories—bitter rivals, separated by background, temperament, and two big rivers—were an equally big reason there was a bit of hope and a new beginning, at a time when there should have been neither. In spite of their rivalry, the two men, their two teams, their two stars, and their city, were carving out a special place in the pivotal decade ahead.

FIVE

A City Steps Up, Two Stars Stand Out

You look for his weakness and while you're looking for it, he's liable to hit 45 home runs.

—Satchel Paige (on Josh Gibson)

"He's gone and done it again!"

So exclaimed the lead sentence on the front page of the *Pittsburgh Courier*, the city's African-American newspaper, just six days into January 1934.

"Gus Greenlee," the article continued, "who has spent more money among Negroes in the Hill district than any other Negro we know, announced early this week that his latest addition to the pleasure seekers of the Hill district will have its formal opening on next Tuesday evening."

And indeed, on the evening of January 9, 1934, Gus Greenlee did greet throngs of friends, excited customers, and a small crowd of entertainers and performers all gathered to celebrate the gala reopening of his famous Crawford Grill. Part of the renovation included a new, "modern dining room" on the second floor. But the most eagerly anticipated part of the reopening involved the extensive work on the downstairs bar, which was undoubtedly the most popular spot throughout the evening's revelry. After all, it had been a historically long wait for a drink. Only weeks earlier, on December 5, 1933, national Prohibition had ended in America. Alcohol was flowing again. Indeed, Christmas had come early for Greenlee. Having tapped his deep political connections, the Grill's owner had an extra reason to celebrate—a reason buried deep in the fifth paragraph of the *Courier*'s article: "Gus," readers were informed, "is the only owner in the lower Hill district with a license to sell liquor."

The King of the Hill, as it were, didn't get his liquor license—or anything else he attained—by waiting in line like a wallflower. And if the *Courier*'s account betrayed a bit of neighborhood pride in their benevolent rogue, well, that was accurate. On both counts.

"Yeah, he's breaking the law with the numbers, and yes, prior to that he broke it during Prohibition," says Rob Ruck, author and a professor of history at the University of Pittsburgh. "But he helped a lot of people out, in terms of paying rent, doctor's bills, starting black businesses, running black political campaigns . . . the numbers guys in the hill—and this is true of other black communities—are often the source of funds that sustained Negro League Baseball."

And sustain he did. Greenlee already owned a variety of commercial properties in and around the Hill District. His was a powerful presence in the Black community. And now his gleaming new Grill on Wylie Avenue established itself as a magnet for a diverse crowd, and as a stop for top performers. Its jazz headliners would include greats like Louis Armstrong, Lena Horne, Art Blakey, and Ella Fitzgerald. Photographs from the period show an often-beaming Greenlee, relaxing in the Grill, cigar set in his toothy grin, an arm around a patron, or posing at a table with friends and colleagues. (And in one, celebrating a birthday with several of his numbers runners.)

But the Crawford Grill wasn't alone. Although it was still the Depression, Pittsburgh's Hill District was nonetheless very much alive. Like all of America, the city was struggling through a punishing period of layoffs and crippling economic uncertainty. The steel mills, limping through slashed work rolls and output, ground on. Yet through the slumping shoulders and spirits, through the gray, smoggy trails from the forest of smokestacks, there was life. There was music and art, sports and literature, and a local Black newspaper that was beginning to have national and lasting impact. Despite the hardships, the energy and heartbeat of the Hill, and its unique community of African Americans, was alive and vigorous. To many, in this the most unlikely of times, it seemed like a true renaissance.

"During the Great Migration, black folks who came to Pittsburgh came largely from the Northern and Eastern parts of the South—states like Delaware, Virginia, North Carolina," explained journalist Mark Whitaker, in an interview with NPR in 2018.* "These migrants were very often descendants of house slaves or 'free men of color.' They arrived with high degrees of literacy, musical fluency and religious discipline, and once they settled in Pittsburgh, they had educational opportunities that were rare for blacks of the era, thanks to abolitionist-sponsored university scholarships and integrated public high schools."

It wasn't the Harlem Renaissance of the 1920s, but then, Pittsburgh wasn't New York.

And vice-versa.

"Pittsburgh is a hugely important industrial metropolis at that time, first half of the century," says Ruck. "It doesn't have a black community that's as big as New York, Philadelphia, Chicago, but it's got a great, central location, along the East-West rail lines, so that makes it particularly important for black performers, teams, speakers, and political figures. Everyone stopped in Pittsburgh."

It sure seemed that way. Just down the street from the Crawford Grill was the Loendi Club.† Founded in 1897 as "The Loendi Social and Literary Club," it was part quiet retreat for the city's influential Black professionals, and part music venue for young stars like Count Basie, Cab Calloway, and Billy Eckstine. It held lectures and gatherings; Black celebrities, from musicians like Duke Ellington and Billy Strayhorn to boxer Joe Louis (and later, Jackie Robinson) visited and rubbed elbows at the Loendi.

And above all, even now—especially now—baseball flourished in Pittsburgh like it never had before. Or anywhere else, for that matter. While rivalries like the Crawfords and Grays ignited passionate divisions, the game itself had long been something that unified and uplifted.

---

* Whitaker, a former editor of Newsweek and former managing editor of CNN Worldwide, is the author of *Smoketown: The Untold Story of the Other Great Black Renaissance*. His family has roots in Pittsburgh's African-American community.

† The club was named after a river in East Africa.

"Pittsburgh's black population almost triples in the first three decades of the twentieth century as a result of the Great Migration," points out Ruck. "And sport there—which is much more organized on a sandlot, neighborhood basis—begins to bring the black community together . . . given the discrimination in every other aspect of life, it offers a source of self-esteem and identity."

And for a generation coming of age in the Great Depression, no sport did that quite like baseball.

"In the mid-1930s," wrote Lawrence D. Hogan in *Shades of Glory*, "Pittsburgh became to black baseball what Harlem had been to black literature and the arts during the 1920s, the catalyst of a renaissance."

Other eastern cities, like Baltimore, Newark, and Philadelphia, were vital to the revival of the Negro Leagues. In the West, Kansas City was also instrumental in the rebirth of organized Black professional baseball in the 1930s.

"But the catalyst was found in the Steel City," writes Hogan. "Pittsburgh became a black baseball crossroads as a result of its central geographic location, the astute leadership of Gus Greenlee and Cumberland Posey, Jr., and the presence of a Georgia-born, Pittsburgh-bred ballplayer named Joshua Gibson."

IT'S ENTIRELY POSSIBLE THAT JOSH GIBSON WAS THE SINGLE MOST feared hitter who ever lived. It's possible that Josh Gibson hit more home runs than any player in history, as well as the longest home run ever recorded. It's also not possible to know any of these things for certain.

Negro League players passed their seasons in a sort of sepia background—both literally and figuratively. Stars shone for those close enough to observe in person. All else was blurred, separate and obscured. If not for an African-American press committed to covering their play, few would know anything about Black baseball. All of which suited white baseball just fine. After all, if a Black ballplayer was known to have officially hit 75 home runs in a season, what team couldn't use him? What team could decline him? *Did* a black ballplayer named Gibson hit 75 home runs in 1931? Might have. Might not have. The records aren't exactly exact. By contrast, owing to major media outlets in every city, plus its own national resources, Major League Baseball's record-keeping was standardized, detailed, and exhaustive. Want to know who hit the most doubles in the American League in 1935? An internet search taking less than 10 seconds reveals it was Joe Vosmik (47). As if to underscore the glaring disparity, the exact same search for the *Negro* League produces this result: "1935 in Baseball." *Major* League Baseball.

Negro League teams were more occupied with simply scheduling games and staying in business. For most of its existence, such was the overriding priority of the Negro League itself. Having enough uniforms, bats, balls, and basic equipment was never a given. Nor was safe and dependable transportation for the team. Rigorously keeping standardized records was an unaffordable luxury. Nor were major white media outlets covering and documenting the games.

But this we know: Josh Gibson changed the way that whites looked at Black baseball players. To watch what Gibson did in his prime in the Negro Leagues made it possible to imagine, a decade later, what Jackie Robinson might do in the major leagues. There was a template. For sure, scores of other Black baseball players of major-league quality had already toiled in obscurity for decades on the wrong side of the color barrier. From Rube Foster and Smokey Joe Williams, to Cool Papa Bell and Oscar Charleston, there were exceptional Black ballplayers who could have instantly and seamlessly assumed spots on virtually any major-league roster. But Josh Gibson was a man apart, a truly breakout talent. Because of Gibson, some whites slowly began to think about the color barrier just a bit differently. Maybe what the barrier blocked from view was worth seeing. Maybe, we're actually *missing* something. Josh Gibson presented the first full, vibrant portrait of a Black superstar baseball player. Yes, that mythic blast may have traveled 500 feet. It may have gone only 420. What's a fact is that the symbolic wall it cleared was being measured now for future assaults. There was more where Gibson came from.

He became synonymous with Pittsburgh, but wasn't born there. His birthplace was Buena Vista, Georgia. As to birth *date*, it was most likely December 21, 1911. His father, Mark Gibson, was a sharecropper who went to Pittsburgh in 1923 in order to find better work, which he found at a steel factory. He sent money back to his wife, Nancy, who three years later brought their children north to complete the family's move to Pittsburgh. The family settled in the Pleasant Valley section of the city.

At 15, Josh Gibson, the oldest of three, was already 6'1" and 200 pounds. He could work a man's job and make money, so he did. He dropped out of school and was hired for heavy labor at an airbrake manufacturing plant, working alongside adult men. If anything qualified as a passion in the quiet but cheerful teen's life, it was baseball. And in his spare time, evenings and weekends, he was already bent on playing as much of it as he could. His first official team for which he was given a uniform was an all-Black nine fielded by Gimbels Department Store. (The store apparently ensured young Gibson's continued place on the team by giving him a job as an elevator operator.) Soon Gibson was playing in a wider Negro Greater Pittsburgh Industrial League, made up of a wide variety of blue-collar teams, one of which was the recently renamed Pittsburgh Crawfords.

In fact, it was Gus Greenlee's purchase of the team and his beefing up its management and scouting that indirectly led to Josh Gibson being officially "discovered." In 1928, the 16-year-old Gibson had been selected to play in the Industrial League All-Star Game. Crawfords manager Harold "Hooks" Tinker was at Pittsburgh's Ammon Field to watch the game.*

"I had two of my Crawford players on that all-star team," Tinker recounted later. "Otherwise I wouldn't have been there. And that's when I saw Josh."

Clearly, Tinker was impressed with what he saw.

"I said, 'This boy is a marvel.' Near the end of the game he hit a home-run and hit the ball out of existence. They didn't even go after it."

But Tinker went right after the 17-year-old who hit it. He signed him to play for the Crawfords, making it Gibson's first semipro contract. There were other good tidings, too, in store for the young man. His girlfriend, Helen Mason, was pregnant, and in March 1929, they were married in Pittsburgh.

The following year, however, the good tidings turned to tragedy. After a miscarriage, Helen became pregnant again, with twins. In August 1930,

---

* Located in Pittsburgh's Hill District, Ammon Field today is Josh Gibson Field.

she went into premature labor, which, it is thought, aggravated an undiagnosed kidney condition. The babies—a boy and a girl—were delivered safely, but Helen died in childbirth.

In the aftermath, devastated and reeling, Josh Gibson seemed able to grasp only the barest fundamentals. Not yet 20, he did seem to grasp that he was simply not able to parent two infants on his own. Fortunately for him, his late wife's parents agreed to take in their newborn grandchildren. And Gibson grasped a bat, which must have seemed dependably solid and familiar, and which he never let go of again.

How Josh Gibson dealt with the crushing emotional pain within would be hard to say. By all accounts, he was never given to a lot of talk. Though physically mature beyond his years by the time he was a teen, there still seemed to be a certain shy, young man quality about him, even as he roared into his 20s with a growing reputation as the most fearsome slugger virtually anyone had ever seen.

"Next to hitting," former teammate Ted Page once said, "I think he liked eating ice cream more than anything else in the world."

No sooner had Gibson begun playing again with the semipro Crawfords, that their rivals, the Homestead Grays, began craning their collective neck at the balls flying out of the yard across town.

"I had never seen him play, but we had heard so much about him," said William "Judy" Johnson, a player-coach for the Grays in 1930. "Every time you'd look at the paper you'd see where he hit a ball 400 feet, 500 feet."

Cumberland Posey just wanted the young slugger to travel however many feet and miles it was across the river to Homestead. And he did. Gibson joined the Grays, and under the patient tutelage of coaches and players like Johnson, he began to become both a real catcher and a well-rounded ballplayer. It didn't hurt to have living legends as teammates. Barely 20, Gibson was able to learn alongside the likes of Oscar Charleston, Bill Foster, and Smokey Joe Williams. And each of these accomplished stars would find themselves watching as intently as their fans, as this quiet young hitter lashed into yet another pitch, driving the ball crazy distances out of one park after another.

Gibson settled in among his teammates and seemed indeed to need little more than baseball to thrive. If there were other things that gnawed at him inside, they seemed to be expelled with the vicious whack of a bat, and a ball banished far, far away.

"He was to be totally sheltered by the game he played and the organization he played for," wrote William Brashler, author of *Josh Gibson: A Life in the Negro Leagues*. "And even though he had to cope with a fickle social and racial climate in the country, he did not spend much time thinking about it or devising ways to change it. If anything got in the way of playing baseball, he avoided it, for his was a single-minded, stifled life, and he wasn't interested in much more."

That was fine with Gus Greenlee. He didn't need Josh Gibson interested in much more than bashing a baseball, anyway. And he had been just as impressed by what he was hearing about with this kid as his rival, Cum Posey, had been. After all, the team Greenlee now owned had him first. The Crawfords' former rookie was blossoming into a genuine star, and Greenlee wanted him back. In 1932, able to tout his brand-new ballpark—and peel off cold, hard cash—Greenlee lured Gibson back over the river. (By this point, Gibson should have had his own bridge.) But Greenlee had another reason to put the young, slugging catcher back in a Crawfords uniform. He was envisioning him as one-half of what looked to be a phenomenal battery of rare, potent talent. He wanted the 21-year-old rising star to catch a 26-year-old pitcher who was already brilliantly carving his own path to stardom: Satchel Paige.

HIS WAS AN EXTRAORDINARY, EXPANSIVE LIFE THAT UNFOLDED IN ONE unlikely adventure after another like a modern *Odyssey*. From barefoot, boyhood poverty in the Jim Crow South, to punishing boyhood loneliness in reform school. From the lush, green, swelter of the tropics, to the waving white wheat fields of the Great Plains. And like a soundtrack to all these far-flung legs of the journey, there was the frenzied din of city stadiums full of screaming fans. Ultimately, in the unlikeliest leg of all, there was passage to the Promised Land of the major leagues, when he really was a latter day Methuselah on the mound. All this in a career so long and so full and so *everywhere*, it makes other distinguished, lengthy baseball careers seem like mere blips by comparison. The one, single constant in the ball-capped blur that was Satchel Paige's life was a long, restless, right arm that for more than 40 years reared back and fired a baseball at what seemed to be a never-ending succession of batters. Indeed, *Maybe I'll Pitch Forever* is both the title of Paige's autobiography, and what truly seemed like his professional goal by the fifth decade of his career.

He was born neither "Satchel" nor "Paige." In 1906, his birth name in Mobile, Alabama, was LeRoy Robert Page. His mom was a washerwoman, his dad a gardener with a penchant for mostly being somewhere other than at home parenting a growing brood of seven kids. "She was the real boss of our house, not dad," Paige wrote.

While Mobile had at one time been relatively tolerant (for the Deep South), Paige's birth coincided with the advent of sweeping new whites-only ordinances, relegating its Black community to the same rigid segregation that was making a cruel and hateful mockery of "separate but equal." Being poor with few opportunities to advance was equally oppressive for all of Paige's Black neighbors.

"Those first few years I was no different from any other kid, only in Mobile I was a nigger kid. I went around with the back of my shirt torn, a pair of dirty diapers or raggedy pieces of trousers covering me. Shoes? They was somewhere else."

By seven, LeRoy was expected to help, by doing some work to bring in whatever he could for the family. He progressed from collecting bottles for pennies, to making 10 cents per bag lugging them for train passengers at Mobile's busy depot. An inventive kid, he rigged up a long stick with a rope, which enabled him to carry multiple bags and make more money per trip. A kid said Paige looked like a "walking satchel tree," and a nickname was born.

"That's when LeRoy Paige became no more and Satchel Paige took over," he wrote.

There would also be one more tweak to his given name. "My folks started out by spelling their name 'Page,'" he would say. "And later stuck in the 'i' to make themselves sound more high tone."

Disinterested in school and with little else to do, Paige enjoyed watching a local semipro baseball team, and found he could throw pretty well himself. ("Only I couldn't afford a baseball," he recalled. "So I took up rock throwing.") He made his school baseball team. Then he made a mistake about which he wrote, "Unless you've gone around with nothing, you don't know how powerful a lure some new, shiny stuff is." He shop-lifted some trinkets. But there was nothing trivial about the punishment: He was sent away to reform school for six years. He was 12.

"He did not have a childhood, what we would consider a childhood," says Pamela Paige O'Neal. A retired teacher in Kansas City and Satchel Paige's oldest daughter, Paige O'Neal, remembers her dad, who was 42 and still playing professional baseball when she was born, as always being busy with his children when he was at home.

"He engaged us in all kinds of activities, he was always teaching. He grew up fast because he had to support his family; it was almost like he lived his childhood through us in a way."

For sure, Satchel Paige was forced to grow up even faster once he was removed from his home, his parents, and his siblings. Yet, looking back, Paige would credit his experience at the Industrial School for Negro Children at Mount Meigs, Alabama, for setting him on his path to great-ness as a pitcher.* Two coaches, Edward Byrd and the Reverend Moses Davis, were the first to see that the tall and gangly 6-foot, 140-pound kid was built to pitch. Few first impressions have ever been more thoroughly validated.

With Byrd's patient but determined guidance, Paige began to harness his natural physical talents. For the first time he learned mechanics. His lanky limbs gained order and form, and he began to develop the sky-high leg kick that would bedevil batters and become his pitching signature. Byrd impressed on the youthful Paige that there was also a mental aspect to pitching, and that he needed to engage his brain as well. The student began to understand that the "game within the game" could help him spot a hitter's weakness, and give him an advantage. He was no longer just throwing a ball. He was *pitching.*

---

* Ironically, Paige's experience was somewhat similar to that of Babe Ruth, who was sent to Baltimore's St. Mary's Industrial School for Boys in 1902, where he became a promising enough ballplayer to leave the school 12 years later with a professional contract.

"You might say I traded five years of freedom to learn how to pitch," Paige wrote.

In December 1923, just shy of his 18th birthday, Satchel Paige was released from Mount Meigs. Back at home in Mobile, he looked for work, any kind of work, but found none. He did find himself sitting and watching the semipro Mobile Tigers work out and prepare for their upcoming season. His older brother, Wilson, was playing for them, and after watching the team finish its practice, Satchel asked the manager if he could try out.

Tired, wanting to get home, the manager only relented because of his brother's connection with the team. What followed was a familiar scene from countless sports movies: the revelation, and the arresting moment of a young phenom's discovery. The ball, as Paige remembered, "popped against the catcher's glove like they was firecrackers." Eyes widened and jaws dropped. Questions were asked. Money was exchanged.

"The manager gave me a dollar and told me to come back with Wilson for the next game," Paige wrote. "I felt like that dollar was a thousand." He also felt that it was the moment he started baseball as a career. LeRoy "Satchel" Paige was launched.

WHILE JOSH GIBSON HAD, IN A SHORT TIME, MADE A ROUTINE OF CROSSing Pittsburgh bridges to play for different teams, some feared he may have burned one on his most recent move. Jumping from the Grays to the Crawfords did not pass without incident. While Gus Greenlee had bested his rival by luring away the young slugger, Cum Posey was livid. In his regular guest column for the *Courier*, he wrote, "As Gibson is very young, he is easily advised," adding that, in this case, Gibson had been "poorly advised." But Posey went further. He vowed that if Gibson did not play for his Grays in 1932, "He will not play in Pittsburgh . . . it is time an example was made of a few players who have no respect for their signed obligations but will jump to any club for a few dollars more."

While Posey could do little about his keen frustration and anger in 1932, the tables, as always, would turn again and again for these hot-headed rivals. Bridges were not so much burned, as seemingly turned around on mid-crossing. Posey would have his own share of satisfaction.

Both Josh Gibson and Satchel Paige would bolt on Greenlee, too, when "a few dollars more" were on the table.

PAIGE MADE A CIRCUITOUS ROUTE TO PITTSBURGH. BUT THEN, PATIENT and predictable straight lines between points were not the Paige way. Zigs and zags, often sudden and impulsive, more often defined the young pitcher's progress. From Mobile, Paige was recruited by the Chattanooga White Sox of the Negro Southern League in 1926. In an indication of how young he still was, his mother, Lula, signed off on his $250 per month contract, of which a large share would go home, and to her. Midway through the 1927 season, Paige's contract was bought out by the Birmingham Black Barons. It was a step up; he was now playing in Rube Foster's creation, the Negro National League. He was green and still learning, but also beginning to show the shooting flashes of pitching brilliance that would coalesce into legend over the next decade. By 1929, he was racking up record-breaking strikeout totals. In one game that season, he struck out 17; in another, he recorded 18—a record that was not tied in the white major leagues until Bob Feller did it in 1938. Paige was becoming enough of a starring attraction and a legitimate gate draw, that it marked the first time in his career that his owner (Birmingham's R. T. Jackson) rented his services out to other clubs for select games. Both owner and pitcher would receive a cut. In the years to come, given Paige's celebrity and ability to draw fans, the rent-a-star practice became irresistible for a succession of his teams' owners.

Over that winter, Satchel Paige made his first professional foray into the Caribbean. (It wouldn't be the last, or the most memorable.) He was paid $100 a game to play for Santa Clara of the Cuban League. Alas, between the food, the language barrier, and the general foreignness of it all, the tropics didn't take.*

Back home for the start of the 1930 season, Paige spent a brief time with the Baltimore Black Sox, then returned midseason to his former

---

* While he won six games in Cuba, Paige made a hasty and unceremonious exit. It might have involved a woman, or it might have involved a local official who mistakenly thought Paige, in cahoots with gamblers, had intentionally thrown a game. Either way, it would also not be the last time he made more of a desperate escape than a dignified departure from a tropical island.

Birmingham team. The Barons' owner continued to lease or rent Paige out to other teams, including the Chicago American Giants and the Houston Black Buffaloes. A year later, with the spreading ruin of the Depression across America, dozens of Negro League teams, barely solvent to begin with, began to go under or disband. The Birmingham Black Barons were one of them. But R. T. Jackson's loss would be Gus Greenlee's gain. Greenlee was also one of the handful of Black baseball club owners who could afford to hire the star who was now Satchel Paige. It was on to Steel City.

"When I got to Pittsburgh, the first place I headed was Gus Greenlee's restaurant, the Crawford Grill," Paige wrote.

Makes sense. After all, the grill's owner (who would evermore be simply, "Gus," to Paige) would be paying his new star pitcher's salary. For a time, the two would work well together, both for the team's collective success, and for their own individual financial rewards, as Greenlee made free use of Paige as a high-price rental. Later on, things became more strained. Greenlee would learn, as other owners did, that for Paige, things like signed, binding contracts were generally regarded as more bendable than binding. For now, though, it was a big, warm welcome all around.

"As soon as Gus heard I was in, he came busting over," Paige wrote. "We're gonna open against the Homestead Grays," he said. "They're the best there is, Satch. You beat them and you're number one right from the start."

Indeed, the Grays were quite possibly the best Black baseball team. Anywhere. Beating them—and his rival, Cum Posey—was at least a part of why Greenlee bought a ballclub to begin with. His newest, high-priced acquisition didn't disappoint—defeating the Grays easily, and striking out 16. Welcome to Pittsburgh, Mr. Paige.

The game also marked the first time two future legends wore the same Crawfords uniform and shared the same bench between innings. Having heard about each other from afar, the two impressed each other in person, and formed an easy bond now as teammates. Even decades later, Paige's praise of Gibson was profound.

"There's never been power like Josh's," Paige wrote. "If I had to rate top hitters, I'd put him ahead of Ted Williams of Boston, Joe DiMaggio of New York, and Stan Musial of St. Louis, and right in that order."

While there were certainly other great talents on the Crawfords—Judy Johnson, Cool Papa Bell, player-manager Oscar Charleston—Paige and Gibson were the two stars who undeniably bookended everything, and everyone else.

"Almost from the beginning of their careers, Paige and Gibson were grouped together," wrote William Brashler (*Josh Gibson: A Life in the Negro Leagues*). "They were exquisite examples of totally different talents—Satchel, the gangling, whip-armed pitcher; Josh, the stocky, mean-eyed power hitter."

Totally different people, too.

"History binds Josh and Satchel at the hip as the two towering figures of the Negro Leagues," wrote Larry Tye, author of *Satchel: The Life and Times of an American Legend.* "But nature left them as mismatched as yin and yang."

Indeed, the differences between Paige and Gibson extended far beyond their physical contrasts. As time went on, their contrasting personalities were vividly evident too. Paige was outgoing and wisecracking. He also was seen by teammates as being all about the star, which he, well, was. His teammates never questioned that the crowds that jammed the park when Paige pitched were there because of him. Fair enough. But there were gripes behind his back. There was the feeling that Paige was in it ultimately for Paige. He seemed to prove it endlessly: Strict travel schedules and being on time to the ballpark were annoyances for others. Satchel Paige would keep his own time and itinerary. He would freely self-promote himself. He didn't tend to pal around with teammates or go out of his way to socialize with them. Stars of his stature, he seemed to suggest, move in other orbits. Or at least that seemed to be the message. Yet teammates cut him slack, too. He was, after all, the pitcher who won the big games for them. Satchel would be Satchel.

"Josh steered clear of the limelight," writes Tye. "Satchel lived in and monopolized it."

Josh Gibson was no less a star. He just *seemed* less so in the ever-spreading glare of the Satchel Paige show. With one mighty swing of his powerful 37.6-ounce bat, Gibson could also be counted on to win games all by himself. Crowds thrilled to see Gibson's exceptional and exciting play too. But where Paige was a showman who naturally commanded (some would say demanded) attention, Gibson was not. He spent time socially with his teammates, joked and palled around, ate, drank, and played poker with them. He was with his team, and *of* his team. Paige, it seemed, was generally just *on* the team. Until he wasn't, and had moved on to greener diamonds.

By any measure, however much these two stars respected each other's talents, even as they were battery mates, any greater bond seemed entirely unlikely. They were just too different.

"Yet Satchel's best friend on the team was Josh," observes Tye. "It was not a relationship of equals: Satchel was the senior partner in the minds of everyone from Gus Greenlee to the media and fans. It was not a mutual admiration society, either. Josh was closer to other teammates and oftentimes felt ambivalent about Satchel, who befriended few others . . . but Satch and Josh spent endless time together, sometimes as roommates, with the Crawfords, on small-town teams, and in winter ball. They were like Butch Cassidy and the Sundance Kid, opposites who fed off and relied on each other."

But before any blazes of glory, there was their very first game—and victory—together to put fully in the books.

"We celebrated like no one ever had after that game," Paige wrote. "Gus just locked the door on the grill and we went to town."

As postgame victory celebrations go, it was more eventful than most. At some point during the festivities, a young waitress at the Grill named Janet Howard sidled up to Satchel Paige and introduced herself. It took. Paige and Howard would end up getting married a couple of years later.* For his part, Gus Greenlee was equally enthused with his new star. After Paige and Howard had set up a first date, he approached Greenlee.

---

* Clearly, Howard made quite a first impression on Paige. Not well disposed to marriage, he once described it as akin to "walking in front of a firing squad without anyone making you do it." Janet Howard was his first marriage; later there would be multiple "firing squads."

"I got me a date and I'm a little short, how about a few bucks?"

"I'll do better'n that," Greenlee said. "Tomorrow you go down and buy yourself a couple of suits and hats on me. And you got a bonus—seven-hundred bucks a month now instead of two-fifty."

Paige was dumbfounded.

"That's right. Seven-hundred," Greenlee repeated. "That ought to keep you happy enough to stay with me."

"For that kind of money I'd go nowhere else," Paige exclaimed.

And in that moment, he might have meant it, too.

Over the next year or so, to say that Satchel Paige pitched for the Pittsburgh Crawfords would be only partly accurate. Over the 1932 season, Gus Greenlee rented out his team's star pitcher for short stints, to various teams across America. The added travel and disjointed, unpredictable schedule didn't seem to bother Paige. In fact, he rather thrived, as he continued to rack up an impressive number of innings, strikeouts, and wins.

Greenlee's—and Paige's—freelancing didn't impress everyone. Among Paige's teammates, there was simmering resentment both for his showboating antics and what was perceived as special treatment. Homestead Grays owner Cum Posey—admittedly a fierce (not to mention envious) rival—was outspoken in his public criticism.

"Gus exploited Satchel throughout the United States," wrote Posey in a 1936 *Courier* column ("Posey's Points"). "And forgot all about such men as Gibson, Matlock, W. Bell, 'Cool Papa' Bell, Oscar Charleston, Perkins, the men who made the Pittsburgh Crawfords."

For his part, it's not as if Josh Gibson also was not out to tap whatever opportunities came up for him to make more money as a ballplayer. No Black ballplayer had the luxury of turning down such things. And for top stars like Paige and Gibson, those opportunities came often. Over the winter following the 1932 season, Gibson went south to Puerto Rico where he'd been offered the job of player/manager for the Santurce Cangrejeros.* He was paid the near-princely sum of $250 a month. But in

---

* A teeming, urban neighborhood of San Juan, Santurce is considered the birthplace of Puerto Rican "beisbol." The island's first official game was played there on January 11, 1898.

most of Latin America, there was an added bonus for visiting Black players for which no price could be attached: dignity.

"I think my great-grandfather loved it in the Caribbean," says Sean Gibson. "It's why he played down there so many times, over so many years. He loved it there, and they loved him back."

All for very good reason.

"Off the field, players were idolized and shown none of the discrimination they saw as a matter of course in the States," wrote William Brashler. "They were treated as celebrities on many occasions, were free to go anywhere, eat anywhere, and do anything. They had no feelings of apprehension or the instinctive hesitation that a Black had before he did anything or went anywhere in white America."

(Not only was the Puerto Rican League welcoming to Black players, the Negro Leagues in turn became home to Latin stars like Martin Dihigo, José Méndez, and Cristóbal Torriente. For some Black players, the lure of what Latin baseball offered was strong enough to keep them there once they had arrived. Willie Wells was a Texas-born standout shortstop who played for several Negro League teams, and was inducted into the Baseball Hall of Fame in 1997. In the early 1940s, Wells stayed on in Mexico for the summer season after playing winter ball there. "I've found freedom and democracy here, something I never found in the United States," said Wells in an interview with the *Pittsburgh Courier*. "Everything I did, including playing ball, was regulated by my color ... here I am a man. I can go as far in baseball as I am capable of going.")

GIBSON DID RETURN TO PITTSBURGH FOR THE START OF THE 1933 season. It was the inaugural season of Gus Greenlee's new Negro National League. It also marked the end of the honeymoon between Greenlee and Gibson's battery mate, Satchel Paige. Whether it was marriage, baseball, or day-to-day living, Satchel Paige was simply too big and too needy a force to stay put for too long. But other factors played their part. Greenlee was heavily invested in getting the newly re-formed Negro League up and running. By the 1933 season, between the shaky finances of the new league and the worst days of the Depression, Greenlee made it clear to Paige (who had asked for a raise) that the free-spending, bonus-giving days were over. Paige was also irked by the new league's tougher rules. Under them, Greenlee threatened to suspend his star pitcher if he continued his vexing habit of keeping his own schedule, being late (even to games he was pitching), and skipping whatever he didn't feel like being part of.

Which, of course, Paige promptly continued to do.

In August that season, Paige emulated Butch Cassidy in a more physical sense—minus the 10-gallon hat and the six-gun—he abruptly packed a bag and rode west. (On a train.) He couldn't have left Pittsburgh and its smoky, gray skies farther behind. He was headed to the big sky and the flat, waving wheat fields of Bismarck, North Dakota, where Neil Churchill was eagerly awaiting his arrival. Churchill, who was white, owned an auto dealership, as well as the Bismarcks, a relatively successful semipro baseball team locked that summer in a tight race with its bitter rival, neighboring Jamestown. Tapping his connection with Abe Saperstein, the owner of the Harlem Globetrotters, Churchill had succeeded in tempting Satchel Paige to come out and pitch down the stretch for the Bismarcks. (Two twin temptations included a salary of $400 per month, and a late-model used car.) Churchill was delighted. Gus Greenlee was furious. Paige also had a traveling companion: his new wife, Janet Howard. But being a husband was not the only new experience for Paige in Bismarck.

"It wasn't until after I signed up with Mr. Churchill that I found out I was going to be playing with some white boys," Paige wrote. "For the first time since I started throwing, I was going to have some of them on my side."

Actually, for that first stint in Bismarck, Paige was playing with almost *all* white boys. It would be a bit of culture shock for both sides. But Paige, ever up for a challenge, embraced it.

"I'd cracked another little chink in Jim Crow," he later recalled proudly.

Cracking the mostly white Bismarcks baseball team was one thing; cracking Bismarck, North Dakota, and finding a place to stay was another.

"Most of the folks there were pretty nice, but there were some of those other kind, like you run into everywhere," Paige wrote. "Because of them it didn't look like such a hot idea having Janet with me. Those mean folks didn't want any colored people around. They didn't want us living by them. 'Sorry, we just don't have any room,' or 'we just rented the place.' That's what they told me, but when I'd pass those places later on, they were still empty."

Neil Churchill did find some temporary housing for Satchel and Janet Paige, and he was genuinely a bit of a progressive out on the plains. But although his team was integrated at a time few semipro teams were, there was still an adjustment period for the Bismarcks' newest arrival.*

"Mr. Churchill wanted me, but those white players weren't too sure they did," wrote Paige. "They just didn't know what Ol' Satch could do."

What he did was win seven games in the month of August, helping the Bismarcks to a 38-12-5 record, and the state championship. By September, Paige had returned to Pittsburgh to finish the season with the Crawfords. A year later, Neil Churchill added several more Black players to his team's roster. He rolled out a red carpet for Satchel Paige, hoping he'd return for another late summer appearance. He didn't. It would be another two years before Paige made his way back to Bismarck. And it would be a season of significance that resonated far beyond the wheat fields of the West.

In 1934, Paige was dominant. So was Gibson, who hit a home run at Yankee Stadium that some observers recalled leaving the park entirely. (Not likely.) But it was mammoth enough to cement his reputation as one of baseball's greatest sluggers ever.† (Negro Leaguer and future major leaguer Sam Jethroe would later marvel, "If someone had told me that Josh hit the ball a mile, I would have believed them.") Paige went 14-2 for the season with 144 strikeouts. And that was just for league games. He also threw his second career no-hitter. (Against the Grays, no less.) Thanks to Gus Greenlee's enthusiastic rental arrangements, Paige also periodically ranged far and wide once again, playing on a western tour with the Cardinals legend Dizzy Dean, and in a baseball tournament

---

* In one memorable incident early on, after Paige and his three outfielders had words in the dugout, they refused to take the field behind their pitcher. Paige proceeded to strike out the side with no outfield, and the feud promptly dissipated. "After that game, I didn't have any troubles in Bismarck," Paige wrote.

† Gibson is commonly referred to as "the Black Babe Ruth." Even while both men were still alive, it was equally common for Blacks to refer to Ruth as "the white Josh Gibson."

sponsored by the *Denver Post*. Selected for the East-West All-Star Game, which was played at Chicago's Comiskey Park, Paige won the game, 1–0. As significantly, the game drew over 25,000 fans, said to be the largest crowd ever for a Black sporting event.

As the 1935 season was set to begin, Paige and Greenlee repeated their dance over diminishing money for the raises Paige perpetually sought. This time Paige essentially walked out. He returned to North Dakota, where Neil Churchill again shelled out the $400 per month (nearly twice what Greenlee was offering) and the used car he'd lavished on his temporary star two years earlier. Churchill had also added several other Negro League players to the Bismarcks. And again, Paige delivered. He won nearly 30 games, going 29-2 for the season, with over 300 strikeouts. In a postseason tournament held in Wichita, Kansas, Bismarck swept in seven straight games. Paige won all of his four games, pitched in relief in a fifth game, and set a strikeout record for the series that has stood ever since.

Like a baseball nomad chasing the endless summer, Paige went out West again over the winter. A promoter persuaded him to front the "Satchel Paige All-Stars," which would play a white all-star team in Oakland on February 7, 1936. The white team included major-league stars Ernie Lombardi, Cookie Lavagetto, and a promising Pacific Coast League star named Joe DiMaggio. The future Yankee Clipper and Hall of Famer got a single hit off of Paige in a one-run win for the white all-stars. (Nonetheless, a scout at the game wired New York and affirmed the kid was the real deal and ready to come east.) Years later, DiMaggio called Satchel Paige "the best I've ever faced, and the fastest."

A new year brought a new approach and a fresh beginning for sparring partners Paige and Greenlee. The owner nearly tripled his star pitcher's salary, offering him $600 a month, the highest in the Negro Leagues. Greenlee no doubt was pleased with the response; Paige went undefeated. Following the season, he joined an all-star team of Negro League players that swept the *Denver Post* Tournament in seven games. Paige won three of them, including the title game, a 7–0 shutout with 18 strikeouts. "Unhittable," was how more and more players summed up the experience of digging in against him.

Like the sudden swirl of infield dirt past shimmering green grass on a hot and hazy summer afternoon, Satchel Paige seemed part real, part mirage. He strode like a lanky colossus to mound after mound, and in the blur of a leg that lifted skyward and an arm that flung down like a catapult, left batter after batter staring wide-eyed at empty air where a ball must have shot through. By the mid-1930s, Satchel Paige was indeed the Negro League's most dominant player. He was, quite likely, the most dominant pitcher in all of baseball. But in the long march back to the major leagues, he was but one part of a powerful, unprecedented force that had been unloosed in Pittsburgh. It was a force that had reordered and reimagined what Black baseball represented. To both Blacks and whites. Paige had now proven that an incomparable pitcher who could overmatch any hitter at any level, could be Black. Josh Gibson had proven that a Black slugger could hit the ball farther out of major-league ballparks than the white sluggers who called those same ballparks home. Together, the two players, like a Gibson blast or a Paige fastball, exploded the lazy lie that Black ballplayers were somehow an inferior product compared to white major leaguers. *Inferior?* There were droves of white major leaguers—some with names like Hornsby, Feller, and DiMaggio— who observed the work of Paige and Gibson with a professional awe that bordered on reverence. But white fans and journalists and baseball people also were having their eyes opened. That was due to the two teams that Paige and Gibson spent years crisscrossing bridges over rivers to play for. It was also because of the two pioneering owners of those two teams. Yes, they were bitter rivals who looked continuously for any edge (legal or not) that might give their team an advantage. They were both known as impassioned and impulsive men with fiercely competitive personalities. But both were equally passionate about bolstering Black baseball, about showcasing the vast talent that deserved to be seen on the same stage as the nation's best. Indeed, Cumberland Posey was big enough to pay deference to his rival, and publicly recognize Gus Greenlee's role in revitalizing the Negro Leagues.

The truth is, both men created something extraordinary. In the 1930s, at alternate times, the Homestead Grays and the Pittsburgh Crawfords were two of the best teams that ever played the game of baseball. Ever.

1935 Negro National League champion Pittsburgh Crawfords, posing in front of the travel bus bought by owner Gus Greenlee: Oscar Charleston, far left; Satchel Paige, second from right; Josh Gibson, fourth from right NATIONAL BASEBALL HALL OF FAME AND MUSEUM

How extraordinary? Consider: During the period that these two Negro League teams shone, there also existed, after all, a Major League Baseball team in the same city—the Pittsburgh Pirates. In the 10 seasons, 1930–1939, the Pirates (one of eight NL teams) never finished higher than second place; they finished in either fourth, fifth, or sixth place, a total of six times.

"Look at the baseball talent in Pittsburgh in the thirties," says Sean Gibson. "They had two great teams—and the major league Pittsburgh Pirates weren't one of them. They were terrible in the 1930s, when the Grays and the Crawfords were some of the best baseball teams ever. When they played games there, the Grays and the Crawfords drew bigger crowds at Forbes Field than the Pirates did!"

Embarrassing for the Pirates, but true. It was not lost on Pirates management what they could do with a Paige, or a Gibson, or, be still foolish heart, both. They could have added in Oscar Charleston and Cool Papa Bell. And they would have almost certainly celebrated a championship. During the 1937 winter baseball owners meeting in Chicago, sportswriter Chester Washington of the *Courier* sent a telegram to Pirates manager Pie Traynor. He pointed out that, between the Grays and the Crawfords, there were several outstanding players "all available at reasonable figures," and all of whom, he added, "would make Pirates formidable pennant contenders." Washington concluded with, "What is your attitude? Wire answer."

The Pirates never answered. They finished fourth that season, 10 games out. The blind, rote racism they maintained—along with virtually all of Major League Baseball—was clearly as much their loss as the Black players who were excluded. But the Pirates were a baseball afterthought in Pittsburgh in the 1930s. It was the Grays and the Crawfords, and Paige and Gibson, and Cum Posey and Gus Greenlee who formed the power behind Pittsburgh's magnificent, magical baseball decade. What these men, these teams, and this city ultimately did was to create something that would, in less than a decade now, ease the passage of one Jack Roosevelt Robinson. They also created something uniquely, perfectly Pittsburgh: a bridge. To Brooklyn.

SIX

Power of the (Black) Press

The people must know before they can act, and there is no educator to compare with the press.

—Ida B. Wells

On September 11, 1932, Robert Lee Vann, owner and editor of the *Pittsburgh Courier*, gave a speech before the St. James Literary Forum in Cleveland. The speech was titled, "The Patriot and the Partisan." Its premise seemed as intellectually reasonable as it was politically blasphemous.

Since Abraham Lincoln's freeing of the slaves, African Americans had forged what had seemed like a permanent bond with the Republican Party. Vann, however, argued that the previous three presidential administrations—all Republicans (Harding, Coolidge, Hoover)—had all dismally failed Blacks. "The Republican Party under Mr. Coolidge was a lifeless, voiceless thing," Vann said. "The Republican Party under Mr. Hoover has been the saddest failure known to political history." (Three years into the Great Depression, the description of Hoover seemed increasingly valid.) Vann praised Black voters who "changed their political philosophy and are selecting the party which they believe will guarantee them the privileges to which every patriot is entitled." He wasn't talking about the Republican Party. The GOP, he argued, had long since lost the spirit of Lincoln, and long since taken the support of African Americans for granted. Continued Black Republican support, Vann argued, was both foolhardy and a waste of time. Then he hammered home his memorable plea for change:

"Go home and turn Lincoln's picture to the wall," he urged. "The debt has been paid in full."

Neither Republicans in general, nor even many Blacks themselves, were quite prepared for how persuasive Vann's exhortation would be. On Election Day, November 8, 1932, African-American voters abandoned the Republican Party in massive numbers, not just in Pennsylvania, but across the country, helping Democrat and former New York governor Franklin Delano Roosevelt to a resounding, landslide victory over Republican incumbent Herbert Hoover. Within four years, Roosevelt and the Democrats would increase their share of the Black vote to more than 70 percent nationally. It would never again be lower.

Was Robert Vann single-handedly responsible for this seismic shift and near total realignment in African-American political support? No. However, if Robert Vann had given the same speech as a respected banker rather than an influential newspaper owner and editor, its effect would have been vastly reduced. The fact is, in 1932, the *Pittsburgh Courier* was America's biggest and most influential Black newspaper. More than a dozen editions of the paper circulated throughout the nation. (Three years later, it would reach a circulation of 100,000 for the first time.)

In giving his speech prior to the election, Vann was mindful of, and confident in, the significance of the platform he occupied. The *Courier* was a bullhorn that reached Black communities far from Pittsburgh. The same was true of the *Chicago Defender*. By the 1930s, America's Black press had matured and grown, and was now gaining and expanding its reach. But it hadn't happened overnight. As with baseball—and virtually every other business, from banks to beauty parlors and barbershops—Blacks were shut out and forced to create "leagues of their own." This included journalism and newspapers. (And later, radio.) Unable to be hired as reporters or editors at white-owned newspapers, Blacks created their own. It was the only way to have issues covered that were of importance and interest to the African-American community. Black baseball (including the Negro Leagues), for example, was rarely covered by white newspapers unless a Black team was playing a local or prominent white team.

But ironically, being largely shut out and ignored by white-owned newspapers had a unifying effect. Many African-American communities

From left to right: Sam Lacy of the *Baltimore Afro-American*, Brooklyn Dodgers pitcher Dan Bankhead, and Wendell Smith of the *Pittsburgh Courier* in 1948
NATIONAL BASEBALL HALL OF FAME AND MUSEUM

increasingly became connected through a Black press they could count on to cover their stories and that they depended on for information and opinion about the issues that affected their day-to-day lives. In raising the consciousness of these communities, the Black press was in itself becoming a collective weapon against racism and segregation. Indeed, by the 1940s, African-American reporters like Wendell Smith, Joe Bostic, and Sam Lacy had not only cemented reputations as great sportswriters, but had also turned their focus and skills squarely on segregation in baseball. Within the next decade, they and other journalists, sometimes working in tandem with Black ballplayers, would ultimately help breach the color barrier. But before the Black press could help to integrate baseball, it would need to find its way through a century of slavery, the Civil War, Reconstruction, Jim Crow, the Great Migration, and two world wars. First, as always, there would need to be pioneers.

The first printing press arrived in America in 1638, and was installed at Harvard College in Cambridge, Massachusetts. Between the clergy and the colonial government, publishing was tightly controlled, and it would be another 50 years before the first newspaper was published.* By 1827, although the clergy were still an influence, the British were long gone when a Black paper, *Freedom's Journal*, finally joined the nearly 900 American newspapers already being published. Neither of its two founders were journalists. Samuel Cornish was a Princeton graduate and a founder of the First Colored Presbyterian Church in Manhattan. John B. Russwurm was born in Jamaica to mixed parents, educated in Canada, and graduated from Bowdoin College in 1826 as the nation's second Black college graduate. From the first issue, the editors made clear the focus would be big. And fearless.

"Blessings of Slavery," the paper bitingly wrote on April 6, 1827. "Mr. John Hamilton of Lanesborough County, Va., was murdered on the 9th ult. by his slaves. Seventeen of them have been committed to the county jail to await their trial." Such explicitly angry editorial content was not without risk.

"Before the Civil War," writes Patrick S. Washburn, author of *The African American Newspaper: Voice of Freedom*, "a black editor who was too outspoken, like some white abolitionists, might be attacked and killed and his press destroyed."

Nonetheless—and decades before the Civil War—Cornish and Russwurm were equally explicit in their overall objective: raising awareness of the immoral scourge of slavery, and advocating for abolition and freedom. "The civil rights of a people being of the greatest value," the editors wrote, "it shall ever be our duty to vindicate our brethren, when oppressed; and to lay the case before the publick."

---

* Not that it went so well. *Publick Occurrences Both Foreign and Domestick* was published in Boston in 1690. The British, claiming its owner lacked a proper license, shut down the paper after only one issue.

Laid out by America's very first Black newspaper, this essentially became the credo for all the major Black newspapers that followed. By the time of the Emancipation Proclamation, more than 20 Black newspapers had been launched in America. Among the most famous was the *North Star*, published in Rochester, New York, by the legendary Frederick Douglass. His paper and the others were vital platforms in spreading the abolitionist cause. In the wake of the Civil War and Emancipation, African-American literacy rates increased dramatically. With that, so did Black newspapers, along with a legion of courageous and pioneering Black journalists. Like the groundbreaking Black baseball players of the same period, these journalists—men and women—would turn out to be true unsung heroes on the path not only to Brooklyn, but to other civil rights breakthroughs before and after that.

In withstanding his brutally stressful, barrier-breaking season in 1947, Jackie Robinson is justly praised for his grit, determined dignity, and quiet courage. (Through it all, it should be noted, he still managed to bat .297, hit 12 home runs, and leg out 31 doubles.) But that same dignity, grit, and courage were easily rivaled a half-century earlier by another skilled, brave Black professional. For her, there was also the stress and daily battle of being a Black groundbreaker. For her, pitching and hitting were of no concern. But lynching was.

Hers was an especially tough start in life. No wonder Ida B. Wells matured into a woman as tough as nails and ever ready to drop the reporter's hammer of truth. She was born into slavery in Holly Springs, Mississippi, in 1862, just a year before Emancipation. When she was 16, both of her parents and infant brother died during a yellow fever epidemic, leaving her (one of eight children) and a grandmother to care for the surviving siblings. Having attended a small Black liberal arts college in Holly Springs, she took a job teaching, working during the day while her grandmother looked after the kids. After her grandmother died, she moved to Memphis, Tennessee, in 1883 with her two youngest sisters. In Memphis, she continued teaching, took summer classes at historic Fisk College in Nashville, and first began to show both the striking outspokenness and

IDA B. WELLS.

Ida B. Wells, 1891
LIBRARY OF CONGRESS

steely resolve for which she would become renowned.* On May 4, 1884, Wells was ordered by a conductor on a Chesapeake & Ohio train to give up her seat in the first-class ladies car. (The Supreme Court had previously ruled in favor of private railroad companies that segregated their passenger cars.) Dragged from the car, Wells brought a lengthy lawsuit against the company. Although she was ultimately unsuccessful, the experience galvanized her interest and passion for writing and journalism.

While still teaching elementary school, she began to attract writing opportunities with several publications, and in 1889 became editor and co-owner of *The Free Speech and Headlight*, a Black-owned newspaper in Memphis. Her pieces attacked the racism and Jim Crow policies of the period with increasing stridency, which led to her being dismissed as a teacher by the Memphis Board of Education. Wells's dismissal turned out to be a lasting gift to great reporting. She was freed to focus her inexhaustible energy, like no one ever had, on laying bare the most horrific legacy of racism.

On March 2, 1892, a dispute began between two kids—one Black, one white—playing marbles outside of a Memphis store. A week later, it ended with three Black men being dragged out of a jail cell in the middle of the night and brutally murdered by a white mob. But for the fact that the victims were friends of Ida B. Wells, their deaths would have gone uninvestigated and unremarked on. In truth, the deaths *were* uninvestigated; they were most certainly not unremarked on. Wells called on Blacks to begin to defend themselves—with deadly force, if necessary. She also exhorted them to simply get up and move from places like Memphis, where a nighttime lynching had become as common as a morning coffee.

"There is, therefore, only one thing left to do," she wrote in *Free Speech and Headlight*, "save our money and leave a town which will neither protect our lives and property, nor give us a fair trial in the courts, but takes us out and murders us in cold blood when accused by white persons."

---

* While her life's work as a journalist was focused on drawing attention to some of the worst acts of racism and segregation, Wells was also a strong proponent of women's rights and independence. At 24 she wrote, "I will not begin at this late day by doing what my soul abhors; sugaring men, weak deceitful creatures, with flattery to retain them as escorts or to gratify a revenge."

Wells turned to reporting on lynching with the cold, hard, detailed fact-telling of an investigative journalist, along with the brutally honest, incisive truth-telling of a fiery editorialist. All of which worried some Blacks, and angered many whites, especially in the South. After her Memphis newspaper office was burned and destroyed, she herself left the city. In time, the incessant death threats forced her to stay away from the South for good.

Less than a year later, investigating and documenting lynchings in Mississippi, Wells published a new pamphlet detailing more of her research, *Southern Horrors: Lynch Law in All Its Phases.* Three years later, she published *The Red Record*, an even more exhaustive history of lynching. She eventually settled in Chicago,* where she married Ferdinand Lee Barnett, a prominent Black attorney and civil rights activist. They raised a family, and continued to fight together and separately for equality and civil rights. She remained rooted in activist journalism, traveled widely, spoke extensively, and was a founding member of the NAACP. Unflinching and outspoken throughout her life, her own introduction to her *Southern Horrors* best captures the human comet that was Ida B. Wells: "It is with no pleasure that I have dipped my hands in the corruption here exposed," she wrote. "Somebody must show that the Afro-American race is more sinned against than sinning, and it seems to have fallen upon me to do so."

Wells was not alone among pioneering Black journalists, editors, and publishers who also fought doggedly for equality, and relentlessly spoke truth to power. In one celebrated incident, that was literally true for William Monroe Trotter.

Trotter was born in 1872 in Ohio, but was raised in the Hyde Park neighborhood of Boston by a comfortably middle-class African-American family. He earned degrees from Harvard, belonged to a Black Boston literary society, and married in 1899. A lifelong teetotaler and active in the Baptist church, Trotter nonetheless made it clear early on that, as an African American, he had little patience for the accommodationist

---

* In 1893 in Chicago, Wells collaborated at the World's Columbian Exposition with the great African-American abolitionist, statesman, and fellow newspaper editor Frederick Douglass. He had been deeply impressed by Wells's reporting and writing on lynching. In a letter to her shortly before he died in 1895, Douglass wrote, "There has been no word equal to it in convincing power. I have spoken, but my word is feeble in comparison . . . Brave woman!"

stance then-popularized by Booker T. Washington. ("Washington's attitude," scoffed Trotter, "has ever been one of servility.") In 1901 Trotter cofounded the *Guardian*, a weekly Boston newspaper that gave voice to some of the period's most militant calls for Black rights. Its strident editorials (most written by Trotter) often acted as lightning rods even within the Black community itself. W. E. B. Du Bois, an erstwhile ally of Trotter, wrote, "I did not wholly agree with the *Guardian*, and indeed only a few Negroes did, but nearly all read it and were influenced by it."*

Ever in opposition to Booker T. Washington (who supported and advised Republican presidents Teddy Roosevelt and William Howard Taft), Trotter had supported Democrat Woodrow Wilson. In the wake of Wilson's openly segregationist policies, that initial support disappointed and dismayed many Blacks. As part of a delegation of African-American political organizations, Trotter met with Wilson at the White House in November 1913. Wilson defended his policies and denied that they were segregationist; Trotter called that "preposterous." But he went further.

"Only two years ago you were heralded perhaps as the second Lincoln," Trotter told the president. "And now the Afro-American leaders who supported you are being hounded as false leaders and traitors to their race."

Wilson demanded Trotter leave the meeting, telling the group that if they ever wished "to approach me again, you must choose another spokesman." To Trotter, he said, "Your tone, Sir, offends me." To others, Wilson accused Trotter of having "sassed" him.

The *Boston Evening Transcript*, while not entirely defending Wilson's policies, wrote that Trotter "offends many of his own color by his . . . untactful belligerency." How exactly the white-owned Boston paper got Black reaction to Trotter isn't clear. There were certainly some Blacks, even admirers of Trotter, who were not comfortable with his extraordinary exchange with the president. Others found it admirable. Either way, there are few in-person examples quite as remarkable of telling truth to the truly powerful.

---

* In 1901, Trotter used his newspaper's platform to aggressively oppose the play *The Clansman* in Boston. That opposition then pivoted to *The Birth of a Nation*, D. W. Griffith's infamously racist film, which glorified the Ku Klux Klan, and which was based on the play.

Trotter's story was ultimately a truly sad one, also. The *Guardian* never achieved financial stability. In 1934, widowed, forced to sell his home and live alone in a Boston apartment, Trotter either fell or jumped from the roof of that building. His landlord found him dead on the sidewalk. It was his 62nd birthday.

Survival for Black newspapers was always uncertain. Sometimes that extended to the publishers themselves. But it always was true financially.

"As if publishing for a black audience was not enough of a financial handicap, black newspapers also had problems obtaining advertisements," wrote Patrick Washburn. "White-owned newspapers began in the 1830s to become more and more dependent upon advertising to make a profit, but most of the early black newspapers contained no commercial advertising. Certainly little, if any, came from white companies."

In time, in certain cities, under certain exceptional owners, a select few Black newspapers were built into successful, influential, and legendary institutions. They were papers that came to define the Black press, and they were home to some of the nation's most gifted and determined writers and reporters.

ON OCTOBER 18, 1924, ROBERT ABBOTT TOOK THE FIELD AT CHICAGO'S Schorling Park. A historic occasion, it was the eighth game of the first Negro World Series, between the Hilldales of Pennsylvania and the Kansas City Monarchs. Abbott's hat was not his own; his glove was borrowed, too. But Monarchs pitcher "Bullet" Rogan was happy to lend both to Abbott, who would throw out the ceremonial first pitch. "The premier black publisher of his time—indeed arguably in all of black history— appropriately took his place at the center of what was arguably black baseball's most important moment," wrote Lawrence D. Hogan in *Shades of Glory*. "By this time, baseball and the press as black institutions were joined at the hip, the growth of either in this pairing influenced significantly by the growth of the other."

He was born in 1870 on the tiny island of St. Simons off Georgia's Atlantic coast. His parents had been slaves prior to the Civil War. After his father died when Abbott was an infant, his widowed mother, Flora, remarried to a mixed-race German named John Sengstacke, who adopted

Robert Sengstacke Abbott, c. 1918

Abbott as his son. Sengstacke was a teacher, and later started a small newspaper in Georgia called the *Woodville Times*. Thus inspired, Robert Sengstacke Abbott learned the printing trade at Virginia's Hampton Institute (now Hampton University). Touring nationally with the Hampton Choir and Quartet, he performed in Chicago in 1893. There, he was enthralled to hear Frederick Douglass speak,* and to encounter his first, large American city with a thriving Black population. Both experiences proved to be formative.

"Already absorbed by 'the plight of my people,' he was both radicalized and urbanized by his experience," wrote Ethan Michaeli, author of *The Defender: How the Legendary Black Newspaper Changed America*. "What he saw in Chicago that summer convinced him that this city was the perfect place to realize his dreams."

Although Abbott did return to Georgia to help on his stepfather's paper, the lure of Chicago and the West was too great. He returned, and received a law degree in 1900 from Chicago's Kent College of Law, where he was the only African American in his class. But practicing his profession was tough. In Chicago, as well as in Indiana and Kansas, he tried unsuccessfully to set up a law practice. Even among Chicago's Black elite, lighter skin seemed to be the preferred professional calling card. A fellow attorney told him that he was "a little too dark to make an impression on the Illinois courts." By 1904, unable to make a living as a lawyer, Abbott's interest turned to the trade he had learned first—printing. He expressed to friends "his belief that what African American people needed was a newspaper that would 'wake them up,'" Ethan Michaeli wrote. Abbott envisioned a paper that would "expose the atrocities of the southern system, and make demands for justice." His friends found it hard to envision Abbott accomplishing that without having any money to invest in such a dicey enterprise. No African-American newspaper, to that point, had turned a profit. Abbott, however, was convinced and resolute in his vision. He was also essentially penniless. Spending the last of his spare change on some pencils and notebooks, Abbott was able to borrow a typewriter.

---

* Speaking at the World's Columbian Exhibition, Douglass received thunderous applause when he said, "There is no 'Negro problem.' The problem is whether the American people have honesty enough, loyalty enough, honor enough, patriotism enough to live up to their own constitution."

Linotype operators of the *Chicago Defender* (photo by Russell Lee, 1941)
WIKIMEDIA COMMONS

On credit, he was able to rent a room from a local Black Realtor and, most importantly, the services of a local printer. Ironically, one of the greatest legacies Abbott would create—the newspaper's name—cost nothing. A friend suggested that Abbott simply echo what he had taken as a personal mission statement: to create a newspaper that would be a "defender of his race." On May 5, 1905, the first edition of the *Chicago Defender* rolled off the press.

The early days were halting and humbling. The paper wasn't much to look at or (at only 300 copies) much to deliver. It consisted of four, six-column pages, resembling his stepfather's *Woodville Times*, and was billed as "The Only Two-Cent Weekly in the City." The printing cost for the paper's first edition was $13.75. Abbott covered it by pounding the street and putting away the pennies he charged. He determinedly sought out advertising wherever and however he could, from local butchers, tailors, hotels, and barbershops. When he still couldn't come up with the small amount of rent for his "office space," his landlady stepped up and offered to let him use her dining room as a newsroom.* Owing mostly to his inexhaustible energy and unshakeable will to grow the paper's circulation, Abbott was able to incrementally increase its size and print numbers. But that also increased his printing bill. One evening, he was short the $25 needed to get out an edition. "I went to several places and tried to pawn my overcoat, but found out it would only bring me 30 cents," Abbott recalled years later. "I had no jewelry, not even a watch I could pawn to give me the necessary funds to pay for the expenses of my paper."

What Abbott had, however, was a strong sense of what his community hungered to hear.

And he worked hard to make his newspaper that voice. After a series of particularly violent and convulsive race riots in Atlanta in 1906 (at least 24 Blacks and two whites were killed), Abbott developed a stronger sense of militancy. "The Atlanta riots, taking place in his home state just one year after he began publishing *The Defender*," wrote Michaeli, "was a formative moment for Robert Abbott, deepening his resolve to make his newspaper a force to combat the pervasive racism of the era."

Refreshing and inspiring to many in the Black community, the paper's more militant tone attracted both new subscribers and those looking to work for Abbott. Among the earliest to join Abbott was Frank "Fay" Young. A night shift dining-car waiter for the Chicago and North Western Railway, Young collected newspapers left behind by passengers. Each morning, he and Abbott would go through them and find leads for their own stories.

Young was a critical part of the *Defender*'s growth and success, eventually becoming regarded as the "dean of black sportswriters." (And Black railway porters would become an integral part of the growth of the Black press in general.)

No single story or issue cemented the *Chicago Defender*'s growing stature like the phenomenon known as the Great Migration. Fed up with the daily indignity of life under Jim Crow, the lack of economic

---

* Indeed, Henrietta P. Lee, a widow active in her church, was something of a surrogate mother to Abbott. Her support was so steadfast and crucial to him both professionally and personally that, years later, Abbott bought Lee a new home in Chicago.

opportunity, and the constant threat of violence, the Great Migration began a massive and long-term shift of Black population in America from the South to the North and West. (In 1916, when the Great Migration began, 90 percent of African Americans lived in the South; 50 years later, 47 percent lived in the North and West.) Initially, with respect especially to lynchings in southern states, Abbott and the *Defender* took the position of demanding federal intervention. The paper castigated President Woodrow Wilson, who was up for re-election that fall. Wilson had previously sent US troops into Haiti, and into Mexico to help apprehend the revolutionary leader Pancho Villa. "If President Woodrow Wilson is so eager to teach the world good morals," the *Defender* editorial argued, "let him begin by placing the U.S. Army in the South; institute a chase of the lynchers as earnestly as the one he is now carrying on in Mexico." At the same time, cotton was collapsing and southern Blacks began to stream to the North for work. Southern business interests began to grasp the grave implications; their traditional source of cheap—and vital—Black labor was up and leaving. "The maltreatment of the whites toward members of the Race is the sole cause of the exodus," wrote the *Defender*. At the same time, with a labor shortage due to World War I, northern businesses pounced, sending recruiters fanning out across the South, encouraging Black workers to move north for guaranteed jobs. Cities like Chicago, Detroit, and Pittsburgh were seeing train carloads of African Americans arriving daily. When some southern municipalities began harassing, fining, and even banning northern labor agents, Abbott had seen enough. He was determined to force the South to reckon with what it had wrought, while encouraging Blacks to vote with their feet in a way they couldn't at the ballot box—to leave the worst of Jim Crow and embrace a better life away from the "Southland," as Abbott called it. He was equally determined that the *Defender* would be the most strident and powerful voice backing the Great Migration. And it was. In late 1916, the paper published a poem, "Bound for the Promised Land," (M. Ward), which included these verses:

From Florida's stormy banks I'll go, I'll bid the South goodbye;
No longer will they treat me so, And knock me in the eye . . .

. . . No cracker there to seduce your sister, nor to hang you to a limb,
And you're not obliged to call 'em "Mister," nor skin 'em back at him.

When the poem was reprinted a few months later, the paper reported that it had been responsible for "causing more men to leave the Southland than any other effort."

And there were other efforts. In the spring of 1917, the *Defender* promoted the Great Northern Drive, a day on which it called for a million blacks to leave the South. *The Defender's* clarion, combative, leading voice galvanized its subscribers, and thousands of new Black arrivals were quickly attracted as new customers. Its circulation reached new levels. As a new decade dawned, and the paper's staff and circulation expanded, it was clear that Robert Abbott's audacious vision was being realized daily. He had indeed become a powerful "defender of his race." And he'd proven his doubters wrong; his newspaper made a steady profit. It had been many years since he'd felt a need to pawn his overcoat to pay expenses.

As successful as the *Defender* was, its chief rival to the east was even more so.

DURING THE 1932 PRESIDENTIAL CAMPAIGN, WHEN ROBERT VANN HAD called on black voters to renounce their traditional Republican support and to get behind Roosevelt, he was confident that he had the standing to take such a position and to make such a request. His *Pittsburgh Courier* was firmly establishing itself as the Black newspaper of record in America. Like the *Defender*, the *Courier* wielded wide and deep influence among Black Americans, and advocated relentlessly for their rights and for social progress. Even more, it would be the *Pittsburgh Courier* that most effectively focused the power of the Black press for the final decade's battle to break baseball's color barrier.

Ironically, much like Robert Abbott, Robert Lee Vann was a child of the South who left, got a good education, trained for a career as a lawyer, but ended up publishing a newspaper. He was born in 1879 in Ahoskie, North Carolina. He went to college at Virginia Union University in Richmond, and got his law degree in 1909 from Western University of Pennsylvania (now the University of Pittsburgh). Unlike Abbott, it was actually Vann's work as an attorney that led him to owning a newspaper. In 1910, he handled the legal incorporation papers for the launching of the *Pittsburgh Courier* by its original founder, Edwin Harleston. Vann contributed some writing, and although he was helpful in attracting some wealthy investors (including Cumberland Posey Sr.), the paper's weak circulation and lack of advertising threatened insolvency, and Harleston left the paper. Robert Vann assumed the position of editor, and set about putting his personal stamp on what was now his newspaper. He seemed to have a knack for marketing and promotion, which attracted advertisers. (Who no doubt were drawn to Vann's exhorting his readers to patronize only those businesses who advertised in the paper.) But his circulation grew because, as with Robert Abbott and the *Defender*, his readers were drawn to Vann's outspokenness on race. In one early editorial, he wrote that the paper's intent was "to abolish every vestige of Jim Crowism in Pittsburgh." Later, the *Courier* led a concerted protest against the nationally syndicated *Amos 'n' Andy* radio show.* Under Vann's leading role, the paper led a drive to get a million signatures on a petition to force the show off the air for what many Blacks saw as its misrepresentation and stereotyping of blacks. The effort failed, but the larger success was symbolized by the *Courier*'s robust growth and deepening prominence. It was by no means the only significant and successful Black newspaper. By the 1930s, in addition to Chicago's *Defender*, other significant Black newspapers included New York's *Amsterdam News*, Baltimore's *Afro American*, Philadelphia's *Tribune* and *Independent*, and the *Kansas City Call*, among many others across the country. But by the 1930s, the *Pittsburgh Courier* would boast both a local and a national edition, 14 separate editions in multiple states, and circulation numbers officially making it America's largest Black newspaper. The *Courier* also offered its readers a remarkably diverse array of contributing voices, consistently raising its quality of journalistic excellence. In the 1930s, it had also begun to distinguish itself among all Black newspapers as a leader in sports reporting. There

---

* The long-running show, which debuted in 1928, featured two white actors: Freeman Gosden played "Amos," and Charles Correll played "Andy." The pair also voiced various other Black characters in addition to their own. In the series' later years, African-American performers took on the show's roles.

were good reasons for the growth in good sportswriting in Pittsburgh. After all, by the 1930s it was home to arguably the two best Black baseball teams the world had ever seen, and quite likely the two best Black baseball players, too. That's a lot to cover.* It wasn't only baseball. Early on, the paper seemed attuned to the ways in which Black sports—and sports figures—spoke to many of the same themes of pride, dignity, empowerment, and battling through adversity that were editorialized regularly. The saga of the "Brown Bomber" was a perfect case in point. Boxer Joe Louis was from Alabama, not Pittsburgh, but many of the *Courier's* readers might have guessed otherwise. Louis won the World Heavyweight title in 1937. But the *Courier* had been covering him for years earlier. In Louis's heyday, the paper often (only half-jokingly) referred to itself as the "Joe Louis paper." In 1935, then-*Courier* reporter William G. Nunn Sr. (he would later become editor) described Louis as "the answer to our prayers, the prayers of a race of people who are struggling to break through dense clouds of prejudice . . . who, though bowed by oppression, will never be broken in spirit." As Patrick Washburn (*The African American Newspaper*), wrote of the *Courier's* Joe Louis coverage, "Readers loved it, and circulation rose to 250,000 by 1937."

The decade or so from the mid-1930s through the mid-40s were something of a golden age for the Black press, as several of the leading Black newspapers spawned equally extraordinary and groundbreaking reporters and editors. They covered ballgames and riots, elections and lynchings, wars and weddings. Although these reporters were writing a quarter-century or so before the full force of the organized civil rights movement of the 1960s, many were already pointing the way in their coverage. For many Black reporters who covered the Negro Leagues, it was Major League Baseball's stubborn racism that seemed to frustrate and

---

* 1937 was a big year for the *Courier's* baseball—and sports—coverage. Headlines were made when both Satchel Paige and Josh Gibson bolted the city—and the States—having been recruited for big money by the Dominican Republic's dictator, Rafael Trujillo. While the Grays' Cumberland Posey and the Crawfords' Gus Greenlee were certainly tough and intensely competitive owners who demanded perfection, Paige and Gibson, to their very real alarm, quickly discovered that Trujillo *really* demanded perfection. Before pitching a deciding game against Trujillo's rival, and having already noticed the armed soldiers at the ballpark, Paige was told by his manager, "Take my advice, and just win." Genuinely nervous—especially after falling behind by a run late in the game—Paige did win. And promptly bolted the island back for the States.

infuriate further with each passing decade. By the late 1930s, an ignominious anniversary was approaching; it would be 50 years since Black baseball players had been cast out and kept out. The Black newspaper reporters who covered the modern Negro Leagues saw firsthand the talent that was being wasted, robbed of its full potential. They saw with their own eyes, and knew who the star Black players were—Paige, Gibson, Charleston, Bell—who would be instant stars in white baseball, too. Hell, the white stars—Johnson, Dean, DiMaggio—saw and said the same thing.

"I'll be darned if old Connie Mack, boss of the old Philadelphia Athletics didn't tell somebody or other he'd give a hundred thousand for me if they'd let him use me," recalled Satchel Paige. "All I had to be was white."

Some Black journalists tired of comparing great Black and white talent. They tired of stating the obvious. If the great DiMaggio himself, one of the best hitters who ever lived, said that Paige was the greatest pitcher he'd ever faced, who was left to convince? There were only so many words to describe the strikingly similar level of skill at first base between a Buck Leonard and a Jimmie Foxx, only so many ways to say that both Judy Johnson or Ray Dandridge would fit into any white major-league infield

anywhere. With Satchel Paige and Josh Gibson, the superlatives began to elude even the most nimble wordsmiths. Reaching for ever-loftier comparisons, some reached beyond baseball entirely.

"With Paige back in the league," the *Courier*'s Chester Washington wrote in 1936, "he may practically be the Moses who will help to lead Negro baseball into the promised land. . . ."

Even if that metaphor had some merit, few were willing to wait another 40 years in the wilderness of the Negro Leagues before a latter-day Moses or

Josh Gibson, 1930s NATIONAL BASEBALL HALL OF FAME AND MUSEUM

Satchel Paige with the Kansas City Monarchs, c. 1941
NATIONAL BASEBALL HALL OF FAME AND MUSEUM

anyone else could lead his people out of exile. Some Black journalists were simply tired of writing variations of that same message repeatedly in their columns, only to be read and agreed with by their Black readers. At a certain point, for someone like Sam Lacy, it felt like the real-life definition of "preaching to the choir." In Boston, fellow Black journalist Mabry "Doc" Koutnze felt a similar frustration. It was why, in 1938, he had asked to meet with Boston Braves head Bob Quinn, the better to make the pitch directly for raising the Black profile in white baseball. A year earlier, Sam Lacy traveled that route first.

SAMUEL HAROLD LACY WAS BORN IN 1903 IN MYSTIC, CONNECTICUT, but was raised in Washington, DC, where his family moved when he was young. It seems prophetic and fitting that Lacy grew up mere blocks from Griffith Stadium, home of the American League Washington Senators. For his was to be a life spent in sports. He pitched and played semipro baseball after college, he coached and refereed youth leagues, but his career was defined as a dogged journalist, as a tough but fair sportswriter and editor who often dispensed with any "professional" distance between his job as a Black reporter and his sense of fairness and justice as a Black man.

"I never thought of myself as a pioneer," Lacy recalled later in life to Jim Reisler, author of *Black Writers/Black Baseball*. "It was just a case of doing what I thought was right."

As a kid, Lacy spent a lot of time at Griffith Stadium, shagging flies during batting practice, running errands for players, and working as a vendor during games, selling popcorn and peanuts in the stadium's right field "colored only" section where, when he wasn't working Senators home games, he sat with his dad—back, that is, when his dad was still attending Senators games. One of Lacy's most searing memories was of the annual team parade to the park on Opening Day one year. He describes his dad as waving a Washington pennant and cheering the players on, when one (Lacy never identified him) spat on his dad's face as he passed.

"That hurt my father terribly," Lacy recalled. "And you know, as big a fan as he had been, he never went to another game as long as he lived."

For his part, Lacy continued to maintain a connection with baseball, and sports, in his hometown. After graduating in 1923 from Howard University, he pitched for DC's semipro Hillsdale club. He also refereed area high school and college basketball games, and coached some local youth teams. But Lacy also was continuing to cover sports part-time for the *Washington Tribune*, a Black newspaper, something he'd begun doing in college. In 1926 he joined the *Tribune* full-time, eventually becoming sports editor. It was not an uneventful tenure. He traveled to Berlin to cover Jesse Owens's gold medal victory under Hitler's baleful scowl at the 1936 Summer Olympics. He covered Joe Louis's title fights, and he was covering the Negro Leagues just as young players like Satchel Paige, Josh Gibson, and Cool Papa Bell were establishing themselves as stars of the game. As he watched such stars, Lacy wasn't the first to be filled with angry frustration at the cold, hard fact that the meteoric rise of a Paige or a Gibson would, in reality, travel no higher and no further than the very earthly but invisible wall that separated Black from white baseball. Sam Lacy, however, was among the few who took their frustration to those on the other side of that wall.

During the 1936 season, Lacy had a front row seat to the greatness of the Homestead Grays, who played their home games at Washington's Griffith Stadium when the Senators were on the road. Lacy had begun trying to persuade Washington owner Clark Griffith to consider recruiting some of the Negro League's burgeoning stars. In his private moments, Griffith must have sighed at the thought of what his team could do with a Gibson, Paige, Johnson, or Leonard. Although the Senators eked out a winning record in 1936, that year was bracketed by the team's more typical season after season of abysmal futility. Given the temptation, who could blame Lacy for trying? In 1937, Sam Lacy was finally given a one-on-one meeting with Clark Griffith.

"I used that old cliché about Washington being first in war, first in peace, and last in the American League, and that he could remedy that," Lacy said later in an interview. "But he told me that the climate wasn't right. He pointed out there were a lot of southern players in the league, and that there would be constant confrontations, and moreover, that it would break up the Negro Leagues. He saw the Negro Leagues as a source of revenue."

In a subsequent column, Lacy shared that, in their meeting, Griffith had said he was also concerned that if the Negro Leagues were disbanded, it would "put about 400 colored guys out of work." For that matter, Lacy wrote, "When Abraham Lincoln signed the Emancipation Proclamation, he put 400,000 black people out of jobs."

Griffith—and baseball—remained unmoved. (Over the next 20 years, the Senators finished only *four* seasons above .500; Satchel Paige recorded at least 100 documented wins in the same period.) Lacy, however, did move, first to Chicago in 1941 where he became assistant national editor at the *Defender*. But with that paper's sports coverage securely ("possessively," Lacy would say) in the hands of longtime reporter Frank "Fay" Young, Lacy returned to the East to join Baltimore's *Afro-American* as a columnist and sports editor. It's where he would stay and work and write and develop a national reputation for the next nearly 60 years. His passionate, persistent opposition to baseball's color barrier would never cease or pause until it fell.

As accomplished and universally respected as Sam Lacy was, he was not considered the best Black sportswriter of his generation. At least not according to Sam Lacy.

"Anybody can be a reporter—a kid coming home from school and telling his parents what happened in class that day is a reporter—but it takes more to be a journalist," Lacy told Jim Reisler in *Black Writers/ Black Baseball*. "Wendell had that something extra. He was always thinking ahead and never quite satisfied with what he had accomplished."

What Wendell Smith accomplished was an expansive and impressive body of work that spanned parts of five decades. An exceptional reporter and writer, he had unique gifts of creativity, observation, and expression. As a legendary Black journalist, he also had arguably the most direct impact on breaking baseball's color barrier than anyone not named Rickey or Robinson.

Born in Detroit in 1914, Smith was raised there, where his dad was a chef for auto manufacturer Henry Ford. Like his colleague Sam Lacy, Smith grew up playing baseball. At Southeastern High School, he pitched and won All-City honors before graduating and attending West Virginia State College, a Black public college in West Virginia. At 19, after pitching a 1–0 shutout in a playoff game, what should have been a moment of triumph and a lasting memory of achievement became instead a sobering experience that marked Smith's path in life. After the game, a scout approached both Smith's own catcher as well as the game's losing pitcher, no less, and signed both to professional contracts. He told Smith he'd dearly like to sign him, too, but alas, couldn't do it "because he was colored." Smith claimed later that the experience was a pivotal influence in his becoming both a sportswriter and a tireless advocate for integrating baseball. On graduating college and leaving his own playing days behind him, Wendell Smith would embrace both of those roles with equal relish for the rest of his life.

In 1937, fresh out of college, Smith was hired by the *Pittsburgh Courier* as a sportswriter. Clearly something took; a year later, his duties at the paper included assistant sports editor, city editor, and columnist.

"His style could be folksy, but it turned direct when he was taking on both major league and black team owners," wrote Jim Reisler. "In addition to writing some of the very first interviews and player profiles of personalities in Pittsburgh's colorful baseball scene, he also fit the aggressive, sometimes angry style of *Courier* Editor Robert L. Vann, who launched the paper on numerous crusades to benefit black America."

Few things angered Smith like the gaping racial injustice that stared back at him as he began covering Black baseball in the late 1930s. As if he needed reminding that little had changed since college when that white scout had spurned him, he was reminded, anyway. Continually, it seemed. As a full-time professional staffer of an established commercial newspaper, he applied for membership in the Baseball Writers' Association of America. He was denied.* Lacking proper (i.e., "white newspaper") credentials, he and his Black colleagues were also barred from the press boxes of most major-league ballparks. Yet, Smith reserved some of his harshest words for fellow Blacks, many of whom turned out to support segregated white teams just the same.

"Why we continue to flock to major league ballparks, spending our hard-earned dough, screaming and hollering, stamping our feet and clapping our hands . . . is a question that probably will never be answered satisfactorily," wrote Smith in a 1938 column. "The fact that major league baseball refuses to admit Negro players within its folds makes the question

---

* Ironically, in 1948 it would be Smith's friend and colleague, Sam Lacy, who would be the first Black sportswriter to gain BWAA membership.

just that much more perplexing. Surely, it's sufficient reason for us to quit spending our money and time in their ballparks. Major league baseball does not want us. It never has. Still, we continue to help support this institution that places a bold 'Not Welcome' sign over its thriving portal. . . ."

In his way, Wendell Smith was echoing a campaign that the *Courier* (and other Black newspapers and organizations) had been pushing since its beginning in Chicago in 1929.

"Don't Buy Where You Can't Work" was meant to put pressure on stores and businesses to hire Blacks by raising the threat of customer boycotts. In the same spirit, Smith was merely pointing out, repeatedly, that every ticket bought at a white ballpark, every hot dog and every bag of peanuts, every cheer for a white ballplayer, represented support for a business that steadfastly refused to hire Black ballplayers.

"We have been fighting for years in an effort to make owners of major league baseball teams admit Negro players," wrote Smith. "But they won't do it, probably never will. We keep on crawling, begging and pleading for recognition just the same. We know that they don't want us, but we still keep giving them our money."

But because of where Wendell Smith worked, there was something doubly frustrating about watching Black fans support white teams. The city of Pittsburgh in the 1930s was home to two of the best baseball teams ever assembled. The major-league Pirates were not one of them. Gus Greenlee had built the Crawfords their own park. Cumberland Posey's Homestead Grays were simply dominant, a team for the ages. Indeed, in just over a decade or so, the Negro Leagues as a whole had grown, and was "Making Progress," as Smith titled another *Courier* column in 1938. All of which only angered him further. How could the strongest case be made for Black players being in Major League Baseball, if Negro League teams themselves didn't enjoy the strongest support from their Black communities? Especially at time when those teams were better than ever.

"Gone are the days when only one or two good players were on a team," Smith wrote. "Now, their rosters are filled with brilliant, colorful, dazzling players who know the game from top to bottom. Negro teams now have everything the white clubs have. Except of course, the million dollar parks to play in, parks that we helped to build with our hard-earned dollars. Nevertheless, we ignore them and go to see teams play that do not give a hang whether we come or not."

Wendell Smith did anything but ignore them. "Smith covered Negro League baseball like a blanket," wrote Jim Reisler. He took great pains to add detail and a reporter's insight to ballgames, and he took great pride in describing what many Black ballplayers were like as people. These were the kinds of up-and-close-and-personal profiles that humanized professional athletes, and that were common features on the sports pages of major white newspapers. But the only place to find such features about Black ballplayers was in a Black newspaper.

"Buck doesn't intend to end up like most ballplayers," Smith wrote in a column about the Grays' great first baseman, Buck Leonard. "He hopes to have a fine business built up by the time his playing days are over, and live quietly down in Rocky Mount as a mortician . . . Buck Leonard is the perfect example of the modern day Negro athlete. Like [Joe] Louis and Louis Armstrong, [Jesse] Owens and all the rest, he's one swell guy."

Both Wendell Smith and Sam Lacy broke new ground in their writing. Both were exceptional journalists, with a gifted eye for context and detail. Notice how Lacy begins a column in which he interviews a manager in the dugout: "[He] shifted the wad of tobacco from one side of his mouth to the other. He poked a squirt of brown into the cinders in front of the St. Louis Browns dugout and rubbed it in with the toe spikes of his right foot." In their writing, both journalists portrayed Negro League players as real people, dealing with many of the same challenges as other Blacks, and at the same time facing frustrations that were unique and compelling. Yes, it was clear from their achievements that such standout stars as Satchel Paige, Josh Gibson, Buck Leonard, Oscar Charleston, Judy Johnson, and Ray Dandridge were ready and able to star in white baseball. And it was frustrating that they were unable to do that. But there were whole rosters of other Black players, everyday players who weren't stars, who simply despaired at the *fact* of the color ban, that no Black player, despite their skill and their promise, could expect to rise to the highest level of the game.

"It will never be," Jud Wilson, third baseman for the black Philadelphia Stars, told Sam Lacy in 1939, "because the big league game, as it is now, is over-run with Southern blood. Fellows from the South are in the majority on almost every team in the major leagues."

But by writing and sharing with their readers this kind of candor as well as the games themselves, these Black journalists were turning Black ballplayers into three-dimensional people who—in their hopes, fears, frustrations, anger—were struggling with the same prejudice and racism that their readers, and every other African American, struggled with. But one thing was different. The best of the Negro League's ballplayers had a very direct and very specific goal: breaking through to play in the major leagues.

As a racial barrier to be overcome, baseball's color ban had immense symbolic value. By the late 1930s, as the Black press grew and expanded, and as voices like Smith's and Lacy's reached more and more readers in the Black community, the issue of segregation in Major League Baseball began to become more familiar and better understood. At the same time, as the Negro Leagues matured and produced talent that clearly could compete in the majors, there grew a keener sense of injustice. Through their writing, columnists like Smith and Lacy saw to that. Through their robust circulations, leading Black newspapers, like the *Pittsburgh Courier*, the *Defender*, and Baltimore's *Afro-American*, were effectively raising their readers' consciousness on the issue of breaking baseball's color barrier, as well as creating a new sense of urgency, and a greater sense of outrage. But deepening outrage in select cities would not be enough.

It was a huge issue, and a growing challenge to a bedrock, national, white institution.

As such, it would require the building of wide national unity among African Americans, which struck many as a daunting task in and of itself. Perhaps too daunting. After all, baseball's color ban was also a thing of bedrock, which had stood then for nearly half a century. Why would new efforts to topple it succeed now? Even many Negro League players themselves viewed the future with resignation.

"It will have to be a universal movement," said Jud Wilson of the Philadelphia Stars. "And that will never be."

But in its efforts to raise deeper awareness and wider support for desegregation, the Black press would find an unexpected ally. Nimble, resourceful, and highly mobile, it was above all an ally that had a vast reach into Black communities nationwide. It was, in fact, the perfect ally at the perfect time.

SEVEN

Porters, New Yorkers, and a Tireless Lefty

Freedom is never granted; it is won. Justice is never given; it is exacted.
—A. Philip Randolph

They worked on the railroad. They didn't lay the rails, drive the trains, or even conduct them. But they worked harder and for longer hours than anyone else. For the passenger public, they would become the familiar face that was synonymous with the golden age of train travel. And with no fanfare, and with no one looking, they helped break baseball's color barrier.

George Mortimer Pullman moved west like so many young men seeking their fortunes in the mid-19th century. He'd grown up in Albion, New York, where his dad, a carpenter, worked on the building of the Erie Canal. As a young engineer in his late 20s, Pullman was eager to help in the building and development of the city of Chicago. And he did, making a name and a success for himself. A savvy businessman as well as an engineer, Pullman was keenly aware of the rapid growth of train travel, and in 1862 in Illinois he established his company to manufacture sleeper cars for railroad trains. Pullman worked with existing railroad lines to carry his cars. They were luxurious for the time (and more expensive), with comfortable sleeping berths, carpeting, draperies, chandeliers, and gourmet food. But what really set the Pullmans apart was a whole new level of superior onboard service. Pullman imagined that the porters who would work his trains would attend to any and all of his passengers' whims as if the cars were rolling luxury hotels. They would offer friendly, impeccable service

Pullman porter checking the list of hours he is to wake people in the morning aboard the "Capitol Limited" bound for Chicago, Illinois, 1942

and attention, and otherwise blend in and be entirely unobtrusive. With emancipation and the end of the Civil War, Pullman settled on his perfect porter: freed, former house slaves who'd worked on southern plantations.

"The pioneering porter, in fact, was not expected to have human proportions at all . . . he was a phantom assistant who did not merit the dignity of a name or identity of any sort. That is precisely why George Pullman hired him," wrote Larry Tye, author of *Rising from the Rails: Pullman Porters and the Making of the Black Middle Class.* "He was an ex-slave who embodied servility more than humanity, an ever-obliging manservant with an ever-present smile who was there when a jacket needed dusting or a child needed tending to or a beverage refreshing. Few inquired where he came from or wanted to hear about his struggle. In his very anonymity lay his value."

Happy to have a salary and steady work, moving about the nation on a luxurious train, the new porters signed on enthusiastically. ("Lincoln freed the slaves," a popular saying went, "and George Pullman hired 'em.") Over the ensuing 50 years, despite the job's exhausting work and challenges, the Pullman porter established himself as an iconic fixture both in train travel and popular culture. He was depicted in movies, books, and train advertisements. But there was nothing glamorous about his work. While George Pullman paid them wages, he expected his porters to essentially fulfill the same role they had on the plantation: servant. As on the plantation, where slaves frequently were called by their master's name, the porters were routinely addressed simply as "George."* Despite their new status as salaried employee, it's not inaccurate to say the porters slaved away on Pullman's trains. With only a three- or four-hour sleep break, shifts sometimes ran 20 hours long, during which time porters might serve food, clean, carry baggage, make beds, and shine shoes. They had to pay for their own food and uniforms, and do unpaid prep work.

---

* In the wake of George Floyd's killing at the hands of a Minneapolis police officer in 2020, Mayor Melvin Carter, the mayor of neighboring St. Paul, had an observation that recalled his grandfather, who had been a Pullman porter. "I think a whole generation would have heard a certain echo in George Floyd's name," Carter told an interviewer. "Echoes of a whole class of black men who were also called, 'George,' whatever their real name happened to be."

Uniform cap for a Pullman porter, 1950s-1960s COLLECTION OF THE SMITHSONIAN
NATIONAL MUSEUM OF AFRICAN AMERICAN HISTORY AND CULTURE

And, as was often observed, they did all this on trains from which they themselves would otherwise have been barred from riding.

In 1925, spearheaded by labor rights leader A. Philip Randolph, the Pullman porters organized into the Brotherhood of Sleeping Car Porters (BSCP). The Pullman company fought back bitterly for over a decade, but ultimately was forced to accept Randolph's, and the porters', effective and successful organizing effort. The Pullman company signed a labor agreement with the BSCP, which became the first African-American union to negotiate a collective bargaining agreement, winning better terms and conditions, with a major American company.

To be sure, some elements of the Pullman porters' working conditions could not be cut out or bargained away. There was a built-in lack of dignity and overlay of raw racism that was never going to fully go away or even meaningfully dissipate. Today's flight attendants on a 40-minute commuter hop are accorded more respect (starting with using their actual names) than most porters were on a five-day cross-country train trip. But amid the hurt, the backbreaking work, the struggle, and the sacrifice, there were silver linings. As the Pullman porters established themselves more firmly in their jobs, the job itself became a building block in the Black community, where Pullman porters were viewed with respect and admiration, and credited with helping create an important portal through which thousands entered the Black middle class. The job, and the uniform, were often handed down between multiple generations. And even a partial list of former Pullman porters includes such famous and groundbreaking African Americans as US Supreme Court justice Thurgood Marshall, former San Francisco mayor Willie Brown, and photojournalist Gordon Parks. By the 1950s and 60s, many of the sons and daughters of Pullman porters would begin to go on to successful careers in fields their parents could only have dreamed of. People like Elaine Jones, who in 1993 became the first woman to head the NAACP Legal Defense Fund, and whose dad worked as a Pullman porter for 20 years. Tom Bradley, who became the first African-American mayor of Los Angeles in 1973, was the grandson of a slave, and the son of a Pullman porter.

Otis Gates III will never forget his first train trip when he was eight. His dad, wanting his three sons to have better educational opportunities, moved the family up from the South to work as a Pullman porter out of Boston.

"I remember the long train ride we took from Chattanooga, to Cincinnati, to New York, to Boston," Gates recalled. "In those days, 1943, if you got on the train, and you were Black, you got on the car which was closest to the steam engine, which was powered by coal, which meant that when the engine started up, you started coughing, 'cause of all the smoke and all the other crap that came back on you."

Gates, a tall man with a bald head, soft, warm eyes, and a quick laugh, has vivid memories of his dad, Otis Gates Jr., who was a Pullman porter for nearly 40 years.

"I remember seeing him leave for a trip, in uniform, with a small overnight bag, and I remember picking him up at South Station.* If he'd

---

* Before he became famous, another African American also had experience working out of Boston's South Station. In the early 1940s, Malcolm Little, later to become Malcolm X, worked the coach car between Boston and New York for the New York, New Haven & Hartford's "Yankee Clipper."

gone on a long trip, he might be gone for a week or longer, like out to Chicago or eventually out to California. He was tired after a trip, but dad looked strong, always. He used to bring home, on a good trip, a fair amount of tips. Pullman porters didn't make a lot of money, they made a small amount, and they depended on the largesse of people who would give them tips. He didn't talk much about the places he went; sometimes he'd talk about how some people were very nice to him. Once that led to a job for me before I went to college."

Otis Gates III, who grew up in Boston's Roxbury neighborhood, did well in school. He went to Boston Latin Academy, then Harvard. After graduation he spent three years in the Air Force, eventually returned to Harvard for an MBA, did consulting, and retired in 2016 after many successful years in real estate. He recalls, with a deep laugh, how it was that his dad came to understand how impressive it was that his son was accepted to Harvard.

"When I first told my dad I got into Harvard, my chest was all pumped out, and he just kind of said, 'Well, that's good.' He just wanted me to get into college, but he didn't know Harvard. Then a while later, he came back from a trip and he came in and he said to me, 'Wow, son, that is some school you got into there!' And I asked him why he said that, and he said he was on the road, and he was shining shoes, and all of these important guys are sitting up there, talking about their sons, and one guy says his son didn't get in to Princeton. And my dad looks up and says, 'My son got into Harvard.' And oh, Jesus, they were all over him about that. So he realized that was somehow something enormous."

But in addition to leaving a legacy for their children, either through a job itself or simply modeling an extraordinary work ethic, it was a nearly invisible effort by many Pullman porters that represented an equally enormous contribution to the cause of desegregating baseball, and advancing the cause of civil rights in general.

By the 1930s, enterprising Black newspaper editors like Robert Abbott of the *Chicago Defender* and Robert Vann of the Pittsburgh *Courier* were looking for any means possible to effectively but economically extend their papers' circulation and distribution.

The South was especially fertile ground for northern Black newspapers, which were seen as being more hard-hitting "race papers," more likely to lead in the battle for racial justice than smaller, local southern Black papers, which often felt less free in how far they could go in reporting and editorializing. In fact, the northern papers were prized like little else.

"'People would come for miles, running over themselves, to get a *Defender*,'" a local Black leader is quoted in *The African American Newspaper: Voice of Freedom*, by Patrick Washburn. "In New Orleans, a black woman said she would 'rather read it than to eat when Saturday comes, it is my heart's delight.'"

For his part, Robert Abbott was especially visionary; he had sensed early on that passenger trains traversing the nation, and all across the South, had a built-in, on-board ally, if he could only forge the relationship.

"The Pullman porter was the perfect emissary for the *Chicago Defender*," wrote Washburn. "He worked in a world of luxury and elegance that gave him a special cachet among many members of the black population. . . some of the better educated and wealthier blacks may have disdained the porter, but to many of America's blacks, the Pullman porter was a man of means and respect."

Indeed, to many Blacks, especially in the South, the Pullman porter was seen as a genuine pioneer, breaking new ground with every mile of track they traveled.

"Robert Abbott knew that for his message to reach a southern audience, he needed the right messengers," wrote Larry Tye. "He found them in Pullman porters. They were emblems of the 'New Negro' Abbott was trumpeting, so who better to deliver his papers across the South?"

Aware of this, and ever enterprising, Abbott reached out to the Pullman porters. He encouraged them—and paid them—to share their stories and file dispatches from the road. The *Defender* published their gossip in a column called "Sparks from the Rail," as well as covering their unionizing efforts in the paper's news section. "They were enlisted as news gatherers and converts to the cause," wrote Tye.

But while Abbott was happy to share the porters' stories from the road, he also wanted them to share the *Defender* on their travels, and help extend its readership to places where he simply could not distribute the paper on his own. And they obliged.

"Porters gathered bundles of *Defenders* before each trip, stored them in their lockers, then left them with contacts along the route," writes Tye. "From there they made their way to barbershops, churches, and individual subscribers in cities and hamlets across the South."

Not everyone shared Robert Abbott's delight in upping the *Defender*'s distribution.

For one thing, a porter surreptitiously taking on and then off-loading an unauthorized bundle of newspapers would have been fired on the spot. In the towns throughout much of the South that the trains ran through, the paper was vilified by white business interests and political powers. Seen as a "race paper" that had already exhorted waves of Blacks to migrate from the South and likely to further inflame those who remained, the *Defender* was routinely confiscated, trashed, burned, and otherwise made to seem as if it was officially banned, even though that was technically illegal. But then, so was lynching.

But the porters found their ways, and the papers kept coming. By 1920, two-thirds of the *Defender*'s paid circulation was outside of Chicago. "They hid them on the trains, and as they rolled south, they would step between cars and throw the papers off at prearranged sites outside city limits, where distributors would pick them up and hand them out," wrote Washburn. "Thus, it was impossible to stop the *Defender*, which made southerners even angrier."

This ingenious and invisible distribution system wasn't limited to the *Chicago Defender*.

In Boston, New York, Philadelphia, and Pittsburgh, local Black newspapers, often hidden in bread baskets or mail sacks, were loaded onto trains by porters. In Baltimore, for example, the *Courier* or the *Amsterdam News* might be offloaded and the *Afro-American* would be swapped on, to in turn be dropped off in Washington or Memphis. And so on and on, deeper into the South. Heading west, reaching out into rural areas and farmland, the newspapers found their way ever farther via the rails. In this way, in smaller and smaller communities far from these papers' urban sources, Black readers became familiar with Wendell Smith, Sam Lacy,

Joe Bostic, and Nell Dodson Russell. Through them, the consciousness of countless African Americans was raised further. They developed a deeper sense of the injustice Negro Leaguers were facing, and gained a greater awareness of the struggle to desegregate Major League Baseball. As Ida B. Wells had said, "the people must know before they can act, and there is no educator to compare with the press." Extending a nearly invisible hand of hugely important help, even as they went about their busy jobs, the Pullman porters became an incomparable ally in the effort to educate.

IF THE PULLMAN PORTER REPRESENTED AN UNLIKELY AND UNSUNG hero in the long battle to break baseball's color barrier, they weren't the only unlikely ones. As the decade of the 1930s drew to a close, some others with unique roles in the struggle came more prominently into view. From Kansas City and the Midwest, and increasingly to New York City, what makes these particular people partly so notable is that not only did they each play significant roles in furthering racial justice and integrating baseball, but, unlike almost all of the key players in that story, they were not Black men.

Nell Dodson never complained much about being behind in the count as she covered baseball games. After all, as a Black woman, she had two strikes against her in a white man's world. She went to an almost entirely white university, but wasn't allowed to live in a dorm. She worked for a Black newspaper, but never earned the fame or byline (or salary) of her male colleagues.

What Nell Dodson did have was the confidence, determination, and guts instilled in her by her father, Walter, who raised her as a single dad after his wife died when Nell was a young girl in Minneapolis. And she was a fearless reporter. While at the University of Minnesota (as a Black student, she was forced to live at home), she began her career as a journalist. She filed stories on campus life as a Black student for the *Spokesman*, a Black newspaper in Minneapolis. In 1935, she began writing a sports column for the paper, which would mark the first of many times her career path was lined with whining males.

"It was okay for a young lady to write about campus dances or visitors from out of town, but writing about sports was not especially welcomed," wrote Donna L. Halper, a media historian, and author of *Invisible Stars: A Social History of Women in American Broadcasting*. "Some men complained to the editor, asking why the newspaper couldn't find a man to write about college sports. The editor, Cecil 'C.E.' Newman, was undeterred. He believed Dodson had potential as a writer; plus, he liked her willingness to learn."

One suspects Newman also liked his new reporter's *un*willingness to be intimidated.

"Since C.E. Newman has been in the newspaper business, he has had a procession of men sports writers parading through his office. Some of 'em have been good, some have been just so-so," wrote Dodson in one of her first sports columns in 1935. "If C.E. could have found just ONE man who would have taken his work seriously, and turned it out regularly, THEN he would have kept that one man on the job. As it is, Auntie Personalities is gonna keep on doing her sports stuff until some male comes along who can turn out what is wanted, when it is wanted, and in the manner wanted. And THAT'S THAT."

Any questions?

"Her only problem," Halper wrote in a 2017 article for Dodson's former paper (now the *Minnesota Spokesman-Recorder*), "was being denied access to locker rooms (an issue that would continue to frustrate female sports reporters well into the 1980s). Otherwise, her thorough coverage of college sports earned the respect of the readers and the players."

In fact, it earned Dodson, still a college undergraduate, a remarkable job offer. In 1938, Baltimore's *Afro-American* hired her as a reporter and columnist. Although it meant leaving school, her dad, and her mentor, Cecil Newman, she moved east to accept the new job. Like her new colleague at her new paper, Sam Lacy, she became adept at not only covering the details of a Negro League game, but also at weaving in her own commentary on the racism, injustices, and the endless, hurtful day-to-day indignities that dogged Black baseball like a pebble in a cleat. Her column, "Lady in the Pressbox," may have been named, in its time, to suggest a "fairer" take on things, but Dodson didn't defer to anyone's expectations, and didn't flinch at writing on what she saw and what she thought, and to hell with having to run into that person at the park tomorrow. She called out Negro League owners who were happy to bank their money, meet their payroll, but stiff their teams of the investment that was sorely needed. She also documented the dramatic pay disparity between Black and white professional athletes, as well as the same woeful disparity between the conditions and facilities in which white and Black athletes trained. She was promoted to sports editor, which was extraordinary for its time, making her one of the very first (if not first) African-American woman sports editor in America. She also reported on entertainment, which led to her next job offer, from the *Amsterdam News*. Further and further from the mostly white, upper Midwest of her youth, Nell Dodson was now a mature and accomplished Black journalist, taking on a new assignment in New York City. As the 1940s began, the forces that would finally move baseball out of its racist past were already there.

ALWAYS A HUMMING AND VIBRANT CITY OF THE WORLD, NEW YORK IN the late 1930s and the start of the new decade was even more so. Then approaching a population of eight million, it represented the most diverse urban center in America. One borough alone—Brooklyn—was home to nearly three million people, and a single one of its neighborhoods (Williamsburg) was larger than the city of Fort Worth (180,000). The 1930s had seen the world's two highest buildings (Empire State, Chrysler) rise out of Midtown Manhattan. Franklin Delano Roosevelt had preceded his first term as president (1933) with one term as governor of New York (1928–1932). During the Depression, FDR's federal reconstruction programs, such as the Works Progress Administration and the Civilian Conservation Corps, found some of their most ambitious and shovel-ready projects in New York City, where colorful Mayor Fiorello La Guardia and his "master builder," Robert Moses, were poised to think big and reimagine the nation's largest metropolis. In 1939, with the Depression's grip loosening and New York coming alive with building and development, the city hosted the World's Fair. But it wasn't just the blur of steel girders being guided into place above, or the chug of steam shovels clawing out yet another block-wide foundation below. From the arts, to sports, to politics, New York was also beginning to reimagine more than just buildings and bridges, but the quality of urban living, also.

In 1939, one of Broadway's hits was *Awake and Sing!* by Clifford Odets. It was not a musical. A searing indictment of the human cost of unbridled capitalism in the wake of the Depression, it followed Odets's first hit, *Waiting For Lefty*, a one-act play about the 1934 New York Taxi Strike. The fact that overtly political theater could succeed commercially may have been something of a surprise; that it was the type of drama that fueled Odets's passion as a playwright was no surprise at all. The dramatist was also a Communist. For that matter, so was one of the city's best sportswriters.

For many good reasons (the names, Stalin, Pol Pot, and Kim Jong-un come to mind), the notion of communism has always been about as appealing in America as typhus. (Of course, McCarthyism sickened a lot of good people too.) So it's easy to forget that there have been times in American history when capitalism has been called more into question. The Great Depression was the most significant of those moments. But then, complete economic collapse, 25 percent unemployment, massive homelessness, widespread hopelessness, a Dust Bowl, bread lines, soup kitchens, and a shanty town in Central Park will make a person question a lot of things. In the wake of the economic wipeout in 1929, when previously hardworking Americans washed away like so much flotsam from a flood, people were desperate for an alternative. The American Communist Party offered one. Mind you, post-crash in the early 30s, FDR's bold programs hadn't yet found full traction. Communism as the governing principle of a major nation was then only a decade or so old. For many American progressives, it was an ideology that still had its showroom sheen and that new car smell. Why not take it for a spin? With the American economy ass-up and in the ditch, simple standard features like a decent job and a place to live sure looked good. Membership swelled during the Depression, and while the American Communist Party never wielded significant electoral influence, it did have a real effect on progressive causes like the labor movement and the struggle for civil rights. For a time, those values and causes themselves attracted to the Communist Party USA well-known Americans like Howard Fast, Bayard Rustin,[*]

---

[*] A major figure of the American civil rights movement and one of the organizers of the landmark 1963 ("I have a dream") March on Washington, Rustin grew up in Harlem where, his biographer John D'Emilio wrote, "he saw that whenever blacks got into trouble, it was invariably the Communists who were willing to defend them."

Tillie Olsen, Woody Guthrie, Pete Seeger, and Clifford Odets. And not least, though less well known, Lester Rodney.

In some ways it's hard to imagine a more unlikely hero in the battle to integrate Major League Baseball than Lester Rodney. He was white, Jewish, and a Communist. Nobody's perfect.

Born in Manhattan in 1911, Rodney's upbringing conjures the quintessentially sad—and sadly common—"before and after" of life in Depression-era New York. His father, Max Rodney (a staunch Republican), had worked his way up from salesman to part ownership in a Paterson, New Jersey, silk factory. Eventually the family moved to a large house in Brooklyn's Bensonhurst neighborhood. Life was good.

Of his father, Lester Rodney would later recall in an interview, "He wanted me to be a member of the Young Republican Club and he even once arranged a date for me with the daughter of the club president."

Sports-obsessed from boyhood, Lester Rodney attended New Utrecht High School, where he ran track, played basketball, and covered sports for the school's newspaper. Then life changed. With the stock market crash of 1929, Max Rodney lost his job, his house, and as his son recalls, "became an old man overnight." Lester Rodney received a partial track scholarship to Syracuse University, but had to turn it down, as he couldn't afford the balance of the tuition. Instead, Rodney worked a variety of jobs, from chauffeuring to lifeguarding, to help support his family. He also took night school classes at NYU, where he came across a copy of the Communist Party's newspaper, the *Daily Worker*. Naturally, he checked out its so-called sports section, "so-called" because the paper's editors made no secret of their distaste for sports, which they considered another "opiate of the masses." Rodney scoffed; what a waste, he thought. He wrote a letter to the *Worker*'s editor, pointing out that, by dismissing the passionate relationship with sports in a place like New York, the paper was also missing out on an easy and significant way to connect with many working people. Not even Karl Marx could rebut that. The Communist *Daily Worker* offered non-Communist Lester Rodney a job, to take charge of their sports page, to cover teams, write about them as he saw fit, and to surprise people that the least likely newspaper in New York suddenly had something significant to say about sports. And that's exactly what Lester Rodney did. And then some.

"I felt that if we were to succeed I had to establish our credentials as an American sports section, not as a paper whose only interest in sports was to grind an ideological axe on this one issue," Rodney told Irwin Silber, author of *Press Box Red: The Story of Lester Rodney, the Communist Who Helped Break the Color Line in American Sports*. "Right from the start, we began doing things that none of the other papers were doing. When the Negro Leagues played in New York, we'd cover them and highlight players we thought were good enough for the Big Leagues. You could call that part of a campaign to familiarize our readers with black players and to break down the silence . . . the other papers, like the *Times* and the *Post*, might have briefly reported on a Negro League game, but if Satchel Paige pitched a shutout or even if Josh Gibson hit the longest homerun ever at Yankee Stadium, they'd never say 'Why isn't this guy playing for a major-league team?'"

But Rodney said it. And he asked that question repeatedly. Relentlessly. He asked it rhetorically at first, in column after column. Later, he asked it bitingly and incisively. He brandished that question like a weapon, openly calling out powerful men who were not used to being so publicly pressured and excoriated. And he was the first to admit that, although he'd been a baseball fan since he was six, it was only after he was a reporter, and exposed to the Negro Leagues, that his own eyes were opened to just how shameful the color ban was, and how equally shameful it was that in his own profession, there was a "huge void that no one is talking about," he told an interviewer years later. "This is America, land of the free, and people with the wrong pigmentation of skin can't play baseball?"

He was a dogged reporter, who covered sports well, and impressed his big-paper peers by his hard work and his keen baseball knowledge. His political views deepened, too, as did his commitment to the *Daily Worker*.

"No other paper said anything about the fact that black players were locked out of Major League Baseball," he told an interviewer years after the barrier fell. "That was the culture of the times. Racism was accepted. And that was one of the things that attracted me to the Communists. What the Communists were doing down in the South were working for black voting rights, putting their bodies where their mouths were."

Lester Rodney in retirement, California, ca. 2000
PHOTOGRAPH BY BYRON LAGOY, WIKIMEDIA COMMONS

Rodney's commitment deepened, too. Both to covering the sport he loved, and to the paper he covered it for. In time, he was carrying two cards that had never, ever been paired on the same person before: an official Communist Party member card, and another as a member of the Baseball Writers' Association.

"I never thought of myself as a 'Communist sportswriter,'" Rodney told Silber. "I was a sportswriter who happened to be writing for a Communist newspaper. By the time *The Daily Worker* was something the players might react to negatively, they knew me as a sportswriter and a person."*

Indeed, part of what often made Rodney's reporting so significant and often newsworthy was his friendly relationship with many players and managers. With very few exceptions, only Black sportswriters were asking tough questions about segregation. Lester Rodney almost single-handedly changed that. It wasn't easy. To many, he was about as welcome as a mosquito. And as persistent.

"Rodney began buttonholing managers, asking them about the color line," wrote Silber.

"The first manager he tackled was Burleigh Grimes of the Brooklyn Dodgers."

His chat with Grimes, a former major-league pitcher, took place as the two men stood in the outfield of Ebbets Field prior to a game in 1937. Their exchange, related later by Rodney, provides insight into how challenging it still was at that time to draw out white major-league personnel on the issue of segregation in baseball—not to mention the added challenge of getting them to comment publicly.

"We started talking about the game and who was going to pitch that day. Baseball chatter . . . and he says, 'Frankly, I could use another pitcher and just one good hitter.' So I say—and I remember these were my exact words—'Burleigh, how would you like to put a Dodger uniform on Satchel Paige and Josh Gibson?' Well, he looks at me like I'd just hit him over the head with a club. You just didn't talk about those things then."

But Rodney persisted. Grimes, who seemed to like the reporter well enough personally, expressed his sincere belief that the ingrained racism, especially in the South, would make it impossible to truly integrate the major leagues. He did, however, also sincerely acknowledge that he knew just how good some of the Black ballplayers were. Rodney pounced.

"'Burleigh,' I say. 'Can I at least write, "I know how good they are"—Burleigh Grimes?' I'm not saying you'll—"

---

* One of Rodney's favorite memories of baseball people reacting to his unusual twin roles—Communist and sportswriter—involved legendary manager, Leo "the Lip" Durocher. "I was chatting with Leo before a game," he recalled, "and he suddenly turns to me and says, 'You know, Rodney—for a #@%!# Communist, you sure know your baseball!'"

Grimes, Rodney recalled, became "livid."

"No, no! . . . I'm not gonna stick my neck out!"

While Rodney failed to coax out more neck from the Dodgers' meek manager that day, he did begin to have success with others. In fact, it was another, better-known manager who made sports headlines with Rodney's prodding. In 1939, Leo Durocher had become player-manager of the Brooklyn Dodgers.

"I put the same question to Leo that I had put to Burleigh Grimes two years earlier," Rodney recounted in *Press Box Red*. "But Leo was different than Burleigh . . . scrappy, more confident. And sophisticated. He felt this thing coming, I'm sure. And what he said was, 'Hell, yes! I'd sign them in a minute if I got the permission from the big shots.'"

So Rodney went after the big shots, too. Over the decades since Blacks had been barred, Major League Baseball owners, team executives, and league officials had consistently pleaded—with a straight face that borders on grotesque for its glaring dishonesty—that, in fact, there was no official ruling of any kind that barred Blacks. There was a technical truth to that lie. Because, of course, a "gentleman's agreement" is bound with a private wink and a nod, not a public announcement and a written decree. Urbane, well-dressed, well-mannered, and well-educated big-league owners like Boston's Tom Yawkey preferred their particular brand of benign racism as they preferred their Kentucky bourbon—smooth, well-aged, well-blended. More subtle, but no less racist.* But some owners had more of a sense of the arc that was beginning to bend, and a bit more of a backbone to say so. Even if they still did nothing to assist in the bending.

"In 1939, I thought the great fight was being won," Rodney recounted to Silber. "That was the year I got my first favorable comment from an owner, when William Benswanger of the Pittsburgh Pirates wrote back to my usual question about the color line saying, 'I don't see why it wouldn't be the same as having black musicians.' Coming from an owner, that was a breakthrough statement."

———

* Yawkey, in fact, was also asked by the *Daily Worker* about hiring Black players. He responded that he had "never given any thought to the matter." Which, in the 1930s, may have been partly true. By the 1940s, it wasn't.

Rodney frequently spoke with, and interviewed Black ballplayers, also. He covered Negro League games regularly, which stoked his primary source of outrage, seeing extraordinary players like Paige and Gibson, who would star on any major-league team, forced to toil in relative obscurity. Still, for the time, it was highly unusual for a white paper, and its white reporter, to give coverage to Negro League games and players. In 1937, Rodney interviewed Satchel Paige, who was in New York with the visiting Kansas City Monarchs. Paige had many ideas he wanted to share about integrating baseball, like polling every big-league fan if they want to see Black players in the major leagues; or having the World Series winner play one game with an All-Star Negro League team at Yankee Stadium. "He wanted this in the papers," recalled Rodney, "but he hadn't gotten anywhere because the papers weren't paying any attention to him. He was an embarrassment to them. Like a bad conscience."

Rodney and the *Daily Worker* paid attention.

"I never met a black player who told me he wanted to stay in the Negro Leagues," Rodney said in an interview years later. "That's ridiculous. If you feel you're the best violinist in the country and you live in Paducah, you don't want to stay in Paducah. Of course, you want to play at Carnegie Hall, for the money and the acclaim."

For its part, the *Daily Worker* realized that part of its social and political goals of ending discrimination and segregation in America were perfectly complimented by its first-ever sports editor, and his own genuine passion about ending baseball's color barrier. The sports section itself grew from a single page to several. The paper adopted Rodney's position as its own official campaign: "Jim Crow Must Go." Young Communist League members would hand out leaflets at ballparks featuring Rodney's columns. At parades and marches in New York and other cities, placards began to appear—held by both Communist Party members and various trade unionists—reading, "End Jim Crow in Baseball," and "Admit Negroes to Big League Baseball." Through Rodney, the *Daily Worker* also forged cooperative efforts with Black newspapers like the *Pittsburgh Courier*, and Black columnists like Wendell Smith who, through the late 1930s, had also been aggressively interviewing major-league sources as part of the *Courier*'s own campaign to focus public attention on segregation in baseball. The two papers began an informal, reciprocal agreement allowing each to reprint the other's stories. The *Daily Worker* enthusiastically reprinted and trumpeted Smith's columns. In 1939, drawing increased attention to baseball's color barrier, Wendell Smith wrote, "In the past five years, this form of sporting segregation has been revealed to the public by the press of the nation." He went on to applaud the courage of half a dozen white sportswriters "who have seen fit to champion the cause of the Negro player." He did not mention Lester Rodney.

In *Press Box Red*, Silber suggested that "Smith's omission may have been given some encouragement by the baseball establishment itself, which clearly was unhappy at the fact that the Communist *Daily Worker* had gained prominence as the foremost crusader on the issue."

"The participation of the Communist party in the integration campaign often allowed baseball officials to downplay the protests," wrote Jules Tygiel in *Baseball's Great Experiment*. "Larry MacPhail, the Yankees president, and the *Sporting News* both charged that 'agitators' motivated by selfish interest produced the clamor for integration."

MacPhail, who distinguished himself as a bitter (and often inebriated) racist to the end, called Rodney and others who advocated desegregating baseball, "political and social-minded drumbeaters." MacPhail could flail and hurl stupid taunts, but the drumbeaters were having an impact. That's the funny thing about a well-beaten drum; it makes noise.

"The success of the Communists in forcing the issue before the American public far outweighed the negative ramifications of their sponsorship," wrote Tygiel. "The crusade waged by the Communists, the black press, and a small coterie of white sportswriters helped to alleviate the apathy that nourished baseball segregation."

It was the defining paradox of Lester Rodney's life: The man who did more to attack baseball's color barrier than any other white sportswriter had guts and passion that were unassailable—as well as political beliefs that were considered, to many, un-American. Ironically, that's exactly the word that Rodney used to describe the color ban.

In the midst of the usual (and visceral) negative reaction to the role of the American Communist Party in anything, from sports to civil rights, it was easy to miss an additional irony that occurred in 1939. It spoke to the

Daily Worker's genuine growth as a savvy sports observer. It was a column that was reprinted from the *People's World*, the West Coast's Communist newspaper. In it, writer Dave Farrell raved about a standout student athlete at Pasadena Junior College: "Of the many fine Negro ball players I've seen in recent years, Jackie Robinson strikes me as having the best chance to cut the buck in organized ball." Thus, in its October 4, 1939, edition, the Communist *Daily Worker* likely became the first American newspaper to call attention to Jackie Robinson as a future major leaguer.

But as 1939 turned to 1940, no sports page scoop from any source or any paper could eclipse the larger news coming from abroad. In September 1939, Hitler's German forces had invaded Poland. Before the year was out, both France and Great Britain were also at war. While it would take another full year before the United States entered the war, neither Lester Rodney nor Wendell Smith, nor anyone else could have known that the same conflagration that would reorder the entire world would, ultimately, influence the reordering of Major League Baseball—and civil rights—as well. For more than 50 years, African Americans had held tight to the goal of breaking baseball's color barrier. Now, they would die for it, too.

EIGHT

Free Enough to Die

We were told there was no segregation here in England—it isn't from the people, they are fine, only from our officers . . .
—CABLE FROM AN AFRICAN-AMERICAN SOLDIER
TO FIRST LADY ELEANOR ROOSEVELT

AS THE YEAR WAS COMING TO A CLOSE IN DECEMBER 1941, EVEN THOUGH the nation was still officially at peace, the US military was beginning to prepare to inevitably join a war that was already raging in Europe and the Pacific. Those preparations did not include any plans to widen the pool of potential recruits. In 1941, the United States counted just under eight million military personnel. Of that number, fewer than 4,000 were African American. (Of that, only a dozen were officers.) From Portsmouth, New Hampshire, to Pearl Harbor, Hawaii, there was a sense of change underfoot, even if it only seemed to apply to combat readiness. There was no change at all underfoot with what applied to Black military personnel. In the Navy, that meant automatically being assigned as a messman, where ship duties included cooking, cleaning, making beds, shining the shoes of white officers, and waiting on them in the officers' mess. ("Seagoing bellhop," is how a messman of the period described his job.) Being an excellent messman offered no incentive; they were ineligible for promotion, and were barred from receiving training in virtually any other specialty (signals, engineering, gunnery). No symbol of their lowly status was apparently too small for the Navy to ignore: The regulation buttons on their mess uniforms were plain, stripped of even the tiny Navy insignia (anchor and chain) that adorned every naval uniform but theirs.

Doris "Dorie" Miller was a messman. Born in 1919 in Waco, Texas, he was no stranger to one of the worst periods of vicious, lethal southern racism; three years before Miller was born, 17-year-old Jesse Washington was lynched and burned alive in front of Waco's city hall. Miller's family struggled during the Depression. In 1939, when Miller wasn't able to find a job, he joined the US Navy to help support his family. He was 19. Two years later, Mess Attendant 2nd Class Miller was serving on the battleship *West Virginia*, based with the Pacific Fleet in Pearl Harbor. On the morning of December 7, 1941, he was below decks on laundry duty. The first wave of Japanese bombs and torpedoes devastated the *West Virginia*; massive explosions rocked the huge ship, which began listing in the water where she was berthed. Miller ran to his battle station, the ship's magazine, where he would be tasked with passing ammo up to the deck. But the magazine was already flooded, so Miller, the ship's heavyweight boxing champ, was sent to the signal deck and ordered to carry the mortally wounded body of the *West Virginia*'s commanding officer to a safer location. Miller was then ordered to help an officer, by feeding an ammo belt for one of a pair of the ship's still-operational antiaircraft machine guns. Noticing that the other gun was unmanned, Miller began operating the gun by himself. He had zero training—and zero authority—to fire the .50-caliber deck gun. But he did. Amid explosions, fire, acrid smoke, sloshing, slippery oil, and low-flying, strafing Japanese fighter planes, Miller aimed his gun and fired relentlessly.

The white officer who was manning the other gun later described Miller as "blazing away as though he had fired one all his life."

Miller only stopped firing when the gun's ammo ran out and the ship began to sink. He then helped pull sailors from the water, saving several lives, and with the final order to abandon ship, was one of the last three crewmembers to leave the *West Virginia*. A hero, he'd been doing someone else's laundry just a couple of hours earlier.

Weeks later, the Navy released several official accounts of heroism as Pearl Harbor was under attack. These reports referred to an unnamed, "unknown" Black sailor who had acted heroically. Eventually, in March

Adm. Chester W. Nimitz, USN, Commander-in-Chief, Pacific Fleet, pins the Navy Cross on Doris Miller, Steward's Mate 1/c, USN, at a ceremony on board a US Navy warship in Pearl Harbor, May 27, 1942. LIBRARY OF CONGRESS

1942, the *Pittsburgh Courier* was able to identify the unnamed sailor as Dorie Miller. Several bills were quickly introduced in Congress to award Miller with the Medal of Honor. Although 16 other sailors (all white officers or petty officers) received the award for their heroism at Pearl Harbor, Miller's commendation was blocked by Navy Secretary William Franklin Knox, as well as a group of southern legislators. The story generated significant press attention, but only a week after the attack, Miller had already put out to sea again. Reassigned to the heavy cruiser *Indianapolis*, the sailor who had fought back and saved lives at Pearl Harbor was a messman again, his lowly battle station once more below deck.

"Mother, don't worry about me and tell all my friends not to shed any tears for me," Miller wrote home from the South Pacific, "for when the dark clouds pass over, I'll be back on the sunny side."

But Miller's actions at Pearl were so genuinely impressive, they would not be overlooked. Pressure from Black newspapers, the NAACP, and others built on President Roosevelt, urging him and the Navy to honor Miller. In May 1941, Roosevelt approved the Navy to award Miller the Navy Cross, given for gallantry during combat, making Miller the first Black sailor to receive it. In a photo that is as striking as it is stirring, legendary admiral Chester W. Nimitz reads the commendation, as Miller stands on the flight deck of the carrier *Enterprise*, a line of white officers looking on. At the same time, the Navy announced that Black recruits who volunteered for service would now receive other specialized training previously denied them. The training was segregated, but so was the rest of America's armed forces in 1941. In addition, pressure mounted to have Miller brought home to go on a war bond tour, just as the other white sailor heroes had done. (Both Wendell Willkie, the 1940 Republican presidential nominee, and New York mayor Fiorello La Guardia urged the Navy to allow Miller to return home.) And he did. Almost a year after the attack, on November 23, 1942, Miller arrived back in Pearl Harbor, and from there was sent to speak across the United States, including his hometown of Waco. He also addressed the first class of Black sailors to graduate from the Navy's new Black recruit program at Camp Robert Smalls on Lake Michigan. Alas, returning back to the Pacific Theater, Miller's next assignment would be his last. On the escort carrier *Liscombe Bay*, he had been promoted to cook, third class. On November 23, 1943, the ship was hit by a Japanese torpedo. A massive explosion sank the ship in less than 30 minutes, resulting in a stunning loss of life: Less than a third of the *Liscombe Bay*'s 900 sailors survived. A year later, his body never having been recovered, Dorie Miller was officially listed as killed in action. His short life was both tragic and inspirational. His heroism—and the unusually public and official recognition of it—seemed to augur at least the possibility of something new for African Americans at the very dawn of World War II.

Dorie Miller was not the first African American to die in combat for his country. In fact, African Americans died with some of the very first shots of the nation's founding. Arguably, the very first casualty of the American Revolution was Crispus Attucks, a dockworker of African and Native American descent, shot and killed by British soldiers in the Boston Massacre on March 5, 1770. Prince Estabrook, a freed slave from Lexington, Massachusetts, enlisted in that town's militia in 1773, and was wounded on Lexington Green, in the American Revolution's first armed battle, on April 19, 1775. Mere blocks from the massacre site on Boston's busy State Street, stands a larger, even more impressive testament to the bravery of Black soldiers. Walking northwest, the streets incline slightly, weaving and wending their narrow way up Beacon Hill. At the top, opposite the State House (built in 1798) on the edge of Beacon Street and the Common, is the famous Robert Gould Shaw Memorial, a huge bronze relief sculpture (by Augustus Saint-Gaudens) depicting the 54th Regiment Massachusetts Infantry, as it departed Boston on its way south to fight in the Civil War.* The soldiers of the 54th were among the first African Americans to train and fight in the Civil War, and the monument was the first in America to honor the heroism of African-American soldiers.

Following the Civil War, Congress established the first regular, all-Black US Army regiments. Formed in 1866 at Fort Leavenworth, Kansas, the "Buffalo Soldiers" of the original 10th Cavalry Regiment went on to become the source of both legend and dozens of descending future Black army regiments that would serve both at home and abroad. Segregated Black units served with distinction in Europe during World War I, none more so than the 369th Infantry Regiment, which had formed originally

---

* The "fabled 54th" was led by Shaw, a young white colonel, and son of passionate New England abolitionists. On July 18, 1863, in the attack on Fort Wagner in South Carolina, Shaw and more than 75 of his men were killed. The battle was depicted in the film *Glory*.

as a New York National Guard regiment. Nicknamed the "Harlem Hellfighters," it was one of the first Black regiments to serve with the American Expeditionary Forces, and spent 191 days in frontline trenches, more than any other US unit. It was also one of the most decorated US units, and was awarded the Croix de Guerre for gallantry in action by the French government. On its return to America, the 369th was the first unit to march up Manhattan's Fifth Avenue.

But in World War I, as in World War II, many African Americans had deeply mixed feelings about serving a country that largely regarded them as second-class citizens. On the one hand, W. E. B. Du Bois certainly wasn't wrong when he observed, "That which the German power represents today spells death for the aspirations of Negroes and all darker races."

In an editorial in 1918, he further exhorted blacks to "forget our special grievances and close our ranks shoulder to shoulder with our own white citizens and the allied nations that are fighting for democracy." On the other hand, journalist A. Philip Randolph (who would go on to found the Brotherhood of Sleeping Car Porters) spoke for many African Americans when he pointed out the cruel irony of being asked to help make Europe "safe for democracy" when the world's largest democracy was distinctly unsafe (or worse) for Black people. "No intelligent Negro," Randolph wrote in 1917, "is willing to lay down his life for the United States as it now exists."

Yet they did. Nearly half a million African Americans served in World War I. Although most were officially confined to support roles (laborers, stevedores, cooks, etc.), about 50,000 black soldiers saw combat in segregated units. About 770 were killed. It was not long before many Blacks questioned whether the sacrifice had been worth it.

"Within four months of the 369th Regiment's triumphal Fifth Avenue parade, there were race wars in the streets of America," wrote Gail Buckley, author of *American Patriots: The Story of Blacks in the Military from the Revolution to Desert Storm*. "The summer of 1919 was known among blacks as Red Summer—'Red' for blood. Seventy-eight blacks were lynched in 1919: ten were veterans, several of whom were lynched in uniform."

A quarter of a century later, with the advent of World War II, the same mix of emotions still existed for most African Americans when it came to volunteering for military service. After all, essentially the same America still existed. Just the same, in the wave of military enlistments following Pearl Harbor, one out of every seven volunteers was Black; ultimately more than 1.2 million African Americans would serve in the Second World War. But it wasn't always easy to square patriotism with racism.

"Negroes did not need us at the NAACP to tell them that it sounded pretty foolish to be against park benches marked 'Jude' in Berlin, but to be *for* park benches marked 'Colored' in Tallahassee, Florida," wrote civil rights activist Roy Wilkins, in his autobiography, *Standing Fast*. "Negroes were not being sent to any concentration camps, of course, but what a thing to be thankful for."

At the start of America's entry into World War II, the fact that one of the very first heroes in the very first hours of armed conflict was a Black man did, indeed, seem like something for African Americans to

"Colored" water cooler, streetcar terminal, Oklahoma City, Oklahoma (1939)
LIBRARY OF CONGRESS

be thankful for. Of course, had Dorie Miller not taken the initiative to man a gun he was not officially allowed to touch, we wouldn't know his name. In 1941, America's armed forces were still rigidly segregated, and opportunities and advancement were nearly as narrow as they had been in 1917. For Blacks in general, a half-century after Separate but Equal, the doctrine's daily, grinding, state-sanctioned racism still clung tenaciously like an invisible manacle. It felt as if there were two battles going on— the new war that needed to be waged against fascism abroad, and the continuing battle against racism at home. Only two months after Pearl Harbor, another unlikely Black hero gave voice to this feeling. He was a civilian, and he brandished only a pen.

"LIKE ALL TRUE AMERICANS, MY GREATEST DESIRE AT THIS TIME . . . IS for a complete victory over the forces of evil which threaten our existence today. Behind that desire is also a desire to serve this, my country, in the most advantageous way."

So began what some have called the most famous letter to the editor ever published by a Black newspaper. It ran on January 31, 1942, in the *Pittsburgh Courier*. It was written by a Black cafeteria worker named James G. Thompson, who was 26, and employed at the Cessna Aircraft Corporation in Wichita, Kansas.

"Should I sacrifice my life to live half American?" Thompson wrote. "Will things be better for the next generation in the peace to follow? Would it be demanding too much to demand full citizenship rights in exchange for the sacrificing of my life? . . . I suggest that while we keep defense and victory in the forefront that we don't lose sight of our fight for true democracy at home. The V for victory sign is being displayed prominently in all so-called democratic countries which are fighting for victory over aggression, slavery and tyranny. If this V sign means that to those now engaged in this great conflict, then let we colored Americans adopt the double VV for a double victory. The first V for victory over our enemies from without, the second V for victory over our enemies from within. For surely those who perpetuate these ugly prejudices here are seeking to destroy our democratic form of government just as surely as the Axis forces."

Handkerchief, "Double-V" Campaign, World War II COLLECTION OF THE SMITHSONIAN
NATIONAL MUSEUM OF AFRICAN AMERICAN HISTORY AND CULTURE

The reaction to the letter was swift and far-reaching. It captured something widely and deeply felt in the Black community.

"Thompson's letter," wrote Patrick S. Washburn (author of *The African American Newspaper: Voice of Freedom*), "had a huge impact. It resulted in the *Courier* immediately launching a high-profile Double V campaign, which ranked historically in importance with Ida B. Wells's vigorous anti-lynching crusade and Robert Abbott's extraordinary call for blacks to leave the South."

The "Double V campaign," regardless of its importance, had its work cut out for it. In the military alone, African Americans like James G. Thompson and thousands of others were met more with double walls of resistance. The same deep, ingrained racism that barred Blacks from baseball, buses, trains, schools, and jobs blocked them from armed service too.

"For black recruits entering the armed forces in 1942, the first enemy was probably Jim Crow," wrote Arnold Rampersad, author of *Jackie Robinson: A Biography*. "Increasingly, black Americans saw two wars taking place. One was with the Axis powers; the other was being fought out at home and overseas with white American notions of racial supremacy."

It didn't help that, in 1940, Secretary of War Henry L. Stimson made clear that he foresaw complete and permanent segregation in the military. Indeed, entire branches of the military—the Marines, Coast Guard, Army Air Corps—remained closed off to Black volunteers simply because they had always been. And if that was not frustrating enough, the windows that the other branches "opened" to Blacks were both laughable and insulting. The Army defended its tiny 10 percent limit on Blacks by arguing that it represented their share of the wider population. The Navy, as Dorie Miller could attest, would put Black sailors on board, but only in severely limited roles with demeaning titles ("messboys"). It was true that some high-ranking military officials, like Army general George C. Marshall, responded positively to the pressure of the Black press. (In 1941, Marshall said he was "not personally satisfied" on progress to curb discrimination in the Army.) Army colonel Eugene R. Householder, however, summed up the military's more prevalent—and de facto official—position when he stated, "The Army is not a sociological laboratory. To be effective it must be organized and trained according to principles which will ensure success. Experiments to meet the wishes and demands of the champions of every race and creed for the solution of their problems are a danger to efficiency, discipline and morale and would result in ultimate defeat."

How rigid and pervasive was segregation in the military? Although its color is red no matter whose body it's circulating in, blood was segregated. The military prevailed on the Red Cross to ban plasma from African Americans. "White men in the service," the directive read, "would refuse blood plasma if they knew it came from Negro veins." (Perhaps not on the battlefield itself, it should be noted.) But the military's directive was brimming with a bitter if not bloody irony. The man responsible for the development of large-scale blood banks, so critical in World War II, was a brilliant American surgeon and medical researcher named Charles R. Drew. He was Black.

Yet, as America's war effort picked up steam, there were some encouraging signs, particularly from someone who outranked both Householder and Marshall, and everyone else in the military. Unlike his predecessors in the White House, Franklin Roosevelt was at least openly concerned about the issue of racism and discrimination as it related to jobs, the military, and the broader war effort. And he shared his anger and frustration with those—employers, military branches—who were holding fast to longtime discriminatory practices. "The American people are united as never before in their determination to do a job and do it well," Roosevelt told the nation in a radio address in October 1942. "We can no longer afford to indulge in such prejudices or practices."

Backing up his words, Roosevelt signed Executive Order 8802, which prohibited discrimination in war industries involving federal contracts. Black employment for both men and women increased dramatically. For her part, the commander-in-chief's wife, First Lady Eleanor Roosevelt, went further. She met freely and often with such Black leaders as A. Philip Randolph and Walter White, and publicly advocated for greater integration in the military.*

The Black press had kept the pressure up with its widespread Double V campaign. And it had yielded results. By the middle of 1942, there were Blacks in the Air Corps, the Marines, the Coast Guard, and the Women's Army Auxiliary Corps. In March 1942, at the Tuskegee, Alabama, Army Airfield, the first four African-American pilots were graduated into the Army Air Force. "These four men," wrote Patrick Washburn, "were idols of the black press, black America's favorite sons."

For many African-American journalists, the Double V campaign was not merely about fighting for dual victories; it was about fighting hard

---

* As African Americans gained more footholds in the Army, even as segregated units, many whites at southern training camps referred to them as "Mrs. Roosevelt's N-----s."

Tuskegee Airmen at a briefing, Ramitelli, Italy, March 1945 NATIONAL ARCHIVES

on dual fronts. And not letting up. "The Negro reporter is a fighting partisan," wrote Percival Prattis, executive editor of the *Pittsburgh Courier* during the war. "The people who read his newspaper ... expect him to put up a good fight for them."

Nell Dodson Russell's wartime columns certainly captured that spirit. "Up until the outbreak of the war, Negroes below Washington weren't supposed to think," she wrote in early 1944. "They were supposed to say, 'Yassuh, Mistah Charlie.' Those days is gone forever as the expression goes. The truth hurts and our press has been printing the truth, bold and ugly as it is."

For the *Courier*'s Wendell Smith, even FDR himself was a fair target for criticism. "He was particularly adamant in calling upon President Roosevelt to adopt a Fair Employment Practice Policy in big league baseball just as he had done in war industries and governmental agencies," wrote David K. Wiggins, author of *Glory Bound: Black Athletes in a White America*. "It was disconcerting to Smith that Roosevelt had never seen fit to issue a statement regarding the exclusion of blacks from major league baseball." Smith pointed out Roosevelt's inconsistency in telling some parts of society to stop discriminating, yet giving "such a discriminating organization as big league baseball a nod of approval."

During World War II, Wendell Smith had extra reason to rail at Major League Baseball's color barrier. As if the previous 50 or so years of being barred from big-league baseball weren't hurtful and angering enough, the war years served to sharpen that anger to an even more painful point. "For obvious reasons, organized baseball was in desperate need of players during World War II," wrote Wiggins. "But major league owners still refused to sign quality black players, who were more than willing to fill the void. Instead of soliciting the services of outstanding black athletes, big league owners would travel all over the world searching for and signing foreign-born players for their ball clubs."

Other owners shopped closer to home. Needing to fill out depleted rosters, they were discriminating shoppers—of everything but actual talent.

"What made the owners' stubbornness particularly ironic was that with so many big leaguers off to war," wrote Irwin Silber, "teams were signing white players of mediocre talent—even including a one-armed outfielder—while ignoring known black stars of the Negro Leagues."

Negro League stars like Satchel Paige and Buck O'Neil were still in their prime in the 1940s, still more than capable of making game-winning contributions to major-league teams otherwise bereft of real talent during the war. For Black sportswriters like Rollo Wilson, the fact that they were ignored even now, while white owners signed up seemingly anyone and everyone else, was deeply insulting.

"A one-armed man, a one-legged man, Cubans, Chinese, Mexicans—anyone except a known colored-man is welcomed into the big leagues at this time."

But by the 1940s, amidst the war and the intensifying campaign to integrate baseball, a single, all-powerful—and resolutely intransigent—target was gaining more attention than the many, separate (and equally intransigent) owners themselves. The *Daily Worker*, in concert with progressive trade unions and civil rights groups, had begun picketing Yankee Stadium, Ebbets Field, and the Polo Grounds in New York, as well as Comiskey Park and Wrigley Field in Chicago. They collected more than a million signatures for a petition to integrate baseball, to be delivered directly to Major League Baseball commissioner Judge Kenesaw Mountain Landis.* (The petition was delivered, and presumably filed away in a folder—or a wastebasket—large enough to hold a million signatures.) Before he left for his own military service in the South Pacific (where he served as an Army combat medic), Lester Rodney opened up his own one-way communication with Commissioner Landis. Shortly before he was drafted, Rodney wrote an open letter headlined, "Time for Stalling Is Over, Judge Landis." It was published in the May 6, 1942, edition of the *Daily Worker*. It read, in part:

> *Negro soldiers and sailors are among those beloved heroes of the American people who have already died for the preservation of this country and everything this country stands for—yes, including the great game of baseball . . . you may file this away without comment as you already have done to the petitions of more than a million American baseball fans . . . yes, you may ignore this. But at least this is going to name the central fact for all to know . . .*
>
> *You, the self-proclaimed "Czar" of baseball, are the man responsible for keeping Jim Crow in our National Pastime . . . Dorie Miller, who manned a machine gun at Pearl Harbor when he might have stayed below deck has been honored by a grateful people. The*

---

* Landis was baseball's first commissioner, serving from 1920 until his death at 78 in 1944. In the wake of the "Black Sox" scandal in 1919, he banned eight players for life, and was credited for restoring faith in Major League Baseball. He also rigidly maintained baseball's color ban.

President of our country has called for an end to discrimination in all jobs . . .

The Louisville Courier Journal *of a month ago, entering the nationwide demand for the end of Jim Crow in our National Pastime said: "Baseball, in this war, should set an example for Democracy."*

What about it, Mr. Landis? . . . the American people are waiting for you . . .

And the first casualty lists have been published.

Yours,
Lester Rodney
Sports Editor, Daily Worker

In truth, Rodney knew better than to hold his breath. Landis did exactly what he had done about baseball's color ban for a quarter of a century: nothing. He did, however, apparently feel a bit more pressure on the subject than he had felt before. He held a press conference in which he said, "There is no rule, formal or otherwise," that bans Black ballplayers from playing major-league baseball. Lawyerly to the last, Landis was telling the truth, while maintaining technical deniability. After all, a "gentleman's agreement" is just that—an agreement, an *understanding*, not a rule. Whether it was formal, informal, semi-formal, or business casual was entirely moot. Nothing changed. African Americans were now going off to war, and dying for their country. Unmoved, white major-league owners still barred them from playing baseball. Two years after Pearl Harbor, in December 1943, those owners convened in New York for their annual winter meeting. Determined to pressure the owners—now during the war more than ever—the Negro Publishers Association requested and received permission from Landis to speak at the meeting. Their surprise guest was their speaker: Paul Robeson. An accomplished actor, singer, political and social activist, and two-time All-American athlete (who also played professional football), Robeson was then in New York starring in an acclaimed Broadway production of *Othello*.

"The time has come that you must change your attitude toward Negroes," Robeson said, addressing the owners. "I come here as an

Paul Robeson playing softball with other members of *Othello* production, Central Park, New York City, 1943 FARM SECURITY ADMINISTRATION–OFFICE OF WAR INFORMATION PHOTOGRAPH COLLECTION (LIBRARY OF CONGRESS)

American and former athlete. I urge you to decide favorably on this request and that action be taken this very season ... the American people will commend you for this action which reflects the best in the American spirit."

Robeson spoke passionately for 20 minutes. When he was finished, the assembled owners (which included Brooklyn Dodgers president and general manager, Branch Rickey) gave Robeson what reports described as "lengthy applause." They asked no questions. They then retired to a private session. And that would be as close as a Black man would come to Major League Baseball for the remainder of the war.

By mid 1943, as the war itself ground on, there were encouraging signs in both the Pacific and European Theaters. With the Allied victory in North Africa, events were lining up for the Normandy invasion that would come just one year later, and that would begin the end. For African Americans, there was a degree of encouragement in the numbers of Black servicemen and women slowly rising in rank in the major branches, even as units themselves remained segregated. The bitter irony was that, even though World War II would represent a genuine pivot point for civil rights gains—including ultimately the desegregation of both the military and baseball—getting there for Black soldiers represented a painful inversion of the "Double V" campaign. For African Americans in uniform, and especially those facing combat overseas, there was instead a "double conflict" to contend with. Not only were they facing a foreign enemy's bullets, but many also faced some of the worst racism they had ever encountered—at home, from their own white countrymen.* Nowhere was this double conflict on more vivid display than, no surprise, in the American South.

Many of the US Army's main training bases were located in the South and West. One of the largest was Fort Hood. Opened in 1942 and located in Killeen, Texas, between Waco and Austin, it was (and remains) a principal armored training center.† The vast and sprawling base, which today covers over 300 square miles, is one of the five largest military bases

---

* Black soldiers also encountered racism overseas, but, again, almost exclusively from many of their own white American comrades in arms. In fact, Black soldiers were stunned to find widespread racial tolerance in France and Great Britain, only to be harassed there, as at home, by racist, white American military personnel.

† The fort is named for Confederate general John Bell Hood, who was born in Kentucky but commanded the particularly hell-bent and gung-ho Texas Brigade, which figured in some of the bloodiest early battles of the Civil War. Today, Fort Hood is among those military bases facing pressure to have its name changed.

in the world. In the early 1940s, it was particularly significant in that it was the main training base for the 761st armored unit. Nicknamed the "Black Panthers," the 761st was the first all-Black tank battalion to see combat in World War II. Assigned to legendary General George Patton's Third Army Armored Division, the 761st helped begin the final Allied thrust out from France in the winter and spring of 1944, helping drive Nazi forces back toward Germany and to eventual defeat and surrender. (Patton initially resisted deploying a Black tank battalion, but by 1944 the critical need for quality, trained armored personnel outweighed his opposition.) The battalion covered 2,000 combat miles and spent 183 days on the front lines, which included the bloody and harrowing Battle of the Bulge, as well as the equally harrowing liberation of some of Hitler's most horrific concentration camps. Having impressed white military superiors (including General Patton) for their grit and courage, the 761st achieved lasting fame, not only for how they performed on the battlefield, but for how they changed hearts and minds off of it as well. Theirs was a remarkable record of valor and success that helped change the lives of all Black soldiers—and African Americans in general.

"The 761st Tank Battalion . . . would become not only the first African American armored unit in the nation's history to land on foreign soil; it would also become one of the first black combat units in the modern Army to fight side by side with white troops," wrote Kareem Abdul-Jabbar and Anthony Walton, authors of *Brothers in Arms: The Courageous Story of WWII's 761st "Black Panthers."* "The unit's actions, and those of their fellow soldiers, would ultimately lead, in 1948, to the desegregation of the American military."

But before the courageous men of the 761st could drive their tanks into Germany, they'd have to ride the buses in Texas.

During training in Texas, even Black soldiers who'd grown up in the segregated South found the level of racism and discrimination hard to stomach. But it wasn't just Camp Hood. Throughout southern military bases, the racial violence was so frequent and so bloody that it sometime seemed there was another front entirely to the larger war. In just the first months of the war, an African-American private was lynched just

Cpl. Carlton Chapman, gunner, 761st Tank Battalion, near Nancy, France, November 1944 NATIONAL ARCHIVES

outside of Fort Benning, Georgia. A couple of months later, in Florida, an argument between some white MPs (Military Police) and Black soldiers resulted in gunfire that killed a Black soldier. The next month, an argument over a bus seat resulted in both a Black soldier and a white MP being shot to death. In 1942, racial friction flared into a full-scale riot with multiple deaths in Alexandria, Louisiana, after Black soldiers reacted angrily to the violent arrest of a fellow Black serviceman. All of these violent and deadly incidents took place at or near American military bases and involved active-duty Black soldiers wearing the uniform of their country. In all of the deadly skirmishing, in all the hail of bullets and the rising body count, none of those involved had yet trained a gun on the actual enemy.

Although, some stateside American soldiers had already seen the Germans up close. By 1943, some American military bases were also being used as detention centers for German prisoners of war. At Camp Hood, toward the end of the war, thousands of German POWs, many of whom had fought in North Africa, were detained. Their presence—and their treatment relative to African-American soldiers—seemed a special added punishment all its own. But not for the prisoners.

"The German POWs had light work detail, and most were allowed to roam through the camp unguarded," wrote Abdul-Jabbar and Walton. "They were permitted to walk in and out of the PX and special services clubs." (From which Black soldiers were banned.) "German prisoners were given more freedom than were the Black American soldiers."

Had German prisoners been escorted for any reason onto a bus around the base or into a neighboring town, they presumably, as whites, would have been able to sit wherever they pleased or were directed. The same was not true for Black soldiers, and that was only part of the cruel challenge they faced with buses. Often getting on one at all was its own ordeal. At many bases, like Camp Hood, buses were driven by civilians. On a day or a night off, buses were essentially the only transportation to get into and back from the local town. Once there, being *in* the local southern town was no picnic, either. For African-American soldiers, nasty cracks, racial taunts, or lack of service were all reminders that their US Army uniform meant nothing if the skin underneath it was black.

War correspondent Ted Stanford of the *Pittsburgh Courier* interviews 1st Sgt. Morris O. Harris, a tankman of the 784th Tank Battalion, March 1945.

As was the case throughout the South, Black soldiers were relegated to the back of the bus. To make matters worse, many white civilian bus drivers had fixed the arbitrary number of six Black soldiers gathered and waiting at a bus stop, before they would stop to pick them up.

"Even a group of five soldiers would be told they had to wait," wrote Abdul-Jabbar and Walton. A Black soldier "wearing the uniform of his country, had no choice but to stand and wait while busloads of white soldiers and white civilian employees came and went."

Black soldiers at Camp Hood came to be especially wary of a late-night, last bus back to base, when the bus was routinely full. Drivers sometimes stopped several miles short of the base, claimed that the bus was overloaded, and ordered Black soldiers off in the dark.

"After a hard day of maneuvers, heading toward the start of another such day, it could feel like a very long walk home."

Reports of such abuse at the bases drew attention, and infuriated the Black press.

"Maybe the War Department's southern brigade has the idea that sending Negro soldiers south where they can get a taste of Dixie 'hospitality' will scare the rising tide of militancy out of the race," wrote Nell Dodson Russell in her "Manhattan Memo" column for the *People's Voice* on January 8, 1944. "It's not scaring us, it's just making us fighting mad."

But in an eerie prefiguring of both baseball and civil rights history, it was one of the newest arrivals at Camp Hood—and newest members of the 761st Tank Battalion—who would end up getting mad enough to make a stand. He had been inducted into the service in April 1942, and sent originally to Fort Riley, Kansas, for his basic training. A national standout in both football and track at UCLA (before withdrawing in order to help support his mother and family), the young officer was already known to most of the men when he arrived at Camp Hood in April 1944. A natural leader of quiet confidence and intelligence, 2nd Lieutenant John Roosevelt "Jackie" Robinson was immediately put in charge of a tank platoon. History began unfolding one click quicker.

Ironically, the men of the 761st had chosen as their motto, "Come Out Fighting." (It was actually a Joe Louis quote.) Their fighting began long before they landed in France and began their long, brutal slog to the German border by way of the Bulge. For Robinson, it had begun even before he arrived at Camp Hood. At Fort Riley in Kansas, at the outset of his basic training, Robinson had quickly scored high as both a marksman and for overall "Excellence" in character. He seemed a natural fit for Officer Candidate School. He applied. And he waited. And waited.

"The men in our unit had passed all the tests for OCS," Robinson wrote in his 1972 autobiography, *I Never Had It Made*. "But we were not allowed to start school; we were kept sitting around waiting for at least three months, and we could get no answers to our questions about the delay. It seemed to be a case of buck passing all along the line."

Robinson—a future major leaguer, no less—had no more luck in trying to join the Fort Riley baseball team, whose coach refused to allow Black players. Thanks to the arrival of boxer Joe Louis for his own Army training at Fort Riley, pressure began to be applied from Washington. Robinson did begin OCS, though his anger and resentment seethed quietly inside as he made his way to his new training at Camp Hood. It was a volatile mix that was soon to be tapped.

On June 9, 1944 (only three days after the Allied Normandy invasion), the 761st Tank Battalion was told to prepare for imminent departure overseas; they were heading for battle. As part of the paperwork, an earlier injury of Jackie Robinson's was flagged. He had injured his right ankle playing football at Pasadena Junior College in 1937. It was now diagnosed as a form of chronic arthritis. Robinson was summarily disqualified for "general military service," although he was still cleared for "limited service." The upshot was that Robinson did not have to fight in any active military theater of operations. Appreciative of how well liked and respected Robinson was, the battalion's commanding officer, Lieutenant Colonel Paul Bates (who was white and universally respected by his Black trainees), asked if he would accompany the 761st to Europe as a morale officer. Robinson agreed to go, but had to go through a medical process to clear the way. It required him to undergo some exams at McCloskey Hospital in nearby Temple, Texas, about 30 miles from Killeen and Camp Hood. After an exam, he was cleared to travel with the 761st, but required to spend a few days at the hospital. On the night of

July 6 he was granted a night's leave. Robinson took a bus back to Camp Hood, dropped by the Negro Officer's Club (which was mostly empty, as his unit was on maneuvers), and left around 11:00 p.m. (without having had a drink) to return to the hospital in Temple. There were few passengers on the bus, and Robinson sat in the fourth row, not the back. As the bus filled, mostly with white civilian workers from the base returning home, the white driver stopped and asked Robinson to move to the back. He refused. He also knew something that the driver may or may not have been aware of: The rules had changed. Just weeks earlier, finally responding to pressure, the military had issued a very lightly publicized new order, prohibiting segregation on all vehicles operating within an American Army base.

"Knowing about these regulations," Robinson wrote later, "I had no intention of being intimidated into moving to the back of the bus." Words and threats were exchanged, and the flustered driver alerted the military police, who met the bus when it stopped. "There's the nigger that's been causing me trouble," Robinson recalled the driver yelling.

The MPs asked Robinson to accompany them to see the duty officer, and he cooperated.

"I was confident that it would be easily established that I had acted well within my rights," Robinson wrote later. "I was naïve about the elaborate lengths to which racists in the Armed Forces would go to put a vocal black man in his place."

Little did Robinson know that those lengths would stretch all the way to a full court-martial. And it might easily have altered history. Although, in some ways, the situation already had.

Within only an hour or so after it began, the bus incident went from bad to worse for Robinson. Captain Gerald M. Bear, who responded to the MPs' call, promptly called Robinson an "uppity nigger." The white civilian stenographer summoned to simply record his official testimony interrupted Robinson to ask, "Don't you know you've got no right sitting up there in the white part of the bus?"

Taken aback, Robinson took vigorous exception. "It wasn't bad enough that she was asking that type of question," he wrote, "She wasn't even pausing long enough to hear my answer."

An officer himself, Robinson felt he was being treated dismissively, and with crudely racist hostility. He grew increasingly worried and frustrated. "As serious as the situation was, I had to laugh," wrote Robinson. "It was so obvious what was happening. I was up against one of those white supremacy characters. Everything would have been all right if I had been a 'yassuh boss' type."

The captain ordered Robinson back to the hospital in Temple, putting him under "arrest in quarters." Arriving at the hospital, Robinson was met by a colonel and some MPs.

"There was talk of a court-martial," Robinson recalled later. "The Colonel advised me that he had been alerted to expect a black officer who had been drunk and disorderly and had been trying to start a riot. It must have been obvious to the Colonel that I wasn't drunk, and when I told him calmly that I had never had a drink in my life, he said that for my own protection I must immediately have a blood test to prove that there was no alcohol in my blood."

It wasn't the only time during Robinson's Camp Hood ordeal that a fair-minded and reasonable person would step in to help him. Although Captain Bear did officially initiate a court-martial, the order needed to be signed by Robinson's commanding officer, Col. Paul Bates, who refused. Higher brass at Hood then had Robinson transferred to a different battalion, whose commander signed the court-martial order. On July 24, 1944, Lt. John Roosevelt Robinson was officially arrested.

Colonel Bates, however, was not done doing what he could to help out his young lieutenant. Bates retained hope that Robinson would still be able to accompany the 761st overseas. That hope, however, was fading quickly. On August 1, the battalion began relocating to Camp Kilmer, New Jersey, to prepare for their ship transport to France. Bates stayed behind at Camp Hood in order to testify on Robinson's behalf.

It's little wonder that Colonel Bates, even long after the war was over, remained an officer who was beloved and respected by the men of the 761st. "The men could never find enough words of praise to describe Paul Bates," wrote Abdul-Jabbar and Walton. "He was fundamentally decent, honest, modest, and compassionate. He saw and treated the men of the battalion with a simple, direct humanity, and they responded in kind . . .

there was nothing he could do to alter the underlying attitudes of other white officers, but he did forbid any direct mistreatments of his soldiers, and he insisted they be given nothing but the highest caliber of armored training. He believed in them."

And Colonel Bates believed strongly, unalterably, in 2nd Lt. John Roosevelt Robinson. Under oath, Bates described Robinson's conduct in uniform as "excellent," and testified that he had both his own and the battalion's respect, and that he would have "utter confidence" in having Robinson lead men into combat. Bates, who "put his career on the line to defend Jackie Robinson on several different occasions," according to Abdul-Jabbar and Walton, also arranged for a number of other members of the 761st to give testimony regarding their own shameful treatment on buses at Camp Hood.

As part of the first of two phases of Robinson's court-martial trial, all of the charges involving his altercation with the bus driver were dismissed. Nine men would hear the case (one was Black); six votes were needed for conviction.

The court-martial trial would turn entirely on what happened between Robinson and Captain Bear after the MPs had arrived . He was charged with behaving disrespectfully toward Bear, and disobeying orders to remain in the receiving area. The stakes were high; at the very least a conviction would mean a dishonorable discharge.

"It became obvious during the proceedings that the prosecution had rehearsed and schooled witnesses—and had done a bad job of indoctrinating them," Robinson recalled later. "My lawyer tricked several of the witnesses into confusing testimony, and luckily there were some members of that court-martial board who had the honesty to realize what was going on."

Robinson also later singled out praise for the Black press, particularly the *Pittsburgh Courier*, which had prominently published letters of support from fellow Black officers. "The Army, sensitive to this kind of spotlight," wrote Robinson, "knew that if I was unfairly treated, it would not be a secret." The trial lasted four hours; Robinson was found "not guilty of all specifications and charges."

The 761st Tank Battalion, meanwhile, with Col. Paul Bates leading his men, would go on to make history, and, more importantly, to make believers, however grudgingly, out of those who still harbored doubts or held onto racist stereotypes about Black soldiers. Through late 1944 and early 1945, and the brutal Battle of the Bulge (the final German offensive before its defeat), the 761st, like the more famous Tuskegee Airmen, played a significant and meaningful role in Allied combat operations even as an all-Black, segregated unit. Their record of continuous and uninterrupted fighting on the front line for over six months (units generally averaged one to two weeks) is still staggering to consider. Their tanks broke through the famed Siegfried line, opening up the crucial corridor for General Patton's troops to finally enter Germany proper. As the end approached, they were one of the first American battalions to link up with the Russian army, signaling the final encirclement of Nazi forces. In May 1945, the 761st helped liberate 85,000 prisoners from Gunskirchen, a subcamp of the larger Mauthausen concentration camp. Sonia Weitz, a 16-year-old camp survivor (she lost her entire family save for her sister to the Nazis), later wrote a poem, "The Black Messiah," about her liberation. One stanza reads:

A Black GI stood by the door
(I never saw a black before)
He'll set me free before I die,
I thought, he must be the Messiah

By the war's end, the 761st Tank Battalion had established a battlefield legacy that could not be ignored. The Army recognized the unit with four campaign ribbons. Individual members of the battalion also were awarded with a total of 11 Silver Stars, 69 Bronze Stars, and 300 Purple Hearts. Their achievements were truly transformative. Eventually. A 761st tank commander like William McBurney had sat with pride and purpose in the turret of his Sherman tank, as he and his unit fought across five countries to victory. He returned home to a country where many still expected him to sit with mute obedience in the back of a bus.

With the conclusion of his court-martial trial, Jackie Robinson was technically now assigned to the 758th Battalion, to which he had been transferred in order to make the court-martial orders official. He asked to be reassigned to the 761st so he could rejoin his own battalion. The request was granted, but it was too late; the 761st Tank Battalion was already headed to combat.

"The court-martial had caused me to miss going overseas with my outfit," Robinson wrote. "I knew that I would be transferred again into some new and strange organization. I was pretty much fed up with the service." The service seemed to sense as much.

In November 1944, Robinson was transferred to Camp Breckinridge, Colorado, where he received his honorary discharge. He was a civilian again. And while it was the same month his buddies from the 761st saw their first action, Jackie Robinson—who had expected to be with them—was still at home, in America. Where he needed a job. Like so much of Robinson's unlikely story, more pieces just seemed to fall into place for where he would ultimately find himself—and as importantly, *not* find himself—less than a year later. As much as he must have thought of Camp Breckinridge as the last sorry spot he had to trudge to before being done with the military, it was also where he found that job. On the base, he had spotted a soldier practicing his pitching. Robinson asked if he could step in and do the catching. Turns out, the fellow pitching, Ted Alexander, had been a member of the famed Kansas City Monarchs of the Negro League.

"He said the Monarchs were looking for players," recalled Robinson. "I was looking for a decent postwar job. So I wrote the Monarchs." The Monarchs wrote back. Jackie Robinson shed his khaki uniform, and within a few months would be wearing a flannel one with the iconic "K.C." emblazoned on the front.

As 1944 drew to a close, there was a gathering and unmistakable sense, in both Europe and in the Pacific, that the overall war effort was now signaling a steady, if still slow and bloody path to Allied victory. It was still dark, the magnitude of death and the unimaginable extent of the Nazi horror not yet even fully comprehended. But as 1945 approached, holiday candles seemed to flicker with just a bit more light than they had

Jackie Robinson with the Kansas City Monarchs, 1945

in years. In many ways, the approaching new year would be one of history's most significant. Some of what would make it so was evident now, even in the fading shadows of a punishing year in which American losses were staggering.* The Allies' fortunes in the war were not all that was changing. As the 761st Tank Battalion fought and fell and bled its way forward, it became a moving metaphor, both literally and emotionally, for the Black experience in the war. And for changes still to come. Substantially influenced by the experience of the 761st, America's military would desegregate within three years. This was, however woefully belated, a powerful validation of the "Double Victory" campaign. But while total victory had been achieved in America's war, only a single battle had been won in the larger African-American fight for justice and equality.

Major League Baseball, and so much else in America, remained segregated. Every tanker, every airman, every single Black veteran returning home was returning—after risking their lives defending it—to a nation that still valued them less than their white counterparts. But in the bitterest of ironies, it was those who would never return home, who did give their lives, that would have one of the greatest impacts on the struggle there. It was the disparity between that sacrifice—that ultimate act of *giving*—and what they were still *denied*, that finally began to change minds in ways few things had before.

And nowhere was that shameful disparity shown in more stark, ugly relief than in Major League Baseball.

"More than any other event, World War II paved the way for the breaking of baseball's color line," wrote author and baseball historian Glenn Stout. "Prior to the war, virtually the only calls for integration of the national pastime came from African American and leftist newspapers. But the war exposed the inherent contradiction and inequality of organized baseball's unwritten policy, providing the unassailable argument that if a man risked dying for his country on the battlefield he deserved the right to play the game."

---

* In the last year of World War II in the European Theater, from June 1944 to V-E Day (June 8, 1945), there were 552,117 US casualties; 104,812 were killed in action. In the Pacific Theater, the final nine months produced the highest casualties of the entire war.

Fifty years of impassioned speeches, personal appeals, petitions, protests, books, essays, articles, letters, interviews, editorials, and lengthy newspaper columns had decried baseball's color barrier. Yet it endured. Now, a single two-page pamphlet with just 10 words and two small pictures seemed to crystallize that "unassailable argument" in a way that a half-century and a sea of words had not. It was a piece of campaign literature for Benjamin J. Davis Jr. Davis, a lawyer, had been moved to join the American Communist Party after his 1933 defense of a young, Black Communist in Georgia accused of insurrection. He later became editor of the *Daily Worker*. In 1943, he was elected to the New York City Council. During his re-election campaign in 1945, he distributed a pamphlet that showed two photos side by side: a dead, Black soldier on the battlefield, and a Negro League pitcher in America. The caption beneath read, "Good enough to DIE . . . but not good enough to PITCH!"

The point was made in a more fundamental and self-evident way than ever before. The ground was shifting. In November 1944, as Jackie Robinson was being discharged from the Army, longtime Major League Baseball commissioner Judge Kenesaw Mountain Landis died at 78. He was replaced by US senator Albert "Happy" Chandler. A Kentucky Democrat, Chandler had previously made conciliatory comments regarding segregation in baseball. Pressed by the *Pittsburgh Courier* if he would allow African Americans to play in the majors, he replied, "If they can fight and die on Okinawa, Guadalcanal, in the South Pacific, they can play baseball in America."

Those words may have been in Jackie Robinson's mind as he made plans to join the Monarchs. Early in 1945, he would don that Kansas City uniform. But it was neither the last uniform he'd wear, nor the last team he'd join in the year to come. It was the next one, after that, that would make history. As for uniforms, every single Black man and woman who'd worn one in the war just ended was now an ally, and unsung hero, in Robinson's quickening march toward Brooklyn.

NINE

Rounding Third, Heading Home

By 1944, we in organized Negro baseball could see quite plainly the handwriting on the wall. The gathering storm of inevitable baseball integration was approaching rapidly, ever more relentlessly.
—EFFA MANLEY (CO-OWNER, NEWARK EAGLES)

THE WAR YEARS HAD BEEN PARTICULARLY TOUGH ON THE NEGRO Leagues. They battled all the same privations, rationing, cutbacks, and shortages that affected most (non-war-related) businesses, including Major League Baseball itself. Like professional white teams, Negro League teams lost many of their best, young players to the war effort. Most Negro League teams, however, were already just making do and just getting by, even before the war. The Kansas City Monarchs, because of their legendary owner and founder, were more fortunate than most. Only a handful of baseball executives are (as of 2020) among the 333 individuals who have been inducted into Major League Baseball's Hall of Fame. J. Leslie Wilkinson is one of them.* More significantly, he became one of the most respected and widely admired figures in the history of Black baseball.

Born in 1878 in Algona, Iowa, Wilkinson grew up to be a promising young pitcher in the state. At 22, however, after a wrist injury, his playing days were over. The young Wilkinson turned to managing, leading an

---

* As of 2020, Effa Manley is the only woman in the Hall of Fame. With her husband, Abe, she co-owned the Newark Eagles, and became a powerful and deeply respected executive and advocate for the Negro Leagues.

all-Black team he had played against and been impressed by. He found he had a talent for both managing and promotion, not necessarily in that order. In time, he also recruited the most talented team of women baseball players he could find. For a white kid from the Midwest in the early 19th century, he seemed to relish a diversity that was uncommon. He put together a team called the All Nations, filled out with Native Americans, African Americans, Asians, Cubans, German Jews, and white Americans. After the First World War, Wilkinson moved his wife and two kids to Kansas City. In 1920, when Rube Foster was organizing the Negro League, Wilkinson applied with a new club he had formed, the Kansas City Monarchs. Foster and several of his associates in the new venture were skeptical and reluctant to admit a white owner. After all, if white baseball owners had hired Black players, there would be no need to start a Negro League. But Wilkinson was clearly different. There was simply no denying his keen business and promotional success, or the fact that he had made a career so far of being an uncommonly fair, tolerant, and progressive owner. Wilkinson's Kansas City Monarchs became charter members of the Negro League. They would go on to become one of the most talented, successful, and legendary Black baseball teams ever. For the decade of the 1920s, the Monarchs had a winning percentage of .665. Over the 28 years of Wilkinson's ownership (1920–1948), the team won 11 league titles and two Colored World Series. In addition to Wilkinson himself, fully *11* former Monarchs players are also in the Baseball Hall of Fame, including Cool Papa Bell, Satchel Paige, and Jackie Robinson. (On Wilkinson being the Negro League's sole white owner, a league historian would later say, "The league was dark, and he stood out, and he didn't care.")

"Wilkie," as he was affectionately known, never lost the adventurous sense of baseball promotion he'd relished as a young manager. In 1929, he hired an Omaha company to design a state-of-the-art, portable lighting system that demonstrated what night baseball could truly look like. It also shed light on a truly savvy businessman; it wasn't lost on his players that lights also extended the workday.

"With those lights, Mr. Wilkinson's teams could get in an awful lot of baseball," wrote Satchel Paige in his autobiography. "I remember once

The 1934 Kansas City Monarchs on a barnstorming trip through Canada, posing in front of the team bus, nicknamed, "Dr. Yak." Monarchs owner J. L. ("Wilkie") Wilkinson stands second from left. NATIONAL BASEBALL HALL OF FAME AND MUSEUM

we played three games in one day. We had a game in the morning and then another one in the afternoon and switched on the lights for a game that same night."

But the keen business was paired with an equally deep sense of fairness and respect. He was the rare businessman and baseball owner with a conscience. He would not book games in places where his team would not be able to find decent lodging or restaurants that would serve them. To increase the comfort level, he bought his team a tourist bus and had it fitted out with sleeping bunks and a kitchen. He insisted that seating at Monarchs game be integrated, and was even known to cut the ropes at various fields that divided "whites" and "colored" seating areas.

"When I got to know him, I realized I was in the company of a man without prejudice, the first man I had ever known who was like that," wrote former Monarchs star first baseman and manager Buck O'Neil. "I was from the South, mind you, so I was unaccustomed to meeting a white man who treated me the way he would his own son."

Satchel Paige himself had reason to feel the same way about Wilkinson.

"If you were down and needed a hand, he'd give you one," Paige recalled in his own autobiography. "He was all the time hiring ballplayers that'd been great and were on their way downhill."

In that, it's possible that Paige had forgotten that he was also referring to himself. After all, at the time he was writing that (1962), he was still three years away from his final major-league game (at age 59). And the "downhill" he had been on had begun a full 25 years earlier. In 1938, pitching in Mexico, Paige had somehow injured his arm, rendering him unable to pitch with any authority or velocity. He was only 32, but unable to pitch as he once had. He returned to the United States, where he desperately sought medical treatment, but without success. He thought his playing days were over. And, without J. L. Wilkinson, they likely would have been. The Monarchs owner, fully aware that the famed pitcher seemed to be done pitching, called Paige and offered him a job. It was clearly more about putting a thankful arm around the player than it was about putting him to work.

"I thought you needed a hand," is how Paige recalls Wilkinson explaining his gesture. Paige was assigned to a traveling squad better known as the "Baby Monarchs," which would soon be renamed the "Satchel Paige All-Stars."

"The squad was a blend of young players on their way up, and oldsters ready to retire," wrote Larry Tye (*Satchel: The Life and Times of an American Legend*). "For Wilkinson, adding Satchel to the mix was a chance to trade on the Paige name to draw fans, pay back other broken-down players who in their prime had helped the Monarchs, and, as a risk taker and a man of faith, to hope against hope that Satchel would regain his grace and skill. For Satchel, Wilkinson's offer was a god-send."

And Paige, humbled and scared by his injury, seemed to fully appreciate the gesture in a way he had never responded before.

"Wilkinson would become close to Satchel in a way that Gus Greenlee never managed," wrote Tye, "and the pitcher would show him a fealty he gave to few others as they cemented their relationship over the next decade."

What's more, Wilkinson's faith and hope in his celebrated but struggling pitcher was rewarded. As sudden and mysterious as the onset of

Paige's injury had been, it just as suddenly and mysteriously disappeared. The arm was back, a taut band that followed through the big, rangy windup, rearing back from near the ground, then whipping up and over to its last second release. Once again, it fired in on a line to batters who once again crouched tense and wide-eyed at the pea-sized blur of a baseball which, once again, stymied the best hitters and helplessly froze most others entirely.

"That hummer of mine just sang a sweet song going across the plate," recalled Paige, in his autobiography, as he recalled his miraculous comeback. "I can't help laughing now when I think how I felt like a kid then, a kid starting all over again."

Satchel Paige was on the road with the Monarchs' traveling team when his arm returned. "We called Mr. Wilkinson that night and told him," he wrote. "'You work yourself back into shape real easy,' he warned me. 'Don't strain that arm. You just stay with the club 'til the season's over and get back in shape. You'll join the Monarchs for the 1939 season.'"

And he did. Unlike his other Negro League stints, he never strayed again. He would play loyally for J. L. Wilkinson, and the Monarchs flourished. He would wear another uniform only when it was that of a major-league team, and only after he had left the Negro Leagues entirely. But that was still nearly a decade away. Before that, in the fall of 1944, J. L. Wilkinson took another chance on another player, this one in great condition, but unlike Satchel Paige, a total newcomer to the Negro Leagues. Also unlike Paige, who Wilkinson had reached out to himself, Jackie Robinson had reached out to the Monarchs and was signed. As the 1945 season got underway, Satchel Paige got acquainted with his new teammates at the Monarchs spring training camp in Houston.

"About the best of the lot was a college boy, a kid named Jackie Robinson," Paige wrote later. "I'd never heard of him before, but he was pretty good—quick on his feet and a good hand at the plate."

For his part, Robinson was considerably less impressed with his introduction to the Negro Leagues than his famous teammate had been impressed with him. He may have needed a job, but his new workplace seemed a questionable fit.

"Up to April, 1945, Robinson had probably never seen an official Negro League game," wrote Arnold Rampersad (*Jackie Robinson: A Biography*). "Nor would he have been romantic about the all-black leagues. Robinson's race pride led him to demand integration, not to glory in separation. His three Army years had only reinforced his contempt for Jim Crow."

But there he was. At that point in time, an entire generation of Negro Leaguers could have told Robinson what to expect. Nevertheless, it seems to have been something other than what he expected.

"I didn't like the bouncing buses, the cheap hotels, and the constant night games," Robinson wrote later. Neither, for that matter, did most of his teammates.

"When I look back at what I had to go through in black baseball," Robinson recalled, "I can only marvel at the many black players who stuck it out for years in the Jim Crow leagues because they had nowhere else to go . . . it appeared it would be years before segregation in baseball was eliminated."

Actually, although Robinson couldn't have known it in early 1945, it would be less than a year.* In fact, he had played for less than a full month with the Monarchs before history's wheels began turning. As often happens with large, looming cultural changes, the wheels seemed at first to spin uncertainly and in the wrong direction. But it was as if unseen hands, some working in unison, some working independently, were now collectively plotting the course and fixing on the ultimate coordinates. From the Midwest to the Northeast, several locations would be grazed by the path of the coming comet of events. Day by day, however, from K.C. to Philly, even as he griped about lousy hotels and endless night games, it was Brooklyn that was invisibly lining up to be Jackie Robinson's True North.

But first, there was Boston.

---

* More than a few Negro Leaguers would later take issue with Robinson's tale of woe on the road, mostly because it was a woefully short tale. When he wrote of what he "had to go through in black baseball," he was referring to his single season in it. By contrast, former fellow Monarch John Donaldson spent 30 years in Black baseball as a supremely talented and highly regarded pitcher. He died poor, in obscurity, and was buried in an unmarked grave. That, is a lot to go through.

It's an irony worth noting that, in the immediate run-up to the fall of baseball's color barrier, three unsung heroes stand out, all of whom, at critical junctures, helped advance Jackie Robinson's journey from risk-taker to groundbreaker—and all of whom were white. There was Col. Paul Bates at Fort Hood in Texas, who played a significant role in helping Robinson win his court-martial case. There was Monarchs owner J. L. Wilkinson who, in taking a chance and giving Robinson a job, was also providing the vital professional platform from which the budding star would be able to showcase his baseball talents. And, there was Izzy Muchnick.

He was born in Boston's famous (some would say infamous) West End in 1908.* Even as a youth, Isadore Harry Yaver Muchnick seemed to be defined by three things: intelligence, athletics, and religion. Indeed, all three would continue to define and guide him throughout his life. One of four children born to Russian Jewish immigrants Joseph and Fannie Muchnick, he was raised a practicing and observant Jew in a neighborhood that was then home to thousands of recent Eastern European Jewish immigrants. (Boston's oldest surviving synagogue, the Vilna Shul, still stands on the west side of Beacon Hill, just on the other side of Cambridge Street from where Muchnick grew up.)

He did well in school, and graduated from prestigious Boston Latin School, where he became the first student there since Benjamin Franklin to receive a double promotion. He attended Harvard College, where he played hockey and lacrosse, and graduated in 1928. In 1932, he graduated from Harvard Law School. He was 21. With such an impressive background, Muchnick had no shortage of suitors for a job, even from several of Boston's most elite and well-established "white shoe" law firms. For these venerable, Yankee firms, however, there was one part of Muchnick's background that did not impress at all: his name. Nonetheless, he did receive job offers, on the condition that he "tidy up" his overly Jewish,

---

* In the 1950s and early 1960s, Boston's West End became a symbol for the pitfalls of the "urban renewal" policy then popular nationally. What had been a bustling, multi-ethnic, and mostly working class neighborhood—only blocks from both city hall and the state house—was replaced by high-rise apartment buildings and more upscale businesses. The razing of the colorful, urban neighborhood has been lamented by many ever since.

Isadore H. Y. "Izzy" Muchnick
COURTESY OF THE RAPPAPORT FAMILY
FOUNDATION

overly ethnic last name. Much-nick refused. So much for making junior partner someday at Hale & Dorr or Ropes & Gray.

As American cities go, Boston was hardly unique in its prejudices of the period. (A few of which, some would say, continue today.) Yet the "Athens of America," as the city is sometimes called, also rivaled ancient Rome for its fierce and festering factionalism, as well as its equally entrenched and pervasive tribalism. ("Here's to dear old Boston," a famous toast goes, "The home of the bean and the cod—where Lowells speak only to Cabots, and Cabots speak only to God.")

Throughout the 19th century, on the doors of Boston businesses, the sign "Irish Need Not Apply" was as common as "Open" or "Closed." By the time Muchnick was starting life on his own in the city, the Irish had succeeded in elbowing past the former Protestant Yankee power structure, and establishing a firm foothold on political office. But racism and anti-Semitism never went out of style in Boston. (Sadly, many of those Irish—who themselves had been victims of a century of prejudice and intolerance—seemed to often have short memories.*)

Izzy Muchnick decided instead to open his own law practice, which he did, in the heart of the city's financial district on State Street. In truth, it seems hard to imagine Muchnick as part of a big, high-powered,

---

* In the late 1930s and early 1940s, it became commonplace in many of Boston's Jewish neighborhoods for residents to be set upon by gangs of mostly Irish-Catholic youths out on organized "Jew hunts." By 1943, with little police intervention or outcry by non-Jewish public officials, widespread violence against Jews in Boston received national attention; both *Newsweek* and the *Atlantic Monthly* magazines reported on it, as did major newspapers in New York. Some of the city's Jewish leaders at the time chose to call out the anti-Semitic attacks for what they were: "pogroms."

hyphenated name–happy law firm. He had been raised in a tradition of social justice and moral responsibility, and the Jewish concept of *Tikkun Olam*, which calls for constructive acts of kindness in order to benefit others, and to literally "repair the world." Muchnick and his wife, Ann, were active in Hadassah, the Jewish women's benevolent organization, as well as HIAS, the Hebrew Immigrants in America Society. But whether it was his experience in sports or at Harvard, Muchnick also felt at ease all around the city and with all types of people. (He would later become friends with the young John F. Kennedy, having helped deliver Boston's Jewish vote in Kennedy's 1952 US Senate campaign in Massachusetts.)

"Being Jewish in 1940s America carried a considerable weight of prejudice, but Muchnick possessed a skill and integrity that allowed him to navigate Boston's difficult, tribal quarters," wrote Howard Bryant, author of *Shut Out: A Story of Race and Baseball in Boston.* "It allowed him to be respected by both the Irish, who controlled city government, and the entrenched Yankees, who dominated Boston's cultural, legal, and financial world. He did this without becoming an outcast from his own community, and such a balance required real political skill."

It was a skill that Muchnick seemed to recognize and embrace in himself, as he began to see politics as a vehicle for doing good and helping others.

"Izzy was truly a pioneer in his way," says Jerome L. Rappaport, a close friend of Muchnick. "So many were engaged in Boston politics, but few saw politics the way he did, to break barriers."

Rappaport, 93, also graduated Harvard Law School at 21. A wunderkind in Boston politics during the 1940s and 50s, he would go on to a highly successful career in business and philanthropy.

"Few people knew Izzy as well as I did," Rappaport recalls today. "He was a good friend, and his reputation for honesty and integrity was absolutely well-earned."

Ironically, Rappaport later was closely involved in the massive West End redevelopment project that bulldozed his good friend's childhood neighborhood. But there is little question about the sincere respect he still maintains for what Muchnick faced and what he accomplished, especially winning a seat on the Boston City Council in 1941.

"Yes, he was representing a heavily Jewish ward," says Rappaport, "but he was so intent on representing his people well, on doing good in general, and he was very conscious of breaking the barrier as a Jew."

No surprise then, that Muchnick viewed other barriers of unfairness and intolerance as targets to be assailed, wrongs to be righted. He pushed for equal pay for women long before it was popular, just as he sought a degree of integration in the city's public schools, well before Boston's busing issue exploded in the 1970s. He also repeatedly called out corruption in city government. All of which earned him few friends. Fighting the good fight often made Muchnick a very lonely and solitary soldier.

"There was something about Muchnick, something both admirable and self-destructive about his unfailing adherence to his principles, for his adherence to a high personal code often conflicted with Boston's insularity," wrote Bryant. "Both of his children would marvel at the number of times their father would align with the underdog, especially in a city such as Boston, with its go-along to get-along political credo."

As the 1940s advanced, Muchnick found himself focusing on a familiar issue: discrimination. As a Jew, he knew what it looked like, and he knew personally what it felt like. But the discrimination and racism against America's Blacks was on a different order. Like many Americans, he was increasingly appalled and angry about their continued mistreatment even after sacrificing their lives for their country in World War II. Unlike most Americans, Muchnick began to realize that he might actually be able to do something about it.

"The duplicity of baseball angered Izzy Muchnick," wrote Bryant. "He was a Red Sox fan, but the game's contradictions conflicted with his worldview. If it was the game that was supposed to represent the goodness of America, the ultimate arena of fairness, how could it be staunchly segregated? How, he wondered, could this impregnable line of segregation—which baseball maintained did not exist—go unchallenged for so long?"

In truth, that "impregnable line" had, in fact, been challenged by many since it was first drawn decades earlier. Yet it stood. Izzy Muchnick, however, was about to challenge it in a way it had never been challenged before. It had started reasonably enough. Muchnick had written the vice president and general manager of the Boston Red Sox, Eddie Collins, requesting that the team take some concrete and public steps to scout and consider Black baseball players for their major-league club. Collins may or may not have discussed the initial requests with the team's owner, Tom Yawkey. Collins was certainly comfortable in his own skin at Fenway Park. After all, he'd had an illustrious playing career as a star second baseman for the Philadelphia Athletics and Chicago White Sox, and had been inducted into the Hall of Fame in 1939. Yawkey, who bought the Red Sox in 1933, had long idolized Collins, and conditioned his purchase of the team on Collins coming to Boston in an executive capacity. As far as Muchnick's queries were concerned, he received nothing but bland and perfunctory replies. Collins, in fact, seemed taken aback by the mere "insinuation" that "all ball players, regardless of race, color or creed have not been treated in the American way so far as having an equal opportunity to play for the Red Sox." "After all," as he wrote Muchnick, "I have been connected with the Red Sox for twelve years and during that time we have never had a single request for a tryout by a colored applicant."

History doesn't record whether or not Collins wrote that with a straight face.

At any rate, neither Yawkey, nor Collins, had any use for, or interest in, what a Jewish city councilor had to say about Black baseball players.* But Izzy Muchnick wasn't a pushover. He was dogged about the battles he chose. And, much to what was about to become Eddie Collins's deep dismay, he had a good lawyer's keen sense of positioning, and a cagey fighter's sense of what punch to throw. The Red Sox had a vulnerability. And Izzy Muchnick had found it.

Once among the most prudish of American cities (the Puritans led to the Watch and Ward Society, which led to the "Banned in Boston" designation), Boston enforced a raft of "Blue Laws," local ordinances that regulated which businesses could operate on Sundays. (Incredibly, until 2003, liquor stores in Massachusetts were not allowed to remain open seven days a week.) One such law pertained to professional baseball. In order for the

---

* Muchnick, it should be noted, also reached out to the National League Boston Braves regarding tryouts for Black ballplayers. Although Braves owner Lou Perini declined Muchnick's request, he did not scoff at his concerns and, in 1950, the Braves would become just the fifth major-league team to integrate.

Red Sox to get permission to play at Fenway Park on Sundays (and the Braves at Braves Field), an annual, unanimous vote of the Boston City Council was required. The vote, and approval, was traditionally a formality. So, Izzy Muchnick would argue, was racism. By 1944, Muchnick had already threatened the Red Sox that, unless they took some concrete action on race, he would withhold his vote to allow Sunday games at Fenway. He was angered by Collins's bald-faced runaround and his patronizing disingenuousness. Proving he could play hardball with a Hall of Famer, Muchnick distributed Eddie Collins's letter to the Black press, leading what had been a local confrontation to gain national attention. Calling out Collins's attitude himself, Wendell Smith of the *Pittsburgh Courier* reached out to Muchnick, who held his fire. For the moment.

But as the 1945 season—and the city council vote—approached, Muchnick dropped the hammer: The Red Sox could hold an organized and official tryout for Black baseball players, or they would lose the privilege of playing baseball games on Sunday at Fenway Park. At the time, Sunday doubleheaders were a longstanding major-league tradition, and a mainstay of a team's schedule. Pre-television, it was also an era when major-league teams depended on ticket sales for the bulk of their annual revenue. Sacrificing all of those games over the course of an entire season would be financially devastating. Tom Yawkey and Eddie Collins were now paying attention.

Collins "had badly underestimated Muchnick's tenacity," according to Howard Bryant. "Collins was used to being in a position of strength when he dealt with baseball issues, but it was clear that he couldn't say a few positive, encouraging words to rid himself of Isadore Muchnick, a man who was determined to see tangible progress."

Backed into it, with no other options, and against their will, the Red Sox agreed to a tryout of some Black ballplayers at Fenway Park.

The Boston Red Sox were not the first major-league team to be approached by African Americans for a tryout. In fact, in 1942, at home in Pasadena, Jackie Robinson himself asked the Chicago White Sox if he could join them for a tryout at their training camp there. Robinson and Negro League pitcher Nate Moreland were allowed to work out with the team. Suffering from a muscle strain, Robinson wasn't at his best. And, even though White Sox manager Jimmy Dykes said, "I'd hate to see him on two good legs," that was the end of it. A year later, under pressure from both the *Pittsburgh Courier* and the *Daily Worker*, the Pittsburgh Pirates agreed to try out a couple of Negro Leaguers, including future Dodgers star catcher Roy Campanella. The players were even sent an invitation, which proceeded to list an eye-glazing list of qualifications, conditions, and provisos. "It contained so many buts," recalled Campanella, "that I was discouraged before I had finished reading the letter." The tryout at Forbes Field never happened.

One of the most significant, if little known tryouts occurred only a week and a half before the Fenway tryout was to take place. On April 6, 1945, Joe Bostic, an African-American sportswriter for the Black newspaper, the *New York Age*, accompanied two Negro League players (pitcher Terris McDuffie and first baseman Dave Thomas) to Bear Mountain, New York, where none other than the Brooklyn Dodgers were conducting their spring training. Bostic's trip was entirely unannounced, and was meant to put Dodgers president Branch Rickey on the spot. It did. Rickey, who was furious and later described the visit as a "stunt," did eventually collect himself, inviting the visitors to have breakfast and allowing the players to work out. Although Bostic had no way of knowing it, Rickey was already actively laying the groundwork for signing a Black ballplayer. And it wasn't going to be McDuffie or Thomas.

Now, less than two weeks later, another tryout for Black players loomed in Boston. Not that it mattered to the Sox, but Muchnick did need to produce some players to presumably show up and actually try out. He resumed correspondence to consult with Wendell Smith of the *Pittsburgh Courier*. Smith had a keen and extensive knowledge of the Negro Leagues, and who some of the most promising young candidates might be. He suggested three players: Marvin Williams, an infielder with the Philadelphia Stars; Sam Jethroe, a speedy center fielder with the Cleveland Buckeyes; and infielder Jackie Robinson, then in only his first weeks of the season with the Kansas City Monarchs. The players were contacted, their teams consented, and all three headed for Boston, where they would be met by both Smith and Muchnick. (The *Courier* agreed to pay their travel expenses.) The tryout would be on Thursday, April 12.

Already wary and deeply skeptical that the Red Sox were going to suddenly sign a Black ballplayer at the start of a new season, the three players arrived in Boston on April 11. The next day, their suspicions promptly deepened when the tryout was suddenly postponed. The Red Sox cited the death of President Roosevelt. While it's true that FDR, 63, did die on April 12 of a cerebral hemorrhage in Warm Springs, Georgia, the news didn't break until early evening that day, leaving the Black players in limbo for most of the day that the actual tryout was scheduled to take place.

Spinning their wheels while waiting for further word at their hotel, the players were told the tryout would be pushed back a few days. Muchnick, mistrustful of Collins to begin with, fumed. Robinson, the most vocally cynical of the three visiting players, contacted Wendell Smith.

"Listen, Smith," he wrote, "it really burns me up to come fifteen hundred miles for them to give me the runaround."

Robinson wasn't imagining things. Fully aware that the players had traveled some distance, and that they were now sitting and waiting in Boston—several *days* after FDR's death—the Red Sox were stalling. They likely felt they could afford to, as the whole affair, embarrassing as it may be, was unfolding outside of public view. In agreeing to the tryout, Eddie Collins had insisted on a total news blackout—no newspaper stories or coverage of any kind, and no reporters or photographers allowed at the tryout itself. Izzy Muchnick—reluctantly, and now regretfully—had agreed.

For his part, Wendell Smith did not feel bound by Muchnick's agreement with Collins.

"This is Boston, cradle of America's democracy," he wrote in his *Pittsburgh Courier* column. "I have three of Crispus Attucks' descendants with me. They are Jackie Robinson, Sammy Jethroe and Marvin Williams. All three are baseball players, and they want to play in the major leagues . . . we have been here nearly a week now, but all our appeals for fair consideration and opportunity have been in vain . . . but we are not giving up!"

In the Cradle of Liberty itself, the press slept like a baby.

"And for much of the week, while no direct mention of the impending tryout appeared in the Boston papers, Collins and the Red Sox put the players off," wrote Glenn Stout (coauthor of *Red Sox Century*) in *Pumpsie & Progress: The Red Sox, Race, and Redemption*.

"The 1945 regular season opened for Boston on April 17 in New York and the Sox were leaving Boston for New York on a 1:00 p.m. train on April 16. Had the Sox been able to delay the tryout for one more day, it likely never would have taken place."

But at literally the 11th hour, the press stirred. On April 16, the morning tabloid edition of the *Boston Daily Record* carried a column under the byline of sportswriter Dave Egan.* "Here are two 'believe-it-or-not items' exclusively for the personal enlightenment of Mr. Edward Trowbridge Collins, general manager of the Boston Red Sox," Egan wrote. "He is living in anno domini 1945, and not in the dust covered year 1865. He is residing in the city of Boston, and not in the city of Mobile, Alabama . . . therefore we feel obliged to inform you that since Wednesday last, three citizens of the United States have been attempting vainly to get a tryout with his ball team. . . ."

"By breaking the edict of silence," Glenn Stout wrote, "Egan apparently broke the door down . . . not until Boston's white, mainstream press took note of the situation did the Red Sox respond to the entreaty from Smith, Muchnick, and the three ballplayers."

Only hours after morning commuters read the column, the three ballplayers, along with Smith and Muchnick, had left their hotel en route to Fenway. As raw as feelings were, as unlikely as it was that it was finally happening, it was impossible to ignore the historical significance of what was about to unfold on the staid, green grass of the venerable ballpark in Kenmore Square.

"Nearly fifty-five years after Cap Anson engineered the removal of the last black major leaguers in the late nineteenth century," wrote Howard Bryant, "the tryout finally took place at Fenway Park at eleven on the morning of April 16, 1945."

And yet, on that sunny morning at Fenway, the Green Monster's spreading shadow was dwarfed by a larger and darker shadow of irony:

---

* Egan, a Harvard Law grad like Muchnick, is best known for perpetually tormenting Sox star Ted Williams in column after column. He was also among the small number of white mainstream journalists who had consistently called for Major League Baseball to integrate.

The very first major-league team of the 20th century to officially try out a Black ballplayer would ultimately be the very last team to actually sign one.

Because so few people were actually there, details of the tryout itself have long remained scarce, dependent on select observations shared later by the participants themselves. Arriving at the park, the players chatted briefly with Eddie Collins, then changed into uniforms provided by the Red Sox. The tryout itself was run by former Sox Hall of Fame outfielder, Hugh Duffy, who greeted the players and had them stretch out before taking the field. ("They were all fine fellows!" Duffy would effuse later.) With word of the tryout having become public, at least a small number of local sportswriters were sitting in the stands. (The *Boston Globe* did not cover the tryout.) Muchnick and Smith were both there, as was then-Sox manager Joe Cronin. (One report later described Cronin as sitting "stone-faced.") Neither general manager Eddie Collins nor Sox owner Tom Yawkey were visibly present as the tryout progressed.* For 90 minutes, the three Black players hit, fielded, and ran the bases. And then, with the same sudden lurch with which it all started, it was all over.

The three players changed in the locker room, and were given standard information forms to fill out. As the Red Sox prepared to head to nearby Back Bay Station to catch their 1:00 p.m. train to New York, general manager Eddie Collins reappeared to say goodbye, and told the three players they would hear from the Sox "in the near future."

"In another life," is perhaps closer to what Collins meant to say. None of the players ever heard anything further from the Red Sox.

By the next day, press reports and quotes on the unusual tryout did begin to pop up.

Mabry "Doc" Kountze, writing for the *Boston Guardian* quoted Hugh Duffy: "We were glad to give them a tryout. They're the same as anyone else . . . Deserve the same chance as anybody." (Describing Jackie Robinson, the ever-quotable Duffy was reported to have cheerfully gushed

---

* Part of the telling and re-telling of the infamous "tryout" invariably includes a disturbing anecdote. A Boston sportswriter who claimed to be present alleged that, at some point during the proceedings, from the shadows of the grandstands, Yawkey was heard to yell, "Get those niggers off the field!" No other eyewitness has ever corroborated the claim, and it has never been confirmed.

to another reporter, "What a ballplayer! Too bad he's the wrong color.") Some years later, recalling the tryout, Izzy Muchnick would say, "I'm telling you, you never saw anyone hit the Wall the way Robinson did that day—bang, bang, bang, he rattled it." Muchnick, briefly running into Joe Cronin as the tryout ended, also recounted the manager being very impressed by Robinson, about whom Cronin said, "If I had that guy on this club, we'd be a world beater."

That was small consolation to Robinson himself, who felt he had done well enough, but had no illusions from the start that he and the other two players had participated in anything other than a humiliating, dressed-up, major-league sham.

"We put our best efforts into it," he wrote later in his autobiography. "However, not for one minute did we believe the tryout was sincere. The Boston club officials praised our performance, let us fill out application cards, and said, 'so long.' We were fairly certain they wouldn't call us, and we had no intention of calling them."

Observing the end results of both the Boston and the Bear Mountain tryouts, Homestead Grays owner Cum Posey was incensed. "The most humiliating experience Negro baseball has yet suffered from white organized baseball," he said. "Any white rookie one-half as good as any of these players would have been kept for at least a week and sent to some minor league club."

Back with the Buckeyes, Sam Jethroe told a teammate that the Boston tryout was "a joke." He described Joe Cronin as "just up in the stands with his back turned most of the time. He just sent some of his men out there and told them to throw some balls, hit some balls to us, and then come back and say we had ability."

The three Black players themselves had been deeply skeptical from the beginning that they were involved in anything other than a charade. Yet even Robinson—arguably the most cynical before the tryout and the angriest afterward—also appreciated the symbolic importance of doing what they did in Boston. Almost eerily referencing events he did not know were only months away, he said of the three players, "We consider ourselves pioneers. Even if they don't accept us we are at least doing our part and if possible making the way clear for those who follow." He added, in what now sounds like striking clairvoyance, "Some day some Negro player or players will get a break. We want to help make that day a reality."

That was the same sentiment that had driven Izzy Muchnick in his battle with the Red Sox to begin with. There had been little political incentive or upside for him. If anything, the whole episode served to cement his reputation as an overly zealous social reformer, attuned to ideals, but heedless of politics.

"Breaking the color line across baseball as a whole, not specifically integrating the local organizations was his objective," wrote Muchnick's two adult children, David M. Muchnick and Frances Muchnick Goldstein, in an essay in 2010. (Both children are now deceased.) "Given the opposition he faced, it was definitely not a simple thing to do; it was simply the right thing to do. And, it was great to get a result that cracked the color line even if it did not shatter it."

Indeed, in wresting a tryout from the Red Sox for Black ballplayers, Muchnick had succeeded where no one had before. True, none of the ballplayers in Boston were offered a job. But only six months later, in Brooklyn, one of them was. And the crack opened a fissure that brought the wall down. Meanwhile, for Muchnick, April 1945 ended with another battle hard-fought, but not hard-won. The color barrier still stood. And Izzy Muchnick, principled but powerless to bring it down (as well as defenseless in how his role would later be twisted), would forever stand as a true, if somewhat tragic, unsung hero.

"The first American politician to disrupt the idea of segregated baseball and emerge with a result," wrote Bryant, "was Isadore Muchnick, the former Hebrew School teacher who could have made a fortune in a Yankee law firm had he only changed his name."

But if some, like Robinson (with good reason) had been cynical from the start about the Sox tryout, others had found some measure of encouragement and hope, if only in the history of the moment and what it might portend. One of those was Mabry "Doc" Kountze, for whom a constructive, positive attitude toward progress on racial issues seemed a part of his DNA. In a way, it was. He had roots in Boston, and felt passionately proud of his city's historic role in being a center of the abolitionist movement during slavery. He wrote for William Monroe Trotter's *Guardian*, and lived the spirit of the paper's mission to advocate tirelessly for racial justice. With the historic tryout, unlikely as it was that the Red Sox would sign a Black ballplayer, Kountze felt uplifted. To him, there was simple but strong symbolism in these three young Black ballplayers, even if only for a morning, taking the field at Fenway Park in major-league uniforms. And in Izzy Muchnick, and his success in forcing the tryout to happen, Kountze saw a "white modern abolitionist."

"If Kountze was aware of the emerging new attitude of Boston, where hostility would replace accommodation, he did not allow it to sap his enthusiasm for the city's old abolitionist spirit," wrote Howard Bryant. "Where others surrendered hope of integration with exasperation, it was Kountze who believed that the relationship between blacks and whites in the city was not a myth, but a powerful example of what was possible."

And that mid-April week in Boston, Kountze had held on to hope. He wasn't naïve. Recalling Jackie Robinson's bus incident and court-martial at Camp Hood, he wrote, "when Jack entered Fenway for his tryout, many saw him as 'just another colored boy,' the same as that Georgia bus driver saw him, even when he wore an army officer uniform. Once again, Robinson and his teammates, were 'in court' being judged by white men." "In Boston," he wrote later regarding the tryout, "we all expected a fair trial at the Hub's Fenway Park. The author, as one of those who participated in the try-out crusade, was already keenly anticipating the end of the color Ban beginning at Fenway Park and Braves Field."

Kountze, of course, was partly right, and his hope was partly rewarded. By April 1945, he was right to "keenly" anticipate the coming end of baseball's color ban. But for all his efforts, all his hope, and all his faith in his city's past progressivism, the fact that it didn't happen in Boston stung him deeply.

"I think this was one of the biggest let-downs the author experienced in his entire career of sportswriting," he wrote. "I could see it happening in Mississippi, but not in Massachusetts."

There was, however, one leading major-league baseball figure who was not a bit let down by what happened in Boston. Far from it. He would have been shocked and actually dismayed had it turned out differently.

After all, he knew the Tom Yawkey and Eddie Collins type of executives. He worked with them. He was one of them. More to the point, he would have been enraged had the Red Sox signed a Black player in 1945. That's what *he* was planning to do. In fact, by the time the tryout was concluded in Boston, Wesley Branch Rickey likely felt he'd had quite enough of these tryouts carried out under pressure. After all, he himself had just experienced the same thing only a couple of weeks earlier at his team's spring training camp, when the two Negro Leaguers had shown up accompanied by journalist Joe Bostic. "Dammit," one can imagine Rickey exclaiming to himself, "How's a white guy supposed to integrate baseball if all these Black players keep demanding we integrate baseball?" It would be morbidly funny if it wasn't pretty much exactly how Rickey actually felt. Only half a century late, and for all the sob stories he'd later share, it was true at that moment that Branch Rickey was very much a man on a mission. And it didn't include "agitators" like Bostic or Muchnick.

"Unbeknownst to Bostic," wrote Neil Lanctot in *Negro League Baseball: The Rise and Ruin of a Black Institution*, "Rickey was already preparing for integration and had no intention of allowing outside pressure to disrupt his carefully designed plans."

While the two players Bostic had brought to Bear Mountain had no appeal in the least for Rickey, the same wasn't true about Boston. Jackie Robinson was a player that was already prominently on Rickey's radar, already the centerpiece of a plan that was coming together in Brooklyn. If, for example, the Red Sox had surprised the world by unexpectedly assigning Robinson to their farm team in Louisville (years later they took that very tack with a Black player, never bringing him up to the majors), Rickey's plans might have been imperiled. In the wake of both Bear Mountain and Boston, Rickey clearly understood that the window was narrowing in which to make his big move. The tryout in Boston seemed to be something of a warning light.

"He met with Wendell Smith immediately afterward, wheels were put in motion, and six months later, Rickey signed Jackie Robinson," wrote Bill Nowlin. "From almost any perspective, that was a reasonably direct result."

Which also makes for a particularly rich irony: In their ham-handed attempt to forestall integration, Tom Yawkey's Red Sox—myopic and hapless as usual—may actually have accelerated it.

In truth, Branch Rickey had been mobilizing for some time for his date with history. A year earlier, in 1944, he had raised eyebrows (and tempers in the existing Negro Leagues) by becoming actively involved in Gus Greenlee's newly formed, upstart United States Baseball League. Initially made up of six Black teams ("a makeshift franchise lineup," according to one description), they were all owned by unhappy former Negro League owners. When the new Hilldale team summarily moved to Brooklyn to become the Brown Dodgers and to play at Ebbets Field, it was clear that Branch Rickey had more in mind than simply some additional revenue for his major-league Dodgers.

"Rickey recognized," wrote Neil Lanctot, "that a black team appearing regularly at Ebbets Field might not only provide income but also prove an important part of his integration scheme, acclimating Brookynites to the sight of black players and perhaps eventually functioning as part of the Dodgers minor league system as a developing ground for black talent."

A final irony surrounded Branch Rickey's final bolt to the finish line, and the fall of the color barrier. In March 1945, New York governor Thomas E. Dewey signed the landmark Ives-Quinn law (named for its creators and co-sponsors, Republican state majority leader Irving M. Ives, and Democratic state senator Elmer Quinn). The law made New York the first state in the nation to forbid discrimination against job applicants or employees on the basis of religion, race, or creed. It was just this new law that, only a month after its passage, Joe Bostic sought to test at Bear Mountain, in having two Black ballplayers ask the Dodgers for a job. And, although Rickey had no use for the players and was peeved by the tryout (he never forgave Bostic), he had great use for the same new law. It would, after all, provide him persuasive legal cover for what he was about to do. On reading the news of the law's signing, Rickey is said to have exclaimed, "They can't stop me now!"

To those who knew Branch Rickey and his career before Brooklyn, the new role of suddenly energized social reformer must have come as a bit of a surprise. If Jackie Robinson seemed to be the perfect person to assume the role which *he* was about to play, Rickey was more of the perfectly imperfect one. Where Robinson's entire life up to that point seemed scripted for the coming moment of inner strength and moral courage, Rickey's seemed, well, less so. Robinson had long maintained a quiet and contained dignity as a Black man, but he was passionate, even fiery when confronted with what he considered unfair, overtly racial slights (such as refusing to move his seat on the Fort Hood bus). For most of his professional career, Branch Rickey—ever bushy-eyebrowed and bow-tied—seemed largely untroubled by prejudice.

"Despite his strong religious convictions, Rickey had shown no indication of remarkable tolerance," wrote Neil Lanctot. "Former major leaguer Bob Berman claimed that Rickey rescinded a contract offer in 1918 after discovering the Bronx high school prospect was Jewish . . . Rickey had remained silent during the integration fight and raised no apparent objection to the segregated seating policy of Sportsman's Park (despite later claiming opposition). Like other organized baseball officials, Rickey was unwilling to alienate white fans and players, particularly in an upper south city strongly opposed to integration."

Sportsman's Park was the longtime home of major-league baseball in St. Louis, where Branch Rickey, prior to 1945, had spent more than two decades of his 30-plus years as a baseball executive. Yes, the times were changing by the time Rickey arrived in Brooklyn's front office in 1942. But so was the location. He was out of the South. And now, for whatever combination of reasons (some known only to Rickey himself), he had determined that he was prepared to challenge and upend a status quo he had long accepted and by which he had abided his entire career. By the summer of 1945, action on an issue that, for decades, Rickey had been content to ignore, was now being planned in terms of mere weeks.

On August 24, prior to a Monarchs game at Comiskey Park in Chicago, Robinson was approached by Clyde Sukeforth, a scout for the Brooklyn Dodgers. Sukeforth told Robinson that he'd been sent by his boss, Mr. Branch Rickey, regarding the Brooklyn Brown Dodgers (of the USBL) who were looking for top players.

"Here we go again, I thought," wrote Robinson later. "Another time-wasting experience. But Sukeforth looked like a sincere person and I thought I might as well listen."

Robinson did listen. And Sukeforth turned out to be both sincere and persuasive. Four days later, on August 28, Robinson found himself in Brooklyn, New York, on the fourth floor of 215 Montague Street, in the offices of the Brooklyn Dodgers, where Clyde Sukeforth ushered Robinson into a dark, wood-paneled executive suite.

"Do you know the real reason you were brought here?" Branch Rickey asked. Robinson repeated what Sukeforth had told him about the Brown Dodgers.

"That's what he was supposed to tell you," Rickey responded. "The truth is you are not a candidate for the Brooklyn Brown Dodgers. I've

Jackie Robinson and Branch Rickey signing Robinson's 1948 Dodgers contract at the team's offices on Montague Street, Brooklyn, New York, where Robinson signed his first, historic agreement with the Dodgers in 1945
COURTESY OHIO WESLEYAN UNIVERSITY

sent for you because I'm interested in you as a candidate for the Brooklyn National League Club." Robinson would later describe the next, initial moments in Rickey's office as surreal and almost dizzying.

"My reactions seemed like some kind of weird mixture churning in a blender. I was thrilled, scared, and excited. I was incredulous. Most of all, I was speechless."

Fortunately, speech returned, which was needed to respond to the torrent of questions from Rickey, on everything from Robinson's personal life to whether or not he felt he had the courage to go through the ordeal, which Rickey assured him was coming. "They'll taunt and goad you," he said. "They'll do anything to make you react. They'll try and provoke a race riot in the ballpark." Rickey removed his jacket and began swinging his arms, yelling obscenities, and acting out the hate, and even the violence, that would surely be waiting for Robinson on the road.

"He knew I would have terrible problems and wanted me to know the extent of them before I agreed to the plan," Robinson wrote later. "I was twenty-six years old, and all my life back to the age of eight when a neighbor girl called me a nigger—I had believed in payback, retaliation. The most luxurious possession, the richest treasure anybody has, is his personal dignity."

Dignity, Rickey made clear, was a luxury Robinson would have to pay for with restraint, not revenge. "Do you think you can do it?" Rickey asked.

"Clyde Sukeforth," Arnold Rampersad wrote, "would remember that 'Jack waited, and waited, and waited before answering . . . we were all just looking at him.'" Now acutely aware of the enormous stakes involved, Robinson clearly pondered with deadly seriousness.

"Could I turn the other cheek?" Robinson recalled wondering as he sat before Rickey. "I didn't know how I would do it. Yet I knew that I must."

When the talking was finished, and history was made, Robinson, Rickey, and Sukeforth were the only three people in the room.

"More than two hours after he entered the dark office on Montague Street, Jack stumbled out into the Brooklyn sunshine," wrote Rampersad. "He had just signed an agreement, dictated by Rickey, that bound him to the Brooklyn Dodgers organization."

Seven years earlier, another proud and courageous Black man, only a few years older than Robinson, had also left a Major League Baseball executive's office, and had also walked back out into a city's sunshine. In 1938, Mabray "Doc" Kountze had wrapped up his own historic meeting with Boston Braves president and part-owner Bob Quinn. Unlike the meeting on Brooklyn's Montague Street, the meeting on Boston's Babcock Street produced no agreement of any kind on anything. Kountze failed to secure a firm commitment from Quinn even on the meeting's hardly controversial subject—making Braves Field more available for paid use by Black baseball teams. Nonetheless, Kountze, a man given to seeing hopeful signs however small or even invisible to others, counted the meeting a positive one. He felt "cordially received" by the older, white baseball executive, and was encouraged by Quinn's detailed knowledge of, and respect for, many Negro League players and owners. And Quinn had also made clear that, in general, as Kountze later wrote, "he favored Colored teams playing in Braves Field, and wished he could have sepia stars like [Cannon Ball] Jackman, and [Berlin]White and Paige and others on his club."

But what would be most memorable about their conversation was something that only became apparent seven years after the meeting. Kountze would then think back and realize that Bob Quinn had sketched an uncannily accurate vision of the future, and had made a very specific prophecy that proved entirely true.

Before coming to Boston, Quinn had been general manager of the Brooklyn Dodgers.

"In Brooklyn, he had seen many top notch Afro-American players and clubs," Kountze wrote later. "He knew Abe and Effie Manley who owned the National (Negro) League Eagles, who played out of Newark and Brooklyn. He said Brooklyn was closer to the actions and abilities of Colored players breaking into the Majors than any other Major League city, and he predicted Brooklyn would be the very first."

And so it was. When he left his late summer meeting in Brooklyn with Branch Rickey, Robinson had been sworn to secrecy. He had little interest in what was left of his first year with the Monarchs, and ended his season a month or so early. By October, Rickey was considering moving

Robinson's public signing into early 1946, and perhaps adding a couple of other Negro League players at the same time. But, as had happened before, it was external forces, not those in Rickey's own heart, which ended up influencing events. In New York City, Mayor La Guardia, running in a tight re-election race, sought a formal agreement from the Yankees, Giants, and Dodgers that they would "uphold the spirit and letter" of the state's recent Ives-Quinn state law forbidding discrimination in hiring. In no uncertain terms, La Guardia was pressuring the city's three Major League Baseball teams to hire Black players.

Rickey would not be scooped. Not content to share a landmark moment he had long been planning to have the sole spotlight for, he decided to act immediately. He ensured he would have not only the historic moment to himself, but the stage as well, since it was set over 300 miles outside of New York City. On October 23, 1945, in Montreal, Canada, Jackie Robinson was officially signed to play for the Dodgers' top minor-league team, the Montreal Royals. After a successful debut minor-league season with the Royals behind him, Robinson was then called up to the parent club, the Brooklyn Dodgers for the coming 1947 major-league season. On April 15, 1947, following the national anthem, Jack Roosevelt Robinson bounded out of the home dugout at an electric Ebbets Field. As if Bob Quinn was punctuating his earlier prophecy with an exclamation point, the Brooklyn Dodgers were facing . . . the Boston Braves.

Wearing number 42, as he strode out to his position at first base amid the din of cheering fans, of broadcasters announcing history, and of exploding flashbulbs capturing it, there were also two inaudible sounds: of a wall falling, and of a cheering that could not be heard with the ear, only with the heart. It rose from those not present physically, but spiritually, those who could not be seen, but were there just the same.

Moses Fleetwood Walker didn't live to see it. And by the time he died, broken and bitter, he could no longer even imagine it. But he was there. Bud Fowler tried his entire life to outrun the shadow of the wall that rose up to deny him in the end at every turn. In life, it seemed that he and his scuffed bat and well-worn mitt had been everywhere, any-where he could hook onto a team, a Black man desperately trying to just play baseball as long as he possible could. Now he was in Brooklyn. Ida B. Wells had written and reported so tirelessly and compellingly on the scourge of racial violence that eyes began to open, if only in horror. She had despaired she would ever see meaningful change. She was there. Even as they worked their regular shifts that historic day, some rolling along the rails within a few miles of Ebbets on their way west or south, the Pullman Porters— who had ensured that those stories of Ida B. Wells and other Black journalists would reach readers all over America—they were there. The Negro Leaguers past and present—those who had come too early and those who were young enough to imagine they might now walk through the door, too—they were there. And the African-American veterans of the war just ended—and those who had given their lives in it—they were there.

On this momentous day, a ballgame was played before a crowd both present and cheering, and another crowd silent and unseen. They watched a game, and they watched a terrible wrong being finally righted. To be sure, even as a Black player bounded onto an otherwise all white field, racism was still alive and well in Brooklyn and clear on across America. So many other barriers remained in place. Many still are. But on this day, some of the hurt and the humiliation were salved. Hope and faith that had long seemed to have run out, were finally redeemed. On this day, the "long arc of the moral universe" seemed to bend improbably toward Brooklyn, touching down on the grass and the dirt of a creaky old ballpark where the familiar white lines would no longer bar a Black ballplayer. And in the bottom of the seventh inning, when Jackie Robinson laid down a perfect bunt and raced toward first base, he was not alone. That invisible crowd was suddenly right there, running right alongside, willing him on. And as Robinson sprinted safely on to second base and caught his breath, they exhaled with him. After all, it had been a long, uncertain journey, and they had helped him get there.

The next Dodger batter doubled.

Jackie Robinson rounded third, and he was home.

EPILOGUE

Waste no tears for me. I didn't come along too early—I was right on time.

—former Negro League star Buck O'Neil

Outside the ballpark, as he left his meeting with Boston Braves president Bob Quinn, Mabry "Doc" Kountze faced, just to his left, the busy blur of cars speeding along on Storrow Drive. Past the cars, he could see down the Charles River all the way to the gray buildings of Boston's skyline in 1938. In the near distance, he could see cars and pedestrians crossing the Cottage Farm Bridge, built just 10 years earlier, connecting Boston and Cambridge. (In 1948, the bridge was renamed the "Boston University Bridge.") As he turned to retrace his steps and head back up Babcock Street, he adjusted the jumbled sheaf of folders and papers in his arms. A diligent journalist, he always made sure he was knowledgeable about his subject, well prepared to discuss it, and ready with questions he sought more information on. With his papers and his glasses, and his bookish, slightly preoccupied manner, he also looked very much like an academic (hence the nickname "Doc"). Turning left on Commonwealth Avenue to begin the just over seven-mile trip back to West Medford, he passed along the busy campus of Boston University, where his academic look and manner fit right in. In truth, Kountze attracted no attention at all. He was entirely anonymous.

Yet at the same time, he was a busy journalist, writing pieces continuously. He was also in contact with others like himself from all over the country, already part of an ongoing, far-flung national effort to integrate Major League Baseball. Kountze would come to realize that many of those involved in the effort were, in some ways, much like him: Black, passionately determined to create social change, but, for the most part, anonymous to the dominant, wider white culture.

For his part, Kountze wrote and reported on sports and racial justice for 50 years and for five newspapers. He wrote two books. He remained forever intent on sharing knowledge that he felt was important to share. "He was really committed, way beyond just baseball," says Shirley Kountze, wife of Doc's nephew, Elmer. "He wanted to make sure people knew about people who were making a difference, and what they were doing."

Mabray Kountze would never have called himself an "unsung hero," but he took a deep, lifelong satisfaction in playing a small role in breaking baseball's color barrier. "As sportswriters, we who 'spoke out,'" he wrote "were all in it, and a part of it, and we knew the very heart of it. There probably has never been, or ever will be, such a sincerely dedicated and nationally united reform crusade again in American sports history."

And as much as he was grateful for Rickey's role, he reminded people all his life that bringing down the color ban was not the work of a single hero, but a 50-year saga involving many different heroes, from many different walks of life, all of whom contributed to a collective victory. And all of whom were unsung, often unknown, in their efforts.

"For example," he wrote, "without Colored baseball players, managers, clubs and even imperfect leagues, there would not have been any Jackie Robinson to draw from to start with. And without the Negro Press and sportswriters to stimulate, encourage, and more widely propagate the ability and progress of Colored Baseball, Black youth might have gone to another sport . . . and of course, the Second World War . . . no one man or group can claim all the credit."

Kountze never claimed any. For him, the sense of solidarity in the effort was reward enough. Long after the color ban fell, he never shied from describing the history behind it bluntly and honestly. There was never any sentimentalizing, not even for his hometown. "All of us were angered by the Red Sox arrogance," Kountze wrote a decade after Robinson's debut, "and keenly disappointed when Brooklyn revealed more courage and democracy than Boston."

Perhaps it was about appreciating a dedicated and tireless straight-shooter, perhaps it was part of shedding a sorry past, but the Red Sox ultimately recognized Mabray "Doc" Kountze's unique stature in Boston, and recognized him in a way he seldom experienced. Kountze became the first Black journalist to receive an official Boston Red Sox press pass. He died in 1994 at the age of 84. Twenty-five years later, I asked Shirley Kountze about the press pass. "I don't know if he ever used it," she said, before pausing. "He was not fond of the Red Sox for many, many years."

As minor (and as overdue) such a gesture as the press pass was, it was more than many of the unsung heroes of this story ever received. Kountze was one of the few who not only lived to see the color barrier fall, but, while still alive, to actually receive some small recognition for his contributions. Sadly, some of the greatest unsung heroes of all—the early Black ballplayers and Negro Leaguers—not only lived and played in relative obscurity long before Jackie Robinson triumphed, but many also remained anonymous even in death. Some of Black baseball's most significant and influential early figures—Moses Fleetwood Walker, Bud Fowler, Sol White—lay for years in unmarked graves. In 2004, seeking to remedy this, and to bestow some deserved dignity and recognition on these men, the Negro Leagues Baseball Grave Marker Project was launched by Dr. Jeremy Krock, an Illinois anesthesiologist, and a lifelong St. Louis Cardinals fan.

"These were great ballplayers who don't deserve to be forgotten, but they have been," Krock told the *New York Times* in 2010. "A lot of these guys, by the time Jackie Robinson made it, they were way past their prime. It was too late for them. And not having a marker on their grave for people to remember them only made it worse."

Today, working with the Negro Leagues Committee of the Society of American Baseball Research, Krock and other volunteers have raised money, purchased headstones, and have properly marked the gravesites of dozens of former Negro League ballplayers.

In 1991, Moses Fleetwood Walker's gravesite was finally marked with a memorial donated by his alma mater, Oberlin College. Such public acknowledgement can be deeply meaningful to these obscure players' descendants, who often grew up with rich stories and legends, but had little that was tangible to touch or point to. "I used to tell people that my great-uncle was the first black major-league ballplayer and they didn't believe me," Sara Freeman, a retired postal worker, told Knight-Ridder Newspapers in 1991. "I was only seven years-old when he died . . . it wasn't until later, after he was gone, that I realized how really important he was. It's nice to know that now other people will understand that, too." In 2016, in Steubenville, Ohio, the Negro Leagues Grave Marker Project laid a new headstone on the previously unmarked grave of one of Walker's former teammates—his younger brother, Weldy.

The role of the Black press was pivotal in changing attitudes and building pressure to desegregate Major League Baseball. Some Black journalists, like Wendell Smith and Sam Lacy, did earn wider recognition in the ensuing years after the color barrier fell. In 1948, Lacy became the first Black member of the Baseball Writers' Association of America. In 1997, he was awarded the J. G. Taylor Spink Award for outstanding baseball writing, earning him a place in the writers and broadcasters wing of the Baseball Hall of Fame. In comparison, no surprise, some of the best early Black women journalists have remained largely anonymous. Skilled and gutsy reporters like Nellie Dodson Russell and Marian Foster Downer of the *Chicago Defender*, as well as Willa Bea Harmon, a pioneering editor for the *Kansas City Call*, all had to face many more obstacles than their male counterparts (black or white), and all still deserve far more recognition than they have received. A bright note, however: Ida B. Wells. Her fearless investigating and in-depth reporting on the scourge of lynchings helped to wake many people up to the horrifying reality of everyday racial violence. In May 2020, 89 years after her death, Wells was posthumously awarded a special citation Pulitzer Prize for her work.

The Pullman Porters, meanwhile, who courageously and ingeniously created their own covert distribution system for much of that writing and for many of those Black newspapers—and without which far fewer Black readers would have rallied to the cause of baseball desegregation—did find a new measure of recognition. Although the last Pullman service ended in 1968, the porters themselves had shed the most humiliating aspect of their anonymity well before. In time, they were allowed to wear individual name tags, no longer forced to be anonymous, and addressed only as "George." (A later study found that of the George Pullman Company's 12,000 porters and waiters, only 362 were actually named George.)

In 1995, in Chicago's historic Pullman District, the National A. Philip Randolph Pullman Porter Museum was founded. A stage play, *Pullman Porter Blues* by Cheryl West, premiered in 2012, and in 2016, President Barack Obama designated the entire Pullman Historic District a National Monument, now overseen by the National Park Service.

While African-American soldiers in World War II were forced to fight in segregated units, the valor exemplified by Black flyers like the Tuskegee Airmen and tankers like those in the 761st armored battalion (the fabled "Black Panthers") led directly to the fall of another color barrier only a year after Jackie Robinson's debut in Brooklyn: the complete desegregation of the US military by President Truman in 1948. Of all the unsung heroes before Brooklyn, none have garnered the lavish attention like some of these legendary Black military outfits. Documentaries and Hollywood feature films have introduced both the Tuskegee Airmen and the Black Panthers of the 761st to whole new audiences. Of course, these were two of what became the most celebrated Black units of the entire war. But the majority of the nearly one million African Americans who served during World War II were often limited to more mundane, support-type roles, like Dorie Miller, the Navy ship's cook who commandeered an antiaircraft gun during the Japanese attack on Pearl Harbor and became one of the war's first full-fledged heroes. In the 2001 movie *Pearl Harbor*, viewers may have wondered who the Black messmate was, portrayed by actor Cuba Gooding Jr., who emerged on deck and began blasting away at the diving and strafing Japanese planes. Whatever anonymity remained for Miller will soon be gone entirely. The Aircraft Carrier CVN-81, a Gerald R. Ford–class nuclear carrier, will be the Navy's newest and most advanced ship, the first carrier ever named for an enlisted sailor, and the first ever named for an African American. It's expected to launch in 2028, and be officially commissioned in 2030. On its shakedown cruise, the USS *Doris Miller* will be completing quite a journey for a once anonymous, below-decks mess attendant from Texas.

Alas, for some unsung heroes, there is a fate worse than remaining largely anonymous: having one's contribution to the cause called into question. And it's a fate that befell Izzy Muchnick, the former Boston city councilor who forced the Red Sox to hold their sham tryout in 1945.

After serving on the city council, Muchnick was elected to the Boston School committee in 1947, where he worked to root out entrenched political favoritism. Over the next seven years, he ran unsuccessfully for both state attorney general, and for a congressional seat from the state's 10th District. He never again ran for office, turning much of his energy to his legal career, and working on behalf of Jewish war refugees. On September 15, 1963, Muchnick, only 55, died of a heart attack in Boston.

His collaborator in the Red Sox tryout, *Pittsburgh Courier* reporter Wendell Smith, saw his career flourish significantly in the years afterward. It was Smith, after all, who had not only recommended Jackie Robinson to Muchnick, but to Branch Rickey as well. The Dodgers hired Smith to accompany Robinson on the road during his groundbreaking season with Montreal in 1946 and, a year later, to stay on in the same role for Robinson's far more eventful, landmark first major-league season. Smith chronicled his travel and experiences in a subsequent book, *Jackie Robinson: My Own Story.* He moved to Chicago where he worked for two white-owned newspapers, the *Chicago Herald-American* and the *Chicago Sun-Times.* In 1964, he transitioned to television, when he began anchoring a sports report for Chicago's WGN. In 1972, he died of pancreatic cancer at 58. Only a month earlier, Jackie Robinson had died at 53.

At some point after Izzy Muchnick died, Wendell Smith had begun to revise some of the history of the infamous Boston tryout. In his retelling of the events, Smith took credit for alerting Muchnick to the idea of withholding his city council vote, and forcing the Red Sox to agree to a tryout for Black ballplayers.

"In February 1945, maybe it was early March, I contacted a Boston councilman by the name of Isadore Muchnick," Smith wrote. "He was white, in his forties. I saw this little piece in the paper where he was running for reelection in a predominantly Negro area and was having quite a hard time getting reelected. I called him and told him he should include in his platform a program, or a threat that he would protest Sunday baseball in Boston if the Braves and the Red Sox didn't express interest in our campaign."

There were several significant inaccuracies with Smith's account. First, the idea for using the city council vote to force the tryout was not Smith's.

("Smith couldn't possibly have known of or understood the workings of Boston's city council," wrote Howard Bryant in *Shut Out: A Story of Race and Baseball in Boston*, "while these arcane procedures were Izzy Muchnick's everyday business.") And as a city councilor, Muchnick never had "a hard time getting reelected." (He ran unopposed twice.) Above all, he most certainly never represented a "predominantly Negro area" in 1945. Or ever.

"Ward 14 remained almost entirely Jewish all of Izzy's life," points out his friend, Jerome Rappaport. "He never had to look for Black votes."

To be sure, by the late 1960s, the Black population did begin to increase significantly in the Mattapan neighborhood of Boston. But not while Muchnick was alive.

"In 1940, Izzy Muchnick's Mattapan district was 99.69 percent white," wrote Howard Bryant. "In 1950, it was 99 percent white. During that year, 439 nonwhites lived among the district's 51,170 residents. . . . In short, there was no Black vote for Muchnick to exploit, nor was there during the 1940s any difficult election year for him."

For Muchnick's surviving family, the mere insinuation that he had been a political opportunist with ulterior motives in taking on the Red Sox was deeply hurtful. That he was no longer alive to defend himself only compounded their pain.

"Muchnick pressured the Red Sox to integrate," wrote Bryant, "because he was the rare person who—like Robinson—often placed principle in front of political or personal pragmatism. He was rarely rewarded for this."

Smith's revisionist history became lasting proof of that. Worse, it was heedlessly accepted and repeated—and never fact-checked—even by established journalists and authors of influential books about Jackie Robinson and the breaking of the color barrier.

"Instead of being known as the first politician to use his clout courageously and confront a resistant power structure," wrote Bryant, "Muchnick emerged as something worse than forgotten, but as the opportunistic, oily politician who sought to exploit both Robinson and the Black struggle for civil rights."

Neither Smith nor any other major author or journalist ever apologized or allowed for the corrected history in connection with their own writing or reporting. Years later, realizing he had the facts wrong in his 1973 book, *What's the Matter with the Red Sox?*, Boston sportswriter Al Hirshberg did apologize to Muchnick's son, David.

"Izzy's motivation with the tryout was totally idealistic—it's who he was," says Rappaport. "He really was an unsung hero in so many ways."

One person close to the Boston tryout story who never questioned Muchnick's motives was Jackie Robinson himself. The two men enjoyed a close friendship for the rest of their lives. When the Dodgers were in Boston to play the Braves, Robinson would routinely visit the Muchnick house for dinner. When he retired, Robinson sent Muchnick a copy of his autobiography, inscribed in part, "To my friend Isadore Muchnick with sincere appreciation for all you meant to my baseball career." In hoping Muchnick enjoyed the book, Robinson added, "Much of it was inspired by your attitudes and beliefs."

There was a bitter irony around the issue of who gets credit for forcing the Red Sox to hold the 1945 tryout. Other than holding a humiliating 90-minute charade led by a 90-year-old former player, the Red Sox weren't forced to do a damn thing. Hire a Black ballplayer? Not only did they take more than another decade to do that (after every other team in Major League Baseball had integrated*), they also took their time hiring *any* Black employees anywhere in their organization, even in menial jobs.

"It also appeared that the team's racist culture emanated from the top," said Walter C. Carrington in an interview in 2019. Carrington, a former US ambassador, who died on August 11, 2020, had been a young lawyer investigating the Red Sox in 1959 for the Massachusetts Commission Against Discrimination. "Tom Yawkey provided financial support to white segregationists in his home state of South Carolina. And Pinky Higgins, the Red Sox general manager, was quoted in the press, vowing, 'There'll be no n------ on this club as long as I have anything to say about it.'"

Give this to Higgins—he was at least an equal opportunity bigot. He was a rabid anti-Semite as well.

---

* On July 21, 1959, Elijah Jerry "Pumpsie" Green took the field for Boston as a pinch-runner in a 2–1 loss to the Chicago White Sox. His appearance, 12 years after Robinson's debut in Brooklyn, meant the Red Sox had finally integrated.

Indeed, ironies connected to race seemed to swirl around the Red Sox for decades, like telltale flies buzzing around something rotten. In later years, especially in relation to Boston's storied rivalry with New York, it became popular to explain the Red Sox perennial inability to win it all (until 2004, they had not won a World Series for 86 years) by referring to the fabled "curse," the supposed bad luck that befell Boston by trading some guy named Babe Ruth to the Yankees in 1920. Alas, the real "curse" lay not with who the team got rid of, but with whom they chose not to hire.

Not only could the Red Sox have signed Jackie Robinson (who likely would have made a difference only a year later when Boston narrowly lost the 1946 World Series to St. Louis), but they also could have put a Red Sox uniform on a young Negro Leaguer named Willie Mays. "Curse of the Bambino?" More like "Curse of the bullshit." In part, what plagued the Red Sox and their fortunes for decades was their accursed racism. (And often really lousy pitching.)

Jackie Robinson certainly saw it that way.

"They are prejudiced," Robinson told the *Chicago Defender* years after the Boston tryout. "Tom Yawkey has owned the Red Sox for a long time and has missed a couple of pennants by a game or two. Maybe if he had a good Negro player on the team he might have won those pennants."

In fairness, with the advent in 2002 of John Henry's ownership of the Red Sox, there seems to have been a tangible break with the past. The team has been active in developing stronger connections with the city's minority communities, as well as hiring more minority coaches and staff. In 2018, in the team's most public acknowledgement of its racist history, the Red Sox took the lead in a successful effort to change the name of the street that runs in front of Fenway's main entrance from "Yawkey Way," back to its original, "Jersey Street." Progress. (The pitching, it should be noted, still generally sucks.)

Lastly, for all the deep pride and giddy jubilation that went along with the breaking of baseball's color barrier, the ripples from this seismic moment had a variety of effects, even on those who cheered Jackie Robinson with all of their heart. Even on those who had been unsung heroes in making it all happen. The Pullman Porters and the Negro Leagues are two institutions—and unsung heroes—that eventually disappeared entirely. But only the Negro Leagues dissolved as a direct consequence of the color barrier falling. Of course, had whites not barred Blacks from playing major-league baseball for half a century, it's unlikely that the Negro Leagues would have formed in the first place. But by 1945, they had been in business for nearly 30 years. The Negro Leagues had provided a critical platform that offered both professional experience for Black ballplayers, as well as showcasing talent that could clearly compete on the major-league level. This was invaluable in the struggle to desegregate. But when the argument was finally won, the inevitable happened. The showcase was suddenly less necessary. Given the new opportunity, Black fans suddenly wanted to see their breakthrough stars on the biggest stage, the one on which they had long been denied—"the show" itself.

"All the people started to go Brooklynites," said Jackie Robinson's former Monarchs teammate, pitcher Hilton Smith. "Even if we were playing here in Kansas City, everybody wanted to go over to St. Louis to see Jackie. So our league began to go down, down, down."

Attracting and keeping fans had never been easy for many Negro League teams. Financial solvency had always been a challenge. But with the fall of the color barrier, and other Black players soon following Robinson into the majors (four more signed in 1947, including Larry Doby, making the Cleveland Indians the first American League team to integrate), attendance throughout the Negro Leagues began a precipitous, irreversible decline. In 1947, the Newark Eagles drew 57,000 fans; a year later, that number had shrunk to a mere 35,000. For the entire season.

It was the same all over the league.

"After Jackie," sighed the Homestead Grays' veteran first baseman Buck Leonard, "we couldn't draw flies."

While happy for Jackie Robinson and the larger victory for civil rights, some Negro League owners, like the Grays' Cumberland Posey, nonetheless lamented the coming collapse of the league he'd worked hard to develop. Effa Manley, who, with her husband, Abe, owned the Newark Eagles, exhorted Negro League fans to turn out, attend games, and save their team. Otherwise, she wrote, "400 young men and their families will be dumped among the unemployed." It happened, anyway.

Within four years of Robinson's debut with the Dodgers, more than 15 former Negro Leaguers were playing in the major leagues, representing more than half a dozen teams. The Negro National League disbanded in 1948. The Negro American League staggered on a bit longer, but by the 1950s, it, too, was essentially all done.

Apart from how the fall of the color barrier broke up the Negro Leagues, there was the somewhat more sensitive question of how many of the Negro Leaguers themselves regarded the role Jackie Robinson had been picked to play, in what had been a moment many of them had quietly longed for their entire careers, but had long since despaired of ever seeing happen, never mind being the one to do it.

Except one.

"They didn't make a mistake signing Robinson," said the Monarchs great Satchel Paige at the time. "They couldn't have picked a better man."

Privately, Paige was bitterly disappointed. He wasn't alone.

"Other seasoned Negro Leaguers were resentful that the young slugger had never served his time in the sandlots and barnyards, eating dust and fending off slurs," wrote Larry Tye in *Satchel: The Life and Times of an American Legend*. "Rather than show deference to the old hands who had, Jackie showed disdain."

For Paige in particular, though, the disappointment was intensely personal.

"Somehow I'd always figured it'd be me. But it hadn't," he wrote years later in his autobiography, *Maybe I'll Pitch Forever*. "Maybe it'd happened too late and everybody figured I was too old. Maybe that was why it was Jackie and not me."

At the same time, ever quick to burnish the Paige mystique, Satchel rationalized in retrospect why he couldn't—no, *wouldn't*—have done what Jackie did.

"Those major league owners knew I wouldn't start out with any minor league team like Jackie was. They'd have had to put me right in the majors and that might have caused a revolution because the high-priced white boys up there wouldn't have had a chance to get used to the idea that way."

Some bravado, perhaps, looking back. Satchel Paige was 41 in 1947; Jackie Robinson was 28. Age, needless to say, was a big factor. So was the fact that Robinson was a college graduate, as well as understated and restrained where Paige was outspoken and more flamboyant. These contrasts, such as they were, clearly weighed heavily for Branch Rickey. And his decision clearly stung Paige, then, and forever after. How could it not? The pick, as everyone knew it would, had come from the Negro Leagues. And Satchel Paige was the greatest pitcher the Negro Leagues ever produced. Even though he often had gone his own way.

"But signing Jackie like they did still hurt me deep down," he wrote. "I'd been the guy who'd started all that big talk about letting us in the big time. I'd been the one who opened up the major league parks to the colored teams. I'd been the one who the white boys wanted to barnstorm against. I'd been the one who everybody'd said should be in the majors."

Yes, they had. A decade or so earlier. Satchel Paige had done everything he claimed he had. He had been a towering figure for Black baseball all through the wilderness years. And now a new era was dawning.

"Satchel Paige had led blackball to the promised land of big-time baseball," wrote Larry Tye. "But like Moses, Satchel was not allowed to enter. Not at first."

Unlike Moses, Satchel Paige did get to finally cross over. On July 7, 1948—Paige's 42nd birthday—Cleveland Indians owner Bill Veeck invited the pitcher to suit up at Municipal Stadium and pitch for him and player-manager Lou Boudreau. When the session was over, Satchel Paige became the seventh Black player in the major leagues.

"I was in the major leagues. The old man'd made it," wrote Paige. "I signed that contract real quick."

But it was some time still before he was finished. Paige, pitching mostly in relief, went 6-1 (with a 2.48 earned run average—second-best in the American League) in helping Cleveland go on to win the 1948 World Series against the Boston Braves. Over the next 17 years, Paige would play parts of six seasons in the majors—two with Cleveland, parts of three seasons with the St. Louis Browns (AL), and one, single game for the Kansas City Athletics (AL) in what was a finale for the ages. Or aged. On September 25, 1965, Athletics owner Charles O. Finley signed Paige to a contract and held Satchel Paige Appreciation Night. At age 59, Paige was 33 years older than his catcher. He shut out the Red Sox for

Satchel Paige with American League St. Louis Browns, c. 1952
NATIONAL BASEBALL HALL OF FAME AND MUSEUM

three innings, recording nine outs on just 28 pitches. He left the game, and the major leagues, to a standing ovation. In 1971, Paige was elected to the Hall of Fame. He died in Kansas City, Missouri, on June 8, 1982. He was 76. Presumably. Paige had teased about his age all of his career. "My birth certificate was in our bible," he told an interviewer once. "And the goat ate the bible. That goat lived to be twenty-seven."

Ultimately though, unlike Satchel Paige, many of the greatest Negro Leaguers and Black ballplayers never did get to cross over. They never did reach the Promised Land, even after the wall had fallen. Their time had passed. For every Roy Campanella, Willie Mays, and Hank Aaron who followed Jackie Robinson into the major leagues, there was a Buck Leonard, Josh Gibson, and Ray Dandridge left to look on helplessly, too old now to embrace the fulfillment of their baseball dream finally opened up before them. The heartbreaking reality that many of the most deserving Black ballplayers of all were still alive—many even still playing—but unable to enter the major leagues represents the most searing indictment of the 50-year disgrace that was the color barrier.

On January 20, 1947, only a few months before Jackie Robinson would take the field in Brooklyn, Josh Gibson died in Pittsburgh, where he had become a baseball legend.

Although Gibson played until 1946, his life had become troubled. He'd been diagnosed with a brain tumor in 1943; reportedly alcohol and drug use became part of his life as well. Gibson, arguably the greatest slugger in baseball history, is often described as having "died of a broken heart." But, as some of his descendants counter, who's to say?

"I mean, people say he was bitter because he didn't make the majors, but how do you know he was bitter about that?" asks Gibson's great-grandson, Sean Gibson. "Those guys played in the Negro Leagues. That's all they knew—it's not like they had the option to play in the majors and they chose the Negro Leagues. The majors weren't letting them in. If Josh died of a broken heart that's because his wife died during childbirth giving birth to his kids."

In 1972, Josh Gibson was elected to the Hall of Fame, part of Major League Baseball's sweeping effort to belatedly celebrate and memorialize Black ballplayers and the Negro Leagues, an effort that continues today also at the Negro Leagues Baseball Museum in Kansas City. Visitors there learn about the great Ray Dandridge. Considered by many to be the greatest third baseman never to have played in the major leagues, he was only 31 when Jackie Robinson signed with the Dodgers. He got as far as the New York Giants Triple-A farm team in Minneapolis, where he mentored a young Willie Mays, and where he watched Mays called up to the major-league club. And where he waited in vain for his own call. Dandridge finished out his career at 42, playing in Bismarck, North Dakota. "Just young enough to get his hopes up, and just old enough to have them dashed," wrote John Holway, author of *Voices from the Great Black Baseball Leagues*, of Dandridge. Alas, it could pass as a poignant baseball epitaph for many great Negro Leaguers who, heartbroken, just missed the moment of integration. But for Dandridge, and other Negro Leaguers, a deeply symbolic, if posthumous victory: In December 2020, Major League Baseball announced it would now include in its official statistics the records of all Negro League players for the years 1920 to 1948. With the understatement of a Josh Gibson tape-measure home run, MLB described the move as "long overdue."

Lastly, visitors to the Negro Leagues Baseball Museum can also learn about John Jordan "Buck" O'Neil. It's hard to miss him; a life-size statue of him sits inside the museum. In real life, he is still dearly missed. O'Neil, grandson of a slave, spent an entire career in the Negro Leagues, most of which was spent as a first baseman for the Kansas City Monarchs, where he was a longtime teammate of Satchel Paige. In 1945, while serving with the Navy in the Philippines, he was sent clippings about a young talent on the Monarchs by the name of Jackie Robinson. Months later, when he was informed Robinson had signed with the Dodgers, O'Neil was overcome with joy. "We started hollering and shouting and firing our guns into the air," he recalled later. "I don't know that we made that noise on VJ Day!" That sense of joy and exuberance summed up O'Neil's long journey through baseball too. He was a good player, and an anchor of the Monarchs for many years. He was also a natural leader. After his playing days ended, he managed the Monarchs. In 1955, he became a scout for the Chicago Cubs. In 1962, the Cubs named O'Neil a coach, making him the first African-American coach in Major League Baseball. O'Neil never got to play in the majors, and was not elected to the Hall of Fame. Yet no former Negro Leaguer worked more tirelessly on behalf of drawing attention to the role of Black ballplayers and what they had done for the game. He was a driving force in the creation of the Negro Leagues Baseball Museum. And through it all, he delighted in sharing his joy for the game he loved, and the stories he never tired of telling. "Sometimes I think the Lord has kept me on this earth as long as he has," O'Neil said later in life, "so I can bear witness to the Negro Leagues."

John Jordan "Buck" O'Neil, Chicago Cubs coach, 1962 NATIONAL BASEBALL HALL
OF FAME AND MUSEUM

And bear witness he did, with warm eyes that gleamed, a smile that
endeared, and a high-pitched laugh that, even as an elderly man, suggested the glee of a kid. In 1994, an entire nation warmed to O'Neil's

upbeat, folksy charm, as he shared stories of the Negro Leagues with his largest audience of all, in the nine-part Ken Burns PBS documentary, *Baseball*. "It's kind of nice to be discovered when you're eighty-two years old," O'Neil laughed.

Buck O'Neil was often asked how he remained so positive, so happy with life, when he and so many of his teammates had been so long ignored and denied.

"How do you keep from being bitter? Man, bitterness will eat you up inside, hatred will eat you up inside," he said. "Don't be bitter, don't hate. My grandfather was a slave. He was not bitter. I learned that from him. And you know what? I wouldn't trade my life for anybody's."

In his 90s, O'Neil accompanied Joe Posnanski, a baseball writer for *Sports Illustrated* and the *Kansas City Star*, on a cross-country trip on which O'Neil was raising awareness of the Negro Leagues. The trip was the basis for Posnanski's 2007 book *The Soul of Baseball: A Road Trip*

Moses Fleetwood Walker gravestone, Union Cemetery, Steubenville, Ohio
COURTESY OBERLIN COLLEGE ARCHIVES

Through Buck O'Neil's America. In it, as O'Neil recollected the wonderful players through the Monarchs' storied history, he referenced Kansas City's Broadway Bridge. "Buck O'Neil often talked about bridges," wrote Posnanski. "He used to say that we often honor the people who cross that bridge—Jackie Robinson, Larry Doby, Minnie Minoso and so on. And we don't often honor those who built the bridge."

In 2006, Buck O'Neil died at the age of 94. On the 10th anniversary of his death, the city of Kansas City renamed the Broadway Bridge the John Jordan "Buck" O'Neil Bridge. When asked if he ever felt regret about coming along "too early," and just missing out on playing in the major leagues, O'Neil said, "Waste no tears for me. I didn't come along too early—I was right on time."

And he was. He came along right on time to finish a bridge begun by Bud Fowler and Moses Fleetwood Walker, a bridge that would one day carry their legacy over the barrier that they, and Buck O'Neil, and so many others after them had helped to topple.

Acknowledgments

While this is my fourth book, it's the first I've ever written almost entirely during a global pandemic. (God willing, that won't be repeated, either.) At Rowman & Littlefield/Lyons Press, thank you, Rick Rinehart, for your steadfast communication and positive outlook during a time when neither was easy to summon. Thanks very much as well to senior production editor Meredith Dias and to copy editor Joshua Rosenberg.

In writing about a time period from which very few persons are still alive, I am very thankful for those whom I was able to speak with directly. Thank you to Jerome Rappaport for his fond memories of his friend, Isadore Muchnick, and to Izzy's son, David. I was able to have one phone conversation with David. Sadly, we were in the process of planning to meet in New York to talk further, when David died in the summer of 2019. Thank you, also, to Paul Linet, for having been good enough to make my introduction to David. With introductions in mind, thank you so much to my colleague Karen Holmes-Ward, whose many and varied friendships and professional connections proved invaluably helpful to me. Thanks, Larry DiCara, whose memory of all things political in Boston's history is as expansive as his warmth and good humor.

I am very grateful to the families of both Satchel Paige and Josh Gibson, and in particular to Pamela Paige, and to Sean Gibson for sharing their family memories.

Memory is also the primary mission of the Negro Leagues Baseball Museum in Kansas City; thanks very much to the museum's vice president and curator, Dr. Raymond Doswell, for his time over several conversations—and for his unfailing patience over many more follow-up questions.

In talking with Otis Gates III, my fascination with the history of the Pullman Porters found a wise and personal connection; thank you, Otis. Thank you to Donna Halper, whose tireless speaking and writing about otherwise little-known great female journalists, especially those of color, has helped keep their memories alive for succeeding generations. Thanks also to Professor Rob Ruck at the University of Pittsburgh, to baseball historians Glenn Stout and Richard Johnson, and to journalist and author Howard Bryant.

A huge thanks to some of the dear and many friends of Mabray "Doc" Kountze in West Medford, Massachusetts. I am very grateful to Adele Travisano, Jay Hurd, and Terry E. Carter, who gave me their time, their insights, and who all still miss "Doc" very much.

Above all, thank you to my family—Anne-Marie, Kyra, and Daisy. I can't adequately express how grateful I continue to be for allowing me to do what I do. Thank you above all.

BIBLIOGRAPHY

Abdul-Jabbar, Kareem, and Anthony Walton. *Brothers in Arms: The Courageous Story of WWII's 761st "Black Panthers."* New York: Crown, 2004.

Alpert, Rebecca T. *Out of Left Field: Jews and Black Baseball.* New York: Oxford University Press, 2011.

Brashler, William. *Josh Gibson: A Life in the Negro Leagues.* Chicago: Ivan R. Dee, 1978.

Bryant, Howard. *Shut Out: A Story of Race and Baseball in Boston.* New York: Routledge, 2002.

Buckley, Gail. *American Patriots: The Story of Blacks in the Military from the Revolution to Desert Storm.* New York: Random House, 2001.

Cooper, Michael L. *The Double V Campaign: African Americans in World War II.* New York: Lodestar Books (Dutton), 1998.

Dunkel, Tom. *Color Blind: The Forgotten Team That Broke Baseball's Color Line.* New York: Grove Press, 2014.

Halper, Donna. *Invisible Stars: A Social History of Women in American Broadcasting*, 2nd ed. London: Routledge, 2014.

Hogan, Lawrence D. *Shades of Glory: The Negro Leagues and the Story of African-American Baseball.* Washington, DC: National Geographic, 2006.

Holway, John. *Voices from the Great Black Baseball Leagues.* Boston: Da Capo Press, 1992.

Kountze, Mabray. *50 Sports Years Along Memory Lane.* Medford, MA: Mystic Valley Press, 1979.

Lanctot, Neil. *Negro League Baseball: The Rise and Ruin of a Black Institution.* Philadelphia: University of Pennsylvania Press, 2004.

Malcolm X (as told to Alex Haley). *The Autobiography of Malcolm X.* New York: Ballantine Books, 1964.

Michaeli, Ethan. *The Defender: How the Legendary Black Newspaper Changed America.* Boston/New York: Houghton Mifflin Harcourt, 2016.

Nowlin, Bill, ed. *Pumpsie & Progress: The Red Sox, Race, and Redemption.* Burlington, MA: Rounder Books, 2010.

Nowlin, Bill. *Tom Yawkey: Patriarch of the Boston Red Sox.* Lincoln: University of Nebraska Press, 2018.

Paige, Leroy "Satchel" (as told to David Lipman). *Maybe I'll Pitch Forever.* Lincoln: University of Nebraska Press, 1993.

Peterson, Robert. *Only the Ball Was White.* New York/London: Oxford University Press, 1992.

Posnanski, Joe. *The Soul of Baseball: A Road Trip Through Buck O'Neil's America.* New York: William Morrow Paperbacks, 2008.

Rampersad, Arnold. *Jackie Robinson: A Biography.* New York: Ballantine Books, 1997.

Reisler, Jim. *Black Writers/Black Baseball: An Anthology of Articles from Black Sportswriters Who Covered the Negro Leagues.* Jefferson, NC/London: McFarland & Company, Inc., 1994.

Robinson, Jackie, and Alfred Duckett. *I Never Had It Made: An Autobiography of Jackie Robinson.* New York: Fawcett Publications, 1974.

Robinson, Jackie, and Wendell Smith. *Jackie Robinson: My Own Story.* New York: Greenberg, 1948.

Rossi, John P. *Baseball and American Culture: A History.* Lanham, MD: Rowman & Littlefield, 2018.

Silber, Irwin. *Press Box Red: The Story of Lester Rodney, the Communist Who Helped Break the Color Line in American Sports.* Philadelphia: Temple University Press, 2003.

Stout, Glenn. "Tryout and Fallout: Race, Jackie Robinson and the Red Sox." *Massachusetts Historical Review* 6, 2004.

Tye, Larry. *Rising from the Rails: Pullman Porters and the Making of the Black Middle Class.* New York: Henry Holt & Co., 2004.

Tye, Larry. *Satchel: The Life and Times of an American Legend.* New York: Random House 2009.

Tygiel, Jules. *Baseball's Great Experiment: Jackie Robinson and His Legacy.* New York: Oxford University Press, 1983.

Washburn, Patrick S. *The African American Newspaper: Voice of Freedom.* Evanston, IL: Northwestern University Press, 2006.

White, Sol. *Sol White's History of Colored Baseball with Other Documents on the Early Black Game 1886–1936.* Jerry Malloy, contributor. Winnipeg: Bison Books, 1996.

———. *Sol White's Official Baseball Guide.* South Orange, NJ: Summer Game Books, 1907 and 2014.

Wiggins, David K. *Glory Bound: Black Athletes in a White America.* Syracuse, NY: Syracuse University Press, 1997.

Wilkins, Roy, and Tom Mathews. *Standing Fast: The Autobiography of Roy Wilkins.* New York: Viking, 1982.

Zang, David W. *Fleet Walker's Divided Heart.* Lincoln, NE: Bison Books, 1998.

NEWSPAPERS

Boston Globe, Boston, MA (1888)

Brooklyn Daily Eagle, New York, NY (1841–1955)

Chicago Defender, Chicago, IL (1916)

Cincinnati Enquirer, Cincinnati, OH (1904)

Dubuque Daily News, Dubuque, IA (1890)

Logansport Pharos Tribune, Logansport, IN (1888)

Louisville Post, Louisville, KY (1888)

New York Age, New York, NY (1919)

New York Times, New York, NY (1886, 1887)

Newark Daily Journal, Newark, NJ (1887)

Pittsburgh Courier, Pittsburgh, PA ("Posey's Points," 1936)

Rocky Mountain News, Denver, CO (1885)

The Sporting Life, Philadelphia, PA (April, 1883, 1888)

The Sporting News, St. Louis, MO (1886, 1887, 1889)

Toledo Daily Blade, Toledo, OH (Aug. 1883)

Trenton Evening Times, Trenton, NJ (1883)

Wilke's Spirit of the Times, New York, NY (1868)

INDEX

About the Author

Ted Reinstein has been a reporter for Boston's ABC affiliate, WCVB-TV, since 1997. His work for *Chronicle*—America's longest-running locally produced nightly newsmagazine—has won multiple broadcast journalism awards. In addition, he is a regular contributor to the station's political roundtable show, and sits on the station's editorial board. He is the author of *New England Notebook: One Reporter, Six States, Uncommon Stories* (Globe Pequot, 2013) and *Wicked Pissed: New England's Most Famous Feuds* (Globe Pequot, 2016), and coauthor (with Anne-Marie Dorning) of *New England's General Stores: Exploring an American Classic* (Globe Pequot, 2017). He lives just west of Boston with his wife and two daughters.

GEORGE RODRIQUE